FREE AND LIVING CONGREGATIONS
The Dream That Would Not Die

Edited by

Marian Quanbeck Christopherson,
Loiell O. Dyrud, and Martin L. Horn

AMBASSADOR PUBLICATIONS

Minneapolis, Minnesota

*The AFLC Heritage Series
consists of writings that reflect
the Lutheran, pietistic, and Scandinavian heritage of
the Association of Free Lutheran Congregations.*

*The writings in this series are of
theological, historical, biographical, or devotional content.*

*The goal of this series is to include
new works, works previously published,
and works not previously translated.*

© 2002 by Ambassador Publications
Board of Parish Education
3110 East Medicine Lake Boulevard
Minneapolis, Minnesota 55441

Library of Congress 2002112594
ISBN 1-58572-046-1

Scripture taken from the New American Standard Bible®
©Copyright The Lockman Foundation 1960, 1962, 1963,
1968, 1971, 1972, 1973, 1975, 1977
Used by permission.

Printed in the United States of America.

Convictions, unless discussed and taught, die. We have much to do in the area of explaining, "Why the Association?"

Our congregations have the initial responsibility in the area of teaching our positions. When our positions are rightly understood, they are loved and command good support from most people. Our people should all be able to give eloquent answers to the question, "Why the Association?" These answers should not pertain to failures of others, but to the Scriptural positions that are held by our church.

—John P. Strand

John P. Strand (1916-1997)

In Memory of John P. Strand

John Peter Strand was born at Carpio, North Dakota, on October 7, 1916, the youngest of eight children born to Norwegian immigrants Peter P. and Petrine (Pedersen) Strand. He was baptized and confirmed at First Lutheran Church, Carpio, and also received his elementary and high school education in the northwestern North Dakota community. A special inspiration to young John was the quiet and consecrated Christian witness of his mother.

His ordination vita tells the story of a spiritual awakening that occurred after he spent three years farming with his father: "Through the faithful work of the local congregation and pastor, and radio evangelism, he was made to see his utter need of salvation, and experienced salvation by faith in Jesus Christ." A call to the ministry had been on his heart for some time, and now he enrolled at Augsburg College, Minneapolis, Minnesota, from which he was graduated with a Bachelor of Arts degree. He also received a Certificate of Theology degree from Augsburg Seminary and was ordained into the ministry of the Lutheran Free Church at Calvary Lutheran Church, Willmar, Minnesota, during the LFC Annual Conference in 1944. The ordination service was conducted by Rev. P. A. Strommen, who preached a message based on Jeremiah 1:4-10.

At a special banquet in 1978, which was held in honor of his service as AFLC president, he recognized his sister Della's assistance during his college and seminary years and said that he would not be where he was if it had not been for her.

During his preparatory years, he was grateful to serve part-time with Rev. Harold Johnson at Columbia Heights, Minnesota, and Rev. J. T. Quanbeck at Nokomis Heights Lutheran Church, Minneapolis. One summer of internship was spent in Everett and Tacoma, Washington, and a second at Grafton and Vang, North Dakota. He was especially grateful to the pastor at Grafton, Rev. Alfred Knutson, for his good counsel and training.

John Strand and Mildred Thorsgard of Northwood, North Dakota, who had met at Augsburg, were united in marriage on

June 23, 1945. Three sons were born to their union: Steven, Michael, and Jonathan.

The first parish to be served by Pastor Strand consisted of Our Saviour's Lutheran Church, Grafton, North Dakota, and Aspelund Lutheran Church of Vang, Walhalla, North Dakota, where he had served his internship. During his eight years there, both congregations grew spiritually as well as physically. In 1952 he accepted a call to be the pastor of the Tioga, North Dakota, parish, consisting of Zion, Temple, St. Olaf, Lindahl, Norman, and Beaver Creek congregations. Pastor Strand's arrival in Tioga coincided with the discovery of oil south of town by only several months, and the ensuing "boom" meant extremely busy years of ministry and outreach. The membership of Zion congregation in Tioga more than doubled in twelve years under his capable leadership, and he was a key influence in the establishment of a community hospital. His churchwide reputation was also strong, and on at least two occasions he was asked to deliver a message at the LFC Annual Conference.

The Tioga congregations had overwhelmingly voted against the merger of the Lutheran Free Church during the referendum of 1961. When the proposed union with The American Lutheran Church was approved by the 1962 Annual Conference, it was an important time of decision for Pastor Strand and his parish. He and several congregational representatives from Tioga were present at an organizational conference in Thief River Falls, Minnesota, on October 25-28, of what would become the Association of Free Lutheran Congregations. There he gave the keynote address, "The Church We Seek," and to his surprise was elected to serve as the first president of this new church body.

Rev. Strand continued as pastor of the Tioga parish until 1964, when he assumed the office of AFLC president on a full-time basis and moved to suburban Minneapolis, Minnesota, where the church headquarters were established. His new ministry responsibilities included the deanship of both the theological seminary and the Bible school when they were first established, and he provided firm leadership for the growing young fellowship until 1978, when he declined re-election and accepted a call to serve as pastor of St. Paul's Free Lutheran Church, Fargo, North Dakota.

In 1982 he announced his retirement, moving to the lake home that he and his wife had built near Remer, Minnesota. Winters were spent in Arizona and Florida, and he experienced a new aspect of involvement by serving a term on the Board of Trustees of the AFLC Schools.

After a long struggle with cancer, John Strand died on July 25, 1997, at his home. A funeral service was held in Trinity Free Lutheran Church, Grand Forks, North Dakota, on July 29, and burial was at Northwood, North Dakota.

Blessed be his memory.

Rev. Robert L. Lee   *March 2002*
AFLC President

Table of Contents

	Foreword – Robert Knutson	xi
1.	Free and Living Congregations An Introduction *Craig S. Johnson*	1
2.	The Lutheran Free Church A Brief History and Recollections *Raynard O. J. Huglen*	11
3.	The Association of Free Lutheran Congregations A Dream That Did Not Die *Robert Lloyd Lee*	27
4.	The Biblical Basis of Congregational Polity The Freedom of the Congregation *Francis Wesley Monseth*	53
5.	Freedom, Life, and the Local Congregation Georg Sverdrup's Theology of the Congregation *Martin L. Horn*	71
6.	The Pastor Servant of the Congregation *Bruce J. Dalager*	107
7.	The Laity Serving in the Congregation *Keith D. Quanbeck*	139
8.	The Annual Conference Next in Importance to the Local Congregation *Loiell O. Dyrud*	185

9. FREE AND LIVING CONGREGATIONS   215
   Writings of Rev. John Strand
      Selections from *The Lutheran Ambassador*

10. FREE AND LIVING CONGREGATIONS   237
    Writings of Rev. John Strand
       Excerpts from *AFLC Annual Conference Reports*

11. HISTORICAL DOCUMENTS OF THE AFLC   257
    Fundamental Principles   257
    Rules for Work   259
    Declaration of Faith   264
    A Statement on the Historical Situation   268

FOR FURTHER READING   283

FOREWORD

What began as a dream became a congregational way of life for thousands of Lutherans. For nearly seventy years, *free and living congregations* were not only our heritage but also the only kind of church structure and polity that we had lived under or experienced. But just as a human body needs nourishment and exercise to stay healthy and strong, so also does a church body or church fellowship. This is especially so if the church organization believes it is primarily a spiritual movement. The church fellowship needs encouragement (nourishment), and it must practice (exercise) what its beliefs and principles are. Because of a lack of one or both of these essentials for a strong and healthy body, this dream became weak and nearly died in the late 1950s to early 1960s.

However, God did what He has often done in times of discouragement and weakness; He raised up leaders, both clergy and laity, to keep this dream and spiritual movement alive. This book is dedicated to one of those leaders, *Rev. John P. Strand*. He was not only instrumental in helping to revive this weak, almost terminally ill movement, but he was one of the giants who provided leadership to this renewed and revived church which became the Association of Free Lutheran Congregations.

I first met John Strand when he served our congregation as a summer seminary intern in 1943. My father, the late Rev. Alfred Knutson, was serving the Grafton, North Dakota, Lutheran Free Church parish at that time. I was a young boy then, and since he often ate meals at our house, he was at times like a big brother to me that summer. More than once, when I failed to come in immediately for supper when my mother called, John would come out and bring me in, with his hand on my shirt collar, reminding me to listen to my mother. I saw him briefly several times over the next nineteen years, but it wasn't until the 1962 organizational meeting of what later became the AFLC that this old, almost forgotten acquaintance developed into a friendship that matured and deepened over the years. My respect and admiration for him grew as well.

John Strand was elected the first president of this new church fellowship, and he served in that position for sixteen years. Since I was elected as a member of one of the boards or committees that were created to oversee the ministries of this new church fellowship, I had the opportunity of working with him for thirteen of those sixteen years. As president, he was an ex-officio member of each board, and he was often at our meetings. He was quick to remind us that our board was to serve the congregation by helping them carry out those ministries they could do better with other like-minded congregations than they could do by themselves. Most of us, pastors and laity alike, had little experience in church-wide positions of responsibility, so we often struggled with writing rules and regulations and forming policies that would guide us in the years ahead. John Strand reminded our board, and I believe the other committees as well, that as boards we existed to serve the congregations; the congregations did not exist to serve the AFLC. I think he reminded us of that at every meeting, or maybe it just seemed that often!

He wasn't interested in our making good decisions as a board, he wanted us to make the *best* decisions. I recall one time when we had prayed over and discussed together for several months before we unanimously agreed as a board that a certain policy was the right thing to do. He asked if we were sure about this, and I replied that I thought it was a pretty good solution to a difficult problem. His comment was that he thought so too, but he wanted us to be sure we had reached the best possible solution. This part of his involvement in the early years of the AFLC is best known by former board members, but it was a valuable contribution to the beginning of the AFLC.

It was, however, as president of the AFLC that John Strand's leadership was most apparent to the congregations. It must be remembered that when the AFLC came into existence, most congregations felt that the freedom of the local congregations had not been a priority for a number of years and had been neglected to the point of being a forgotten part of our local congregational life. Many individuals and congregations had a real fear and mistrust of church leaders. So there was a need for them to be reassured that this new AFLC would give them back the freedom they felt they had pretty much lost.

It became obvious, almost immediately, that John Strand was their defender. He was passionately committed to the freedom of the local church. To individual congregations and in church-wide comments, he vigorously stated that the local congregation was the right form of the Kingdom of God on earth. In any dispute or disagreement, he bent over, more than backwards, for the rights of the congregations. In one of the early years of our AFLC, a local congregation was divided into different factions with the pastor right in the middle of the mess. It was obvious to any who were aware of the problem that all parties needed to share the blame. I asked John if he had given any advice to them. He said he had. I told him it didn't seem to have done much good; maybe he should give some more counsel, only make it stronger or firmer this time! He replied that the congregation would do what it wanted, that they would have to live with their decision, and that they had the right to be wrong. Yes, he knew congregations made mistakes, but he also knew that church leaders and church-wide boards made mistakes too. Since no one has perfect judgment, it was his firm belief that decisions that affected local congregations should be made by the congregation with a minimum of outside counsel or advice.

It is difficult to put into words, for those who didn't know John, just how fervently and passionately he believed in the freedom of the local congregation.

Some of you will remember an address that General MacArthur gave to the cadets at West Point shortly before his death in which he challenged them as future army officers to do their duty and to be faithful and loyal to themselves, to each other, and to their country. The last part of that speech closed with this line: *"my last conscious thoughts will be of the corps, and the corps, and the corps."* I am quite sure that John Strand's last thoughts were of his Savior and Lord and of his love for his family, but I know that from the time he was a young parish pastor until the last years of his retirement, his first and last word in any discussion or debate on church polity was *the congregation, the congregation, the congregation.* This love for and commitment to the local congregation was essential to the early growth and confidence our congregations had in this new AFLC. The churches knew that John Strand was their man.

But Pastor Strand didn't only desire for our congregations to be *free*, he longed even more for them to be *living*. To local congregations and in church-wide events, his sermons exhorted and challenged his listeners to live God-pleasing lives. Live for Christ by obeying Him and keeping His commandments. He did this not with a list of do's and don'ts but by asking us to serve Him out of gratitude and thankfulness for what God through Christ had done for us. Many pastors at ordinations and installations heard him tell them not to dwell on what *man must do* but rather on what *God has done*. There was never a hint of works-righteousness or legalism in his approach to holy living. God had done it all, and our love and faith and trust in Christ and His finished work on the cross should be the motivation for serving and following Him all the days of our lives. This is something the church needs to be constantly reminded of–keeping our eyes on Jesus, the author and perfecter of our faith. Looking at ourselves will only bring defeat and discouragement. John knew he was a sinner, with daily shortcomings, failures, and sins, but he kept his eyes on Jesus, found forgiveness there, and put his trust and confidence in Him. Let us ever remember that while *free* congregations are our heritage, it is of no eternal value unless we are *living* congregations as well.

It is my prayerful desire and hope that the readers of this book will come to better understand our heritage of free and living congregations. And while it may bring personal satisfaction to those of us who were part of the struggle if readers would come to appreciate the trials and difficulties that are part of our past, it is more important that this understanding of our past would create a desire to see this noble experiment in congregational life continue for future generations.

Robert Knutson *March 2002*
New Luther Valley Lutheran
McVille, North Dakota

FREE AND LIVING CONGREGATIONS
The Dream That Would Not Die

We believe in living congregations, where the Spirit of God does His gracious work of creating saving faith in the hearts of repentant sinners, and calling them to use their gifts for Christ.

We believe in free congregations, congregations that are free to serve their Lord as they are guided by the Spirit though the Word of God. The Word and Spirit are the only authority over them.

—John P. Strand

1

Free and Living Congregations

An Introduction

Craig S. Johnson

Georg Sverdrup came to the United States from Norway in 1874 with a vision of what a biblical congregation should be. That ideal was the impetus for the beginning of the Lutheran free church movement and continues to spark that movement today. Sverdrup believed a structure in which congregations were directly under the authority of the Word and Spirit of God and free from the control and domination of pastoral, synodical, or outside authority, would be the best environment for encouraging congregations to strive toward the biblical ideal. But what is the ideal?

The perfect congregation will never exist in this life, for each congregation is made up of sinful human beings. But this does not mean that we set our sights low or that we give up striving to be the congregation that God desires.

Sverdrup continually focused on what needed to be done in order to bring about the ideal congregation. Sverdrup "never claimed that it was an easy task . . . but he was convinced that it should be the main goal of Christian work."[1] The goal of the biblical New Testament congregation became a lifelong obsession with Sverdrup. "But Sverdrup, on the basis of his New Testament studies, caught a vision early in life of what the congregation was really meant to be. And so great and glorious was this vision to him that henceforth he could scarcely think or speak of anything else."[2]

Two adjectives dominated Sverdrup's description of the

ideal biblical congregation and his vision of what it could be: "free and living." But what does Sverdrup mean by these two terms? First, the *free congregation* is a congregation that is free from human authority, whether that authority is the state, the synod, or even the pastor or church council. Second, the free congregation is also a congregation that enjoys spiritual freedom, that is, freedom from worldliness and the power of sin. By a *living congregation*, Sverdrup means a congregation where true spiritual life predominates over sleepiness and worldliness. In a living congregation, those who are spiritually alive exercise their spiritual gifts in ministry both in and outside of the congregation.

At the time of the Protestant Reformation, the common people were not permitted to read and study the Word of God on their own. Only the scholarly and religious leaders could do so. Martin Luther saw the error and tragedy of keeping the Word from believers. He responded to the need by translating the Bible into German, a translation the common person could read and understand.

In a similar way, Georg Sverdrup saw that the local congregation needed to be in the Word and should be given every opportunity. A hierarchical authority is not required for the interpretation of Scripture nor is it the exclusive domain of the pastor. The local congregation can go to the Word itself.

Fundamental Principle 5 states, "The congregation directs its own affairs, subject to the authority of the Word and the Spirit of God, and acknowledges no other ecclesiastical authority or government above itself." The congregation is under the Word, not under some additional authority. The congregation is free to go to the Word for direction and wisdom.

A result of this freedom is a responsibility on the part of the congregation to be in the Scriptures. Believers are not to simply wait for others to study the Bible and give them an interpretation. The ideal congregation diligently studies the Word itself. It strives to be a people of the Word. It opens up the Bible, expecting God will speak and give direction.

What God has said in His Word determines the congregation's purpose and plans much more so than dictates from any human authority. The congregation respects what is said by others, but it respects the Bible the most.

A model of congregational behavior is presented in Acts 17:11: "Now these [the Bereans] were more noble-minded than those in Thessalonica, for they received the word with great eagerness, examining the Scriptures daily, to see whether these things were so" (NASB). The congregation is free and expected to examine the Scriptures on a regular basis to see what is true. According to Rev. John Strand:

> The only authority above the congregation is the Word and Spirit of God. If they do not recognize the authority of the Word and Spirit of God, they are not a congregation. Here, too, they are free to interpret the Scriptures, interpreting Scripture with Scripture, not being bound by the interpretations of others.[3]

The freedom of the local congregation to go directly to the Word of God may seem frightening to some. It may appear safer if a central authority does all the interpreting of the Word, and all the local congregations follow without questioning. Or it may seem best to have only the pastor and leaders interpret the Word, and the congregation must obey whatever they are told. The danger, however, that may come with freedom is not alleviated by more centralized authority. It is dealt with by greater confidence in the Spirit of God and through more time spent by all the members of the congregation in God's Word.

The Apostle Paul was used by God to plant numerous congregations. He remained in contact with the congregations, encouraging and instructing them, but the congregations were free. He left them on their own, knowing they were not really on their own. They had received the Word and the Spirit of God. That was sufficient. They did not need him.

Congregations should be encouraged to exercise their freedom, to go to the Word to find guidance, to depend on the Word for strength, and to test false teaching against Scripture. This applies to all congregations, no matter how old or young, large or small they may be.

> Or even if they are infants, infants can only be taught truly by exercising their infant faculties. Dependence does not train for independence, slavery does not educate men for freedom. Moreover, they have the Holy Ghost to strengthen and to guide them. Christians are not only what they are by nature, they are a Spirit-bearing body. It is not a question merely of our faith in them: it is still more a question of faith in the Holy Ghost. We look too much at our converts as they are by nature: St. Paul looked at his converts as they were by grace.[4]

So, too, we must look at our congregations in light of God's grace. Apart from grace, we would have no reason for confidence in how they may handle freedom. We would have no cause to treat them with honor. But we look at the congregations in light of what God has done. For Christ loved the Church and "gave Himself up for her; that He might sanctify her, having cleansed her by the washing of water with the word, that He might present to Himself the church in all her glory, having no spot or wrinkle or any such thing; but that she should be holy and blameless" (Ephesians 5:25-27).

The local congregation—even though it may be far from ideal, even though its faults at times seem glaring and its shortcomings frustrate and disappoint us—is still the bride of Christ. We are to be aware of how she falls short, but to also pray for eyes that see the work Christ is doing in and through her.

Seeing the congregation through eyes of grace should lead us to respect her. This involves respecting the decisions she makes. A local congregation may do something different from what an individual or another congregation feels is best. Other congregations can advise and offer counsel on the basis of experience, but they should be hesitant to condemn the other congregation's actions unless clear scriptural teaching exists.

Congregations are free to pursue God's unique calling for them. Each congregation is part of the body of Christ. God's specific plan and purpose for one congregation may be quite different from what it is for a sister congregation. A belief in the freedom of the congregation carries with it the understanding that not every congregation will look exactly the same or operate in the same exact manner, but each congregation should respect the other.

Each congregation has the privilege, the freedom, and the responsibility to seek out its calling from God through the Word and the Spirit.

Sverdrup believed the ideal congregation is not only free, but also living. The two are closely tied together. The freedom of the congregation is intended to encourage life. A free congregation, Sverdrup believed, has greater opportunity for spiritual life than one that is bound under human authority. On the other hand, problems result when a congregation has freedom but does not have life. A congregation that is not truly living may use its freedom to engage in all kinds of foolish and dangerous practices.

Human beings can, and often do, form organizations. People can write a constitution. They can elect officers. They can erect a building and have meetings. A living congregation, however, is not something mere mortals can bring into being. What Jesus said regarding an individual's spiritual life is true regarding congregations as well: "That which is born of the flesh is flesh; and that which is born of the Spirit is spirit" (John 3:6).

Free and living congregations are a spiritual movement. They begin with a moving of God's Spirit, and they are dependent on God's Spirit in order to continue on. Without God's Spirit, they are not living. They are nothing more than humanly constructed organizations.

Since the living congregation is birthed by the Spirit, it means the planting of a congregation comes about not simply because some individuals believe it would be a good thing for one to exist. The living congregation comes about because of God's leading. What is true of a family home is true of a congregation as well: "Unless the Lord builds the house, they labor in vain who build it" (Psalm 127:1).

A spiritually alive congregation "can never be achieved by setting up synodical machinery or adopting constitutions."[5] It can, however, become a reality by the work of the Spirit. Sverdrup "believed that if the Holy Spirit were given a chance, he both could and would bring the congregation to life."[6]

The Spirit brings the congregation to life and keeps the congregation alive. A free church is held together by the Spirit, not by the law.[7] The congregation is dependent upon the Spirit for preserving life. The ideal congregation works hard. The members organize well. They strive to learn and grow. But they always remember their need for the Spirit of God in order to remain a living, spiritual movement.

The Apostle Paul was inspired by God to ask the Galatians, "After beginning with the Spirit, are you now trying to attain your goal by human effort?" (Galatians 3:3, NIV). The same question must be asked of congregations. Do we think we can become free and living by human effort? That high goal cannot be achieved by the most brilliant minds, the most loyal dedication, or the greatest effort. It can happen only when the Spirit is working through God's people.

Recognizing the need for the Spirit's presence for life to be maintained led to *Fundamental Principle 4*, which states,

> Members of the organized congregation are not, in every instance believers, and such members often derive false hope from their external connection with the congregation. It is therefore the sacred obligation of the congregation to purify itself by the quickening preaching of the Word of God, by earnest admonition and exhortation, and by expelling the openly sinful and perverse.

In seeking life and purity, the congregation does not look to its structure. It relies on the preaching of the Word of God. As the Word is proclaimed and the sacraments are rightly administered, God works in the hearts of people. The living congregation knows the Word must continually be taught if life is to continue to exist and grow.

A congregation has life only if those who make up the congregation have life. The congregation can have a great heritage, associate with living congregations, maintain the rituals of the church, give the outward appearance of being a vibrant congregation—and yet be dead if the members of the congregation do not have life that comes from God.

This being the case, it is important for the congregation to encourage each of its members to use his or her spiritual gifts in God's service, to actively participate in reaching the world with the Gospel of Jesus Christ, and to daily live and grow in Him. Sverdrup believed that "if a genuinely free and living congregation were to come forth, then all members had to take up their calling."[8]

> Sverdrup thought a true congregation was a fellowship of working Christians who used the means and gifts of grace for the salvation and edification of themselves and humanity. In such a context there would be no attempts to restrict and control lay activities and other gifts of grace. The emphasis would rather be on allowing room and freedom for the full exercise of such gifts.[9]

The living congregation encourages its members to demonstrate and nurture the life Christ has created in their hearts by serving and bearing fruit for Him. A living congregation in some ways resembles a team where everyone is in the game and everyone is involved. It is like a symphony where each has an instrument and each has a part to play. It is not to be a performance where a few put on a show and the majority come to watch. The living congregation sees that the work of the congregation is "to prepare God's people for works of service, so that the body of Christ may be built up until we all reach unity in the faith and in the knowledge of the Son of God and become mature, attaining to the whole measure of the fullness of Christ" (Ephesians 4:12-13, NIV).

The living congregation knows God brought it into existence for a purpose. According to Sverdrup,

> The important thing is to bring as many as possible to salvation in Christ through sincere repentance and living faith. . . . The intention is not to turn the congrega-

tion into a mission field, but rather to make it an evangelizing force in the world, both at home and abroad.[10]

A congregation that is alive wants to see others alive as well. It has experienced the difference Jesus makes. It wants to demonstrate that difference so that others might know it for themselves. "Sverdrup more than once pointed out that the real sign of a living congregation is love for souls, an earnest desire that all the lost be saved."[11]

Georg Sverdrup came to America with a vision. He believed a congregation that was free to be in and under the Word of God could experience and share spiritual freedom with others. He longed to see congregations given life by God and wanted them to share that life with those who were dead in sin. He was convinced that by God's grace, a local congregation could be a powerful force for Christ in the world. He confidently believed, "According to the Word of God, the congregation is the right form of the Kingdom of God on earth" (*Fundamental Principle 1*). May that vision, that high view of the congregation, continue.

The following chapters will explore Sverdrup's high view of the congregation and how these concepts were established in the Lutheran Free Church in 1897 and have continued in the Association of Free Lutheran Congregations since 1962.

NOTES

[1] James S. Hamre, *Georg Sverdrup: Educator, Theologian, Churchman* (Northfield, Minnesota: The Norwegian-American Historical Association, 1986), 145.

[2] John Stensvaag, *Do You Really Want the Congregation? . . . Georg Sverdrup For Our Day* (Reprinted, Minneapolis: Ambassador Publications, 1987), 1.

[3] John P. Strand, "President's Message," *1965 Annual Report of the Association of Free Lutheran Congregations*, 9.

[4] Roland Allen, *Missionary Methods: St. Paul's or Ours?* (Grand Rapids, Michigan: 1962), 125.

[5] Stensvaag, *Do You Really Want the Congregation?* 6.

6 Stensvaag, *Do You Really Want the Congregation?* 5.

7 Hamre, *Georg Sverdrup*, 94.

8 Hamre, *Georg Sverdrup*, 154.

9 Hamre, *Georg Sverdrup*, 157-158.

10 Francis W. Monseth, *Georg Sverdrup: Champion of the Free Congregation* (Minneapolis, 1997), 29.

11 Stensvaag, *Do You Really Want the Congregation?* 4.

Christ came to establish God's kingdom. This kingdom was not only a spiritual reality in the heart, but it was also a new community, which He called a congregation. All the apostles and all the first Christians, driven by the Spirit, worked for this form of God's kingdom, the congregation. There is no other form of God's kingdom mentioned in the New Testament.

—John P. Strand

2

The Lutheran Free Church

A Brief History and Personal Recollections

Raynard O. J. Huglen

The roots of the Lutheran Free Church go back to tens of thousands of Norwegian immigrants who came to America in the last half of the nineteenth century. At first, most who came were single men, but there were some families with children also. Some came with a sense of need for spiritual things and quite early made an effort to arrange for Christian services to be held, congregations to be formed, a church building erected, and the calling of a permanent pastor in their settlements. The kind of congregation established and the pastoral service secured usually depended on what the majority were used to in the old country and what they felt was right to transplant in the new land.

Norway had a state church system (and still does) in which the government had control over church affairs such as erecting buildings, paying the salaries of pastors, and choosing the bishops. Some immigrants wanted to continue a hierarchical system in America, even though the United States government could not be involved, as had been the case in Norway. The Constitution of the United States forbade it.

Others who came to take up life in the new world sought to develop a different idea. They foresaw a new opportunity now, since the church was no longer under government control. This allowed for self-government in the churches, albeit under the Word of God and the Holy Spirit. This, it seemed to them, was more in agreement with the Early Church pattern of the New Testament.

For the purpose of a brief history of the Lutheran Free Church, two closely aligned figures stand out as proponents of a "free church." They are Georg Sverdrup and Sven Oftedal, who were professors of theology. They were not alone in this vision of a free church among Norwegian-Americans. Another who held it was Elling Eielsen, and other men who built up the Hauge's Synod as well as church groups which pre-dated the LFC or existed at the same time.

Sverdrup, Oftedal, and others also had a vision for "living congregations." By this they meant congregations in which members had a personal relationship with Jesus Christ, a conscious, living faith which influenced daily life and compelled them to reach out to those who didn't have that.

Histories of the Lutheran Free Church and biographies of Sverdrup include something of the influences in Norway which helped to mold the spiritual movement which found form in America. Dr. Melvin Helland writes of "The Norwegian Matrix,"[1] that is, that from which something originates. Dr. Eugene L. Fevold uses the expression "Roots in Norway"[2] to tell of the factors which motivated Sverdrup, Oftedal, and others to work for a Lutheran free church in the United States.

These writers tell of the spiritual revival which took place through the gifted, consecrated lay preacher, Hans Nielsen Hauge (1771-1824). In 1796, at home on the farm in southeastern Norway, Hauge had an experience akin to that of John Wesley in London, who felt his heart "strangely warmed." Following that, he felt called to speak first to his family and then at house meetings to those who would listen. This humble man traveled much of Norway, largely in an eight-year period, and through the power of the Holy Spirit alone, was the human means of bringing great spiritual awakening to a land where the church was beset by the deadness of rationalism. Clergy and other church officials, although not all, laid roadblocks for Hauge. The Conventicle Act of 1741 forbade lay preaching and declared that all religious public gatherings should be under the direction of a parish pastor. Hauge was accused of violating this law even though he tried to observe it as much as possible, but he also felt compelled under the higher call he felt God had placed upon him.

A second influence in Norway affecting Sverdrup and others was the Johnsonian awakening, so called because the theological professor Gisle Johnson (1822-1894) was the prime figure in it. And it should be noted that in some respects he was a contemporary of Sverdrup, who was born in 1848. In fact, Sverdrup studied under Johnson.

Dr. James Hamre, who wrote a biography of Sverdrup, says that the Johnsonian awakening fostered an awakening among the clergy "that helped to reconcile them to some degree with the Haugean movement."[3] The Johnsonian revival, as had the Haugean, produced a great increase in pious living as new Christians sought to avoid even the appearance of worldliness.

Sverdrup did, however, regard Gisle Johnson as being weak in the matter of lay activity, particularly lay preaching. According to Professor Andreas Helland, who studied under Sverdrup, Johnson understood that every true Christian is to be a witness of Jesus, but he was not certain if the Fourteenth Article of the Augsburg Confession permitted lay preaching.[4]

Of the influences in Norway that helped to shape the Lutheran Free Church in America, there remains yet a third, and that was mentioned earlier. That was the state church milieu or environment which existed in the old country. It had existed since the coming of Christianity to Norway in the eleventh century and continued under the Protestant Reformation, which introduced the Lutheran church. Not only was the state church hierarchical, but also the clergy was elevated socially above the ordinary people.

Some Norwegians were restless with this situation, among them Sverdrup and Oftedal. They had become acquainted with one another in Norway and shared ideas. They wished and worked for reform, for a greater independence for the local congregations. No wonder, too, that they looked favorably upon the call which invited them to come to America to work in a society where the opportunity of a "free church" existed to a greater degree.

In 1873, Oftedal came to the fledgling Augsburg Seminary, which had been founded in 1869 in Marshall, Wisconsin, and then later transplanted to Minneapolis, Minnesota, in 1872. Sverdrup followed in 1874, and thus ensued 33 years of close comradeship between these two professors who were opposites in some ways but complemented each other to a remarkable degree.

Without attempting to write a history of Augsburg Seminary, suffice it to say that this school became the vehicle through which Sverdrup and Oftedal were able to advance their idea of theological education and what a congregation ought to be, free and living. This they did, first through the Norwegian-Danish Conference (until 1890), the United Church (until 1893), the Friends of Augsburg (until 1897), and the Lutheran Free Church (from 1897 and on). Augsburg's motto was "The Word Became Flesh." In an 1877 report to the annual convention, Sverdrup explained the significance of this motto:

> The motto of the school–"the Word became flesh"–he stated, reflected the conviction . . . that what would truly gather the Norwegian people together was . . . the preaching of God's Word in its truth and purity in the language of the people.[5]

Sverdrup's concept of theological education was that it be "a training of pastors that is in harmony with the Christian congregation, that corresponds to its nature and spirit, and that answers to its needs."[6] The Norwegian term is *menighetsmaessig presteudannelse* and means "a ministerial education in conformity with the origin, nature, and goals of the free and living congregation in America. Such an education would produce a pastor who truly understood the free church and who would work for its well-being."[7] Around the turn of the twentieth century, the Augsburg Seminary catalog included the following statement on how Lutheran Free Church pastors were to be trained:

> Spiritual life and Christian character are considered of infinitely higher importance than mere knowledge. No amount of reading, no memorizing of facts, no mental or intellectual ability are of any real value to the Christian

minister without personal experience of saving grace and firm and manly conviction of the truth as it is in Jesus.[8]

To that end, Augsburg would provide a well-rounded education, including instruction in various languages, but the Scriptures were to be central in all that was done.

Augsburg Seminary's program and ideals led to the founding of the Lutheran Free Church in 1897 after several years of support by a loyal group of adherents called the Friends of Augsburg. The rupture with the United Church was complete. Augsburg would be both an instrument of the affiliated congregations and their heartbeat henceforth, always with the goal of building up free and living congregations.

The Freedom of the Congregation

Generally understood to be the guiding spirit behind the *Fundamental Principles* of the Lutheran Free Church (and later of the Association of Free Lutheran Congregations), Sverdrup set forth his basic assumption in the very first principle: "According to the Word of God, the congregation (local church) is the right form of the kingdom of God on earth."[9]

In his discussion of this principle, Sverdrup wrote, "Next to the question of the individual soul's salvation there is no more momentous question than that of the congregation."[10] And as to the independence of the local congregation, he explains:

> We mean that in the New Testament there isn't any other talk about any bishopric over or in more than one congregation, or anything about any papacy, or anything about any department of ecclesiastical affairs or anything about any church rule or council or synod. There is one congregation at each place where there are Christians and that congregation has its elders or bishops, but there is no "church rule" over others of any nature.[11]

Notice that he speaks of human authority.

Pastor Clarence J. Carlsen, author of *The Years of Our Church*, explains: "This does not mean that our congregations recognize no law whatsoever and reject all authority. They are bound by the authority of the Scriptures and the Spirit of God. These constitute the highest authority of all."[12]

Sverdrup was careful to spell out the limitations placed upon conferences, committees, and officers in a Lutheran free church. They cannot "impose any obligations or restrictions, exert any compulsion, or lay any burden upon the individual congregation, but have the right only of making recommendations to, and requests of, congregations and individuals" (*Fundamental Principle 11*). In explanation, Sverdrup wrote, "Free cooperative work without coercion is the churchly and Christian way. Without doubt, it is also this which leads to the best results."[13]

To sum up, Sverdrup and Oftedal always stressed that the church body is only a human instrument while the congregation is of divine origin.

Throughout its history, to 1963, the Lutheran Free Church lived under this church polity. Her *Rules for Work* document, with few changes, is being used by the Association of Free Lutheran Congregations. The *Rules* endorse a minimum of organization and an Annual Conference short on technicalities.

In the last years of her life, the Lutheran Free Church adopted delegate representation for her Annual Conferences, the makeup of which was determined according to congregational size. In legal action after the formation of the Association of Free Lutheran Congregations, the court seemed to see this delegate system as a sign that the Lutheran Free Church had become more a synod than an association of congregations. The point is arguable in light of the *Fundamental Principles* (note *Principles 5, 10,* and *11*), which were established to protect the freedom of the congregation.

Living Congregations

While Sverdrup was indeed concerned about sound theology, it cannot be denied that he feared a dead orthodoxy, that is, where there is an emphasis on correct doctrine but which lacks a living fellowship with Jesus and a sense of the "joy of the Lord."

In that connection, it can be pointed out that Sverdrup did not believe that a congregation is necessarily "pure," that is, that it is made up only of truly believing persons. Indeed, he believed that if a man is moved by the Spirit to seek membership, he should be received, even if he is not yet at peace with God.

He also noted that members may have grown lukewarm in the faith or have fallen away from the Lord. Such people need to be called back to repentance and restoration. *Fundamental Principle 4* calls for "quickening preaching of the Word" in order that purification may take place. Such preaching rightly divides the Word of truth, presenting the Law to awaken conviction of sin in the heart and the Gospel to declare God's love in Christ and to extend the invitation to receive forgiveness. Quickening preaching is preaching under the guidance of the Holy Spirit to meet individual hearers, members or otherwise, according to their needs.

Sverdrup was strong in emphasizing that believers are saved in order to be useful. In writing about *Principles 5* and *6,* he summarized this way:

> Consequently, this is the right form of the congregation in the world: a people of believing, praying and *working* persons, who receive all they need from the Lord for *their tasks*, the faith and life and gifts, and who therefore acknowledge this wholly and fully, that they belong to the Lord with all that they are, and all that they have, so that they are all the Lord's *servants*, men and women, created by Him unto *all good works*[14] (emphases mine).

The Lutheran Free Church throughout her history maintained an emphasis on the need for self-examination on the part of church members in accordance with the admonition of St. Paul: "Examine yourselves, to see whether you are holding to your faith" (II Corinthians 13:5, RSV). The church occupied a middle position between the two "eternal securities." On the one hand, there was that of some Reformed theology which held that once a sinner was saved he could never really be lost again. On the other hand, there was the belief among not a few Lutherans and others who practice infant baptism that once a child was baptized, the chances of that person falling out of fellowship with Christ were almost too slight to be mentioned. There was, for all practical purposes, an eternal security.

Between those two positions, the Lutheran Free Church held to the conviction that all members and nonmembers alike who attended preaching services should be challenged concerning their relationship to the Lord–baptized or not.

This concern is shown in the articles in the book of family devotions, *Light and Life*, by pastors and lay people of the Lutheran Free Church, published in 1944. Again and again appeals such as these occur: "Have you this gift of peace?"[15]; "The Lord wants to save you. He stands before you and asks, 'Do you want to be saved?'"[16]; "But today He is standing outside your heart's door knocking and asking you to let Him in."[17]; and "Will you come now, as a sinner, as an unrighteous person, confessing your sins unto Him?"[18]

Clarence J. Carlsen wrote:

> The Lutheran Free Church has never accepted the viewpoint that the membership of a congregation necessarily consists of true Christians only. It has rather proceeded on the premise that unbelievers and hypocrites may have been accepted into the congregation and that there may be members who once were true believers but who have fallen away from God. For this reason, as well as in order to win the outsider, evangelistic meetings and evangelistic preaching are stressed in Lutheran Free Church congregations.[19]

Among evangelists greatly used by God in the earlier days to awaken and revive were O. M. Anderson, a layman, and Rev. Peter Nilsen. In the mid-years of the church, Rev. Jens

Halvorson can be mentioned. There were others, including parish pastors and lay preachers, who had the gift of calling people to repentance and faith.

We also need to speak of the spiritual work among the young people of the church. Luther League Federation conventions and Bible camps were effective, through the Holy Spirit, in calling youth to greater consecration to Jesus Christ and, in some cases, to call them back to the faith, if there had been a falling away.

Conclusion

In under sixty-six years of existence, or under seventy if the years of the Friends of Augsburg are counted, the Lutheran Free Church attempted "to build an effective and orderly Christian fellowship with a minimum of human organization"[20] and to be "a searching test of faith in the power and Spirit of God."[21]

As a rather small church body (membership reached 90,000 baptized and the number of congregations over 330), the Lutheran Free Church operated under a relatively united spirit of agreement. With some exaggeration, to be sure, everyone knew everyone else. The congregations took pride in Augsburg College and Seminary in Minneapolis and Oak Grove High School in Fargo (North Dakota), world and home missions, as well as other aspects of Christian work such as Deaconess Hospital, Minneapolis. A publishing company and a retail bookstore were also maintained.

Through the years, there were some who spoke out in favor of uniting with other Lutherans to form larger organizations. These efforts did not come to anything until the 1951 Annual Conference at Bethany Lutheran in Seattle, Washington, when it was first brought up, and the leadership in the Lutheran Free Church began to take a generally favorable attitude toward the issue. The chief argument was that a larger body had much to offer the Lutheran Free Church, and the latter could add its leaven to the whole.

Three referenda were held. The last one, under different guidelines from the first two, was successful, and the Lutheran

Free Church merged with the American Lutheran Church in February 1963.

The Association of Free Lutheran Congregations was begun by Lutheran Free Church members who held a minority opinion and who saw in their action a better possibility of perpetuating the ideals of Sverdrup, Oftedal, and others for free and living Lutheran congregations.

Personal Recollections in the Lutheran Free Church

As someone born into the Lutheran Free Church and who served almost ten years as a pastor in that church before the merger of 1963, I have been asked to write down some personal memories and impressions. Let the reader keep that in mind in what follows.

When one grows up in an organization, one often just accepts the fact and does not ask any questions. My father (R. J. Huglen) was a pastor in the LFC. An immigrant from Norway, he became identified with the LFC in the early 1900s while on the West Coast, eventually being ordained in Wisconsin in 1915. When he passed away at a relatively young age, the church president wrote of him, "He was a man with a clear vision and deep understanding of the Guiding Principles of the Lutheran Free Church." Another pastor wrote, "He loved and was loyal to the Lutheran Free Church."

Mother was born at the time of the Augsburg controversy and into a congregation which soon identified itself with the Friends of Augsburg and the LFC.

From early childhood, although I did not speak Norwegian, I became acquainted with two Norwegian words pertaining to the church. One was *"aarsmote,"* the other *"aarsberetning."* Dad would be going to the *"aarsmote,"* the Annual Conference, in June. It was very important to him, and he missed only one when he made a trip back to Norway in 1921. *"Aarsberetning"* was the annual report of the LFC and was a much-valued book of information about what was going on in the church fellowship.

Then, of course, there were the church papers: *Folkebladet*, the Norwegian-language publication, and *The Lutheran Messenger*, in English. For the Sunday schools, there was *The Child's Friend*. These were honored parts of the reading material in our home.

My first annual conference was in Thief River Falls, Minnesota, in 1938. I was too young (ten years old) to really comprehend what it all meant, but I have three remembrances. One day I sat in the balcony of Trinity Lutheran, a borrowed Norwegian Lutheran church (ELC), and heard part of a business session. (Trinity was used because there was no LFC church in the area large enough to hold an annual conference.) I have no recollection what the topic under consideration was, but I know my dad took part in the discussion. Second, perhaps the same day, I was outside on the sidewalk on the north side of the church. The LFC president, Dr. T. O. Burntvedt, a classmate friend of Dad, gave me a playful "kick in the pants." Third, I remember the ordination service was held in the city auditorium on Sunday afternoon. Dad was one of the pastors taking part in the service and laid his hand on the head of A. L. Hokonson, who would later be a pastor in the AFLC.

By my confirmation time, Dad had already been with the Lord for several years and couldn't give the counsel and guidance a father would want to give a young son. But I had not only my wise and good mother but also a pastor who drew out my Christian faith and encouraged me to give expression to it publicly. Through Sunday school, weekly prayer meetings (they were called that rather than Bible studies in those days), and periodic evangelistic series, as well as evangelical Sunday preaching week by week, others and I were challenged to walk with the Lord, or if we were not in fellowship with Him, to return to Him. Had I had greater knowledge then, I would have known that this was typical of LFC congregations.

When I graduated from public high school, it was taken for granted that I would attend Augsburg College, our church school, which my father, a great uncle, one of my sisters, as well as other relatives had attended. This came about even though financially it wasn't an easy matter, even in those years.

In a sense, Augsburg was all that I could have hoped for. In another sense, it wasn't. I found that not all students were spiritually motivated, as I understood the term. Some didn't reveal any interest in the spiritual program at the school. And there were all variations of experience. It was just after World War II, and there was a large influx of men present to take advantage of the GI Bill. Some were twice my age.

But a warm Christ-centered fellowship was there for those who wanted that and for all who could be encouraged to become a part of that. And so there were, in the boys' dormitory, for instance, house devotions three nights a week and an all-dormitory devotion on Thursday nights. On Monday evening after supper, there was an all-school prayer meeting in the chapel. Thursday nights there was a midweek service in the chapel with a guest speaker or a talk by one of the students. Every school day morning there was a twenty-minute chapel service led by the college president, with a talk by a faculty member, student, or visiting guest from the Twin Cities or beyond.

In both the school semesters each year, there was a Spiritual Emphasis Week with a speaker from outside the school. In addition to LFC pastors, in my time we also heard such men as George Aus of Luther Seminary, Conrad Thompson, A. W. Knock, and C. M. Hanson. Some of us prepared a good deal in prayer for these meetings by gathering at 6:30 in the morning and then a half-hour before the evening services. These were times of renewal, and we prayed for openness to consider God's claim on our lives.

There was a Luther League and Mission Society on campus. Both these groups put on programs in city churches and places further out upon invitation. Courses in religion were required in the freshmen and sophomore years.

In 1947, Augsburg College employed a campus pastor for the first time. At least at first it was a half-time position, the other half involving teaching in the religion department.

My second Annual Conference was in Minneapolis in June 1950. I was attending a summer session at the University of Minnesota and could attend only the evening and Sunday services of the conference. At the Saturday night service at Trinity

Lutheran, I heard Pastor John Strand preach. He was already known as a strong preacher. Pastor Fritjof Monseth led the service. These were two men I would later come to know well and who played such an important part in forming the AFLC.

Following graduation in 1950, I entered Augsburg Seminary, located on the same campus, to prepare for ministry in our church. This was in response to a call from the Lord which I had felt for a long time. Besides the three years of class work, there were two summers of internship, one in a four-point Minnesota parish and the other in a single Iowa church.

My ordination took place in 1953 at Trinity Lutheran, Ninth Street and Twentieth Avenue South, Minneapolis, the "mother church" of the LFC. We were eleven men ordained that day, nine of us from Augsburg and two from the church in Canada. It was a special, sacred day. The church president, Dr. Burntvedt, was the ordainer. We men had presented ourselves to serve the Lord Jesus and our church.

I served two multiple parishes in the LFC in Montana and South Dakota. No great claims can be made, but I sought to conduct ministry as I had been taught and had seen it practiced by my father, in my home church at Newfolden, Minnesota, and on internship. Fellow district pastors were an encouragement, and we enjoyed working together in Bible camp and Luther League ministries on a district level. National or regional youth conventions were a highlight of the year.

It was the custom each fall for the president of the LFC or the stewardship secretary to visit each district for a stewardship session on a particular day. One-half of the day was a Women's Missionary Federation meeting with a special guest, perhaps the president of that organization or the executive secretary.

I would have enjoyed spending a lifetime working in the church body into which I was born and where I was raised and educated. But early in my ministry there was an effort to move the LFC toward union or merger. One argument was that the LFC had much to offer the larger fellowship. Others of us contended that we were too small to make much impact and would instead be influenced in ways that were contrary to our heritage.

Over a period of years, the debate went on, often in a spirit of good will, but sometimes not. I have a great admiration for those who dared speak up in annual conferences to express their concerns. The majority at last prevailed, and a merger with the American Lutheran Church was consummated. Those of us in the minority decided to continue a fellowship as close as possible to what we had known.

The rest, as we say, is history. I have always had great love and affection for those who stood together and dared to walk the "old paths."

NOTES

[1] Melvin Helland, trans. *The Heritage of Faith: Selections from the Writings of Georg Sverdrup* (Minneapolis: Augsburg Publishing House, 1969), 9.

[2] Eugene L. Fevold, *The Lutheran Free Church: A Fellowship of American Lutheran Congregations, 1897-1963* (Minneapolis: Augsburg Publishing House, 1969), 3.

[3] James S. Hamre, *Georg Sverdrup: Educator, Theologian, Churchman* (Northfield, Minnesota: The Norwegian-American Historical Association, 1986), 16.

[4] Andreas Helland, *Georg Sverdrup: The Man and His Message 1848-1907* (Minneapolis: The Messenger Press, 1947), 32.

[5] James S. Hamre, "Georg Sverdrup and the Augsburg Plan of Education," in Norwegian-American Studies 26 (Northfield, Minnesota: The Norwegian-American Historical Association, 1974), 171.

[6] Andreas Helland, *Georg Sverdrup*, 154.

[7] Hamre, *Georg Sverdrup*, 117.

[8] Hamre, *Georg Sverdrup*, 120.

[9] The wording of *Fundamental Principle 1* in this chapter is the wording originally used in the LFC. The wording of *Fundamental Principles* used by the AFLC have been changed slightly. The wording for the *Fundamental Principles* in succeeding chapters will be the wording used by the AFLC unless otherwise noted.

[10] Georg Sverdrup, "The Congregation," *Professor Georg Sverdrups Samlede skrifter i udvalg*, ed. Andreas Helland; trans. John Horn (Minneapolis, 1909-1912), 3:266.

[11] Georg Sverdrup, "The Congregation," *Samlede skrifter*, trans. John Horn, 3:266-267.

[12] Clarence J. Carlsen, *The Years of Our Church* (Minneapolis: The Lutheran Free Church Publishing Company, 1942), 46.

[13] Georg Sverdrup, "Domination by the Church Body or Free Cooperation," *Samlede skrifter*, trans. John Horn, 3:289.

[14] Georg Sverdrup, "Congregational Self-Government and the Use of the Gifts of Grace," *Samlede skrifter*, trans. John Horn, 3:283-284.

[15] Fritjof B. Monseth in *Light and Life: A Book of Family Devotions*, ed. T. O. Burntvedt and Sverre Torgerson (Minneapolis: The Lutheran Free Church Publishing Company, 1944), February 27.

[16] Editors, *Light and Life*, April 2.

[17] Robert Krueger in *Light and Life*, November 18.

[18] John Hjelmeland in *Light and Life*, April 5.

[19] Carlsen, *The Years of Our Church*, 45.

[20] Bernard M. Christensen, "What Is the Lutheran Free Church?" *The Lutheran Messenger* 24, no. 12 (April 10, 1941): 5.

[21] Christensen, "What Is the Lutheran Free Church?" 5.

It was a fearful and bewildered group that gathered in Thief River Falls, Minnesota, in October 1962. They had some convictions, but little experience, and were empty handed. Fearful of merger developments taking place, they determined to proceed to build a fellowship of free congregations. Was history to show them to be fools, or would they know some measure of success under God's blessing? No one knew with any great degree of certainty. With simple faith in God, the decision to organize the Association was made. The results bear witness that this decision was under God's grace and blessing, and according to His Will.

—John P. Strand

3

The Association of Free Lutheran Congregations

A Dream That Did Not Die

Robert Lloyd Lee

A dream was born over one hundred years ago in the hearts of some Lutherans who had recently arrived in America. Frustrated by rigid traditions of authoritarian church government in their northern European homeland, yet encouraged by a powerful surge of spiritual awakening, they dreamed of a fellowship of free and living congregations under the authority of the Word and the Spirit of God. They sincerely believed that the New World offered the opportunity for a new beginning, a rebirth of New Testament Christianity. Augsburg Seminary in Minneapolis, Minnesota, was a center for this movement, and Professor Georg Sverdrup, who put the dream into words, wrote: "Is it really wrong, then, when the days are evil and the night is approaching, to lift up our eyes and mind from the confused and dwarfed present, and to turn to the true, real picture of the congregation which the New Testament gives us?"[1]

Thus the Lutheran Free Church was established, "an experiment in extreme ecclesiastical democracy and decentralization,"[2] because these pioneers were convinced that dreams can come true. It was not a synod, nor even a denomination in the strictest sense of the word, but a spiritual movement with a brief list of rules for work and twelve guiding principles, the first of which declared: "According to the Word of God, the congregation is the right form of the Kingdom of God on earth."[3] The goal of this faith venture was to accomplish together what congregations cannot do best alone, including training pastors, promoting home and world missions, publishing Christian literature, and supporting children's homes and other works of mercy. Choosing not to become an incorporated church body, the LFC instead incorporated each of its common endeavors separately in order to guarantee their independence.

The new church fellowship grew in membership and ministries during the decades that followed, but the dream of the founders grew dim. A recent study suggests that this development is common to all denominations, using the term "historical drift" to describe the inherent tendency of human organizations to depart from their original vision over a period of years.[4]

"Despite its disavowal of the synodical type of polity, the LFC more and more functioned like other Lutheran church bodies," declared Eugene Fevold in his authorized history of the church body.[5] A major departure from the original vision of a spiritual movement occurred in 1959-60 when a delegate system for the annual conferences was approved. A new generation had emerged who had never experienced the struggles of their forefathers to build a fellowship of free and living congregations. The Lutheran Free Church had become in the minds of many of its members simply one of several smaller Lutheran synods within American Lutheranism, though somewhat differently organized, instead of a spiritual movement with a unique mission. The conviction grew stronger that the LFC's destiny could best be fulfilled in a union . . . really a reunion . . . with other Lutherans.

Many LFC members welcomed the movement toward a merger of Lutherans in America after World War II, and there were official representatives involved in the negotiations that resulted in the formation of The American Lutheran Church (TALC) in 1960 by the Evangelical Lutheran Church, the American Lutheran Church, and the United Evangelical Lutheran Church. The Lutheran Free Church was prevented from participating in the organization of this new church body, however, since church-wide congregational votes in 1955 and 1957 rejected the proposed union, even after a vigorous promotion by the church leadership. In spite of the two failed attempts, it still seemed that a majority of the congregations favored merger, and a final referendum in 1961 narrowly approved the resolution. The union agreement was confirmed by the 1962 Annual Conference, meeting in historic Trinity Lutheran Church, Minneapolis, where the LFC was born.

A chart of the three referendums reveals some interesting comparisons and conclusions:

	First Referendum	Second Referendum	Third Referendum
Total Vote	11,992	13,442	17,585
Total "Yes" Vote	7,926	8,258	10,756
% of Total Vote	66.1	61.4	61.2
Total "No" Vote	4,066	5,183	6,827
% of Total Vote	33.9	38.6	38.8
Congregations	327	337	329
Voting "Yes"	210	190	201
% Voting "Yes"	64.2	56.4	61.1
Voting "No"	117	147	128
% Voting "No"	35.8	43.6	38.9

First of all, in each of the votes, only a small minority of the eligible membership participated. There were 56,552 confirmed members listed in the 1961 Annual Report of the Lutheran Free Church, for example, and only 17,585 voted in the final referendum. Secondly, it is important to note that the first referendum followed a one-vote-per-congregation rule, and required a 75 percent vote for approval. When merger negotiations were reopened for a second referendum, the annual conference approved two strategic changes in procedure, lowering the requirement for passage to a two-thirds majority and tabulating the votes of each congregation by confirmed membership. The reason for this change was the fear that a number of smaller congregations would have the power to defeat the merger resolution.[6]

The final referendum was held in the fall of 1961. According to the new method of calculation that allocated to each congregation one to ten votes according its membership, there were only 1218 votes cast, 845 for the proposed union and 373 opposed. Thus the final merger referendum was approved by a vote of 69.4 percent, instead of the 61.1 percent vote indicated in the chart above, which would have been the result if the original procedure had been followed. It should also be observed from the chart that the popular vote for merger in the last referendum was the lowest percentage of all three. Thus, it might be said that, instead of a few smaller congregations blocking the merger, a few larger ones were responsible for its passage, in spite of the lower percentage of the total vote that was cast in favor of it.

Anecdotal evidence suggests that dubious tactics may have been used in some instances to advance the merger agenda. Stories are told of pastors who previously proclaimed their opposition to the proposed union accepting calls to parishes that had voted against it and then proceeding to vigorously promote the merger because their minds had changed. There were rumors of strong pressure directed against one prominent anti-merger pastor by church officials, who allegedly said that they would hold him personally responsible if the referendum failed.

Other questionable strategies can be documented. In numerous instances, the merger vote was scheduled for a meeting after the Sunday worship service, often for the first time in a congregation's history, a procedure protested by those who believed that this would swell the numbers of voters who simply followed the pastor's leading without studying the issues. One pro-merger pastor resurrected an old constitution that had never been translated from Norwegian nor amended, and on the basis of it denied the right of voting to all the women. Another discovered that one of the congregations in his parish had an old constitution that did not specify a voting age, so he invited the youth group to the meeting and encouraged them to vote. When one North Dakota congregation discussed the issue before the vote, the merger opponents were granted five minutes each to express their concerns, while the pro-merger pastor received an unlimited amount of time to rebut them. This writer visited with a non-LFC pastor who served as an agent for two TALC district presidents by receiving interim assignments near communities where there was merger conflict, and he boasted of his involvement in the division of two congregations. While it would be unfair to suggest that there were not occasions when the sinful nature of the merger opponents prevailed, the above tactics employed by even well-meaning merger proponents would be difficult to defend.

Regardless of the tactics or differences in tabulation, however, it seemed clear that a majority of LFC congregations looked forward to a future as part of a new church organization. This was a significant shift from the past. In 1949, the LFC had officially rejected church union overtures, and in the fall of 1954, Dr. B. M. Christensen, president of Augsburg, attended several district meetings and reported in *The Lutheran Messenger* that he encountered considerable opposition to merger, especially among the middle-aged and older lay people in the numerous smaller congregations.[7] Thus the passage of the last referendum represented not only a change of heart among the laity and clergy of the LFC, but a momentous victory for church leaders such as presidents T. O. Burntvedt and John Stensvaag, as well as Dr. Christensen, who all had so actively promoted merger.

Not everyone in the Lutheran Free Church was persuaded by the message of the merger proponents. There was still a remnant for whom the dream of their forefathers was a living reality, and they shared grave concerns about the possible consequences of the proposed union. One of the concerns was polity. Those who favored the continuation of the Lutheran Free Church feared a loss of congregational freedom in the new church body and discerned a growing high-church ecclesiasticism within Lutheranism as a whole. "The priestly element is gaining and the prophetic element is waning,"[8] warned a prominent LFC pastor, who also expressed the widespread concern that congregations in the merged church would be pressured toward uniformity in liturgical practice with the emphasis on a highly formal worship service.

A second concern was piety. The Lutheran Free Church had a heritage of revival, rooted in seasons of spiritual awakening that swept through Lutherans in Germany and Scandinavia, often identified with the movement called *Pietism*. This evangelical emphasis stressed experienced salvation and a personal faith in Christ, expressed in consecrated service and a lifelong struggle against all sin and worldliness. Christianity means that there is a life to be lived, proclaimed the pietists, and there was special concern over such issues as a growing tolerance for social drinking and the acceptance of dancing on the Lutheran college campuses. Also, while the saving grace of God's work in baptism was always clearly affirmed, there was a fear among the opponents of merger that a sacramentalist spirit which seemed to teach eternal security by virtue of infant baptism would surely undermine a cherished LFC *Fundamental Principle*:

> Members of the organized congregation are not, in every instance, believers, and such members [in the original document, the word *hypocrites* was used instead of *members*] often derive a false hope from their external connections with the congregation. It is therefore the sacred obligation of the congregation to purify itself by the quickening preaching of the Word, by earnest admonition and exhortation, and by expelling the openly sinful and perverse.[9]

The third area of concern was theology. The American Lutheran Church was a member of the World Council of Churches (WCC), which represented a liberal ecumenism that was alarming to many within the LFC. Fears were expressed that Communism, promoting an anti-American bias within the organization, controlled some of the WCC member churches. There was a growing awareness, too, that a new approach to the Bible (which some labeled *neo-orthodoxy*) had gained a foothold in the Lutheran colleges and seminaries, questioning the literal interpretation of scriptural events such as the Genesis account of creation as well as some of the miracles. Some advocates of this new scholarship taught that the Bible was not the Word of God but that it contained the Word of God, a clear challenge to the doctrine of inerrancy and infallibility on a theological level and a confusing message to those in the pews who seemed to be hearing that their Sunday School and confirmation instruction was incorrect. There was a growing fear that the faith of students was being undermined instead of strengthened at Augsburg, the birthplace of the Lutheran Free Church, and this was accompanied by a growing sense of betrayal.

Church leaders denied that there were any substantive changes, but E. Clifford Nelson, an authority on American Lutheranism, verifies the concern. The LFC participated in the formation of the American Lutheran Conference in 1930, a conservative cooperative organization of Lutheran denominations that positioned itself theologically between the more liberal United Lutheran Church and the conservative but separatistic Missouri Synod. The conference produced a doctrinal statement called the Minneapolis Theses, which clearly expressed a commitment to the inerrancy and infallibility of Scripture. In his discussion of the developments that led to the formation of The ALC, Nelson refers to the *old Lutherans* who still affirmed the conservative doctrine of inspiration as stated in the Minneapolis Theses and the *neo-Lutherans* who had abandoned it. He concludes:

> By 1956, when the proposed constitution of the new American Lutheran Church was voted on by the Evangelical Lutheran Church, several if not most of its professors of theology were teaching a view of Scripture at variance with the statement on the Bible in the new constitution. That is, while church administrators sought to uphold "old Lutheranism," many college and seminary professors were teaching "neo-Lutheranism."[10]

Carl Chrislock, author of a history of Augsburg College, refers to a shift in emphasis within the religion department that began during the late 1950s:

> Entering freshmen discovered a striking difference between "Basic Bible" at Augsburg and their Sunday School classes at home–frequently the latter had implicitly if not explicitly accepted the Scriptures as "infallible" and "inerrant" both in a scientific and historical sense, while the former proceeded on the assumption that the Bible was, among other things, a human document with a history of its own. . . . Subsequent courses in the religion curriculum often intensified the shock. . . . Ultimately most students found these insights liberating, but a segment of the constituency believed the Augsburg religion department had become a nesting place for heretics, either of the "neo-Orthodox" or "modernist" variety.[11]

Those who shared the above concerns and sought to continue under the principles of the Lutheran Free Church started to find one another. Area rallies were scheduled in 1961 to discuss concerns about the merger and the need to renew a commitment to free and living congregations, the first in July at Maple Bay, Minnesota, and the second in August at McIntosh, Minnesota. Other rallies followed in the coming months at Thief River Falls, Minnesota; McVille, North Dakota; Spicer, Minnesota; and Willmar, Minnesota. A notable feature of these meetings was the presence of concerned pastors and laypeople from The ALC, who encouraged their Free Church friends to stand firm on their convictions. One of these pastors, Rev. H. C. Molstre, McIntosh, Minnesota, would later become the first non-LFC pastor to join the newly organized association.

In October 1961 an Information Committee and a Steering Committee were formed, the first for the purpose of disseminating material in opposition to the proposed union, and the second to investigate the possibility of a new federation of free congregations if the union should be approved. This action was taken in the midst of the referendum (from September 15 to November 15), which was too late to substantially influence the voting. The issue of a new federation was a divisive one, and several of the pastors were firmly opposed to any preparations for a new fellowship, still hopeful that the referendum might be defeated or, if not, then that the union agreement would be rejected by the annual conference. A list of forty-eight pastors was compiled, including those who either publicly or privately expressed opposition to the merger, and the Information Committee sought to provide prayerful encouragement as pressure mounted for them to change their convictions and materials that might strengthen those convictions.

Twenty-one pastors[12] agreed to include their names on a letter that was sent to all LFC congregations and pastors, entitled, "Will You Be Violating Your Constitution?" The issue addressed in the letter was based on a statement in the Model Constitution that only by a process requiring a two-thirds majority vote at the annual meeting of the congregation could the document be amended. Since the constitution also stated that the congregation was affiliated with the Lutheran Free Church and endorsed its Guiding Principles and Rules for Work, this affiliation could not be changed by a majority vote during a referendum. In other words, the signers of the letter were convinced that each congregation would have to vote by a two-thirds majority to change its constitution in order to join the merged church and that it would therefore be illegal to delegate this authority to the annual conference of the LFC.

A mimeographed booklet entitled "The Outcry" found a positive reception in many parishes and included a lengthy article by Rev. A. L. Hokonson, Everett, Washington, that had been refused for publication by *The Lutheran Messenger*, the official LFC magazine. Distribution of the booklets was coordinated by Rev. Richard Snipstead, a young Canadian LFC pastor who had recently accepted a call to serve a parish in northern Minnesota. Providing energetic leadership to the opponents of merger, he later edited a newsletter whose eight issues provided an important forum for those who shared his concerns. Rev. Karl Stendal, Minneapolis, Minnesota, also published two pamphlets, "Thoughts on the Merger" and "What Kind of a Church Do You Want?" which were widely circulated.

Some recall a planning meeting of pastors and laymen in the spring of 1961 in a western Minnesota cabin owned by G. H. Forthun, a Valley City, North Dakota, layman, where the participants ended the day on their knees before God in prayer, seeking His guidance for the future. Others mention a meeting in a Minneapolis hotel during the last LFC conference after the merger resolution was finally approved. There were those whose convictions wavered during the months that followed, as several pastors and congregations who opposed merger now felt constrained to be certified into The ALC because of the conference decision or family ties. Yet a remnant remained firmly convinced that the dream for a fellowship of free and living Lutheran congregations must not be forsaken; rather, it was as relevant as ever to the needs of the hour, or even more so.

The time for opposing the merger had passed, concluded a growing number of pastors and lay people, and the time to reorganize an association of Free Lutheran congregations had come. The unofficial headquarters for this movement was the Powers Hotel in Fargo, North Dakota, where the prayer and planning sessions for an upcoming conference were held. An area rally was held in the school auditorium at Winger, Minnesota, on July 12, which was attended by over two hundred people from northern Minnesota and eastern North Dakota. Though not invited, LFC Vice President Luthard Gjerde was present to represent the denomination and to discourage congregations from withdrawing, making it clear that the leadership would strongly oppose the movement to organize a new association.

The dream was renewed on October 25-28, 1962, when almost three hundred men and women from 76 LFC congregations in seven states and two Canadian provinces registered at a special conference in Thief River Falls, Minnesota. The host congregation for this conference was Our Saviour's Lutheran Church, Rev. Marius Haakenstad, pastor, but the church sanctuary soon proved too small for the crowds in attendance, including many who did not register, and the sessions were moved to a nearby school auditorium. Temporary officers were Rev. Fritjof B. Monseth, Valley City, North Dakota, chairman (later elected as vice-president), and Rev. Richard Snipstead,

Greenbush, Minnesota, secretary.

"Press on Towards the Goal" (Philippians 3:1-16) was the theme of the conference, and the keynote address, "The Church We Seek," was delivered by Rev. John P. Strand, Tioga, North Dakota, who was later elected as the first president of the new association. Rev. Raynard Huglen, New Effington, South Dakota, delivered an essay entitled "A Statement on the Historical Situation" and also read a "Declaration of Faith," which was adopted. The following resolution was overwhelmingly approved: "that we as a Conference continue The Association of Independent Congregations under The Lutheran Free Church Guiding Principles."[13] A Board of Administration was elected, consisting of Rev. Julius Hermunslie (chairman), Spicer, Minnesota; Rev. Hamar Benson, McVille, North Dakota; Rev. Morris Eggen, Granite Falls, Minnesota; Mr. Harvey Dyrud, Newfolden, Minnesota; and Mr. Ole K. Ose, Thief River Falls, Minnesota. Mr. William Svanoe, Edina, Minnesota, was appointed to serve as treasurer.

There had been an expectation that other like-minded Lutherans were waiting to see what the Lutheran Free Church would do, so it was especially encouraging to have several guest pastors at the Thief River Falls conference. Rev. Allen Blegen, Chicago, Illinois, a pastor of The American Lutheran Church and representative of a conservative movement within his synod as well as editor of a newsletter called *The Word Alone*, greeted the assembly and warned against dangerous trends in theology, calling on true Christians to "occupy until He comes" though it be costly and difficult.[14] Other visitors who greeted the conference were Rev. Chester Heikkinen, a former Suomi Synod pastor from Minneapolis, Minnesota, and Rev. B. T. Gabrielson, a pastor of The ALC from Seattle, Washington, both of whom encouraged the LFC remnant to believe that others would be joining them.

The most controversial resolution concerned the name: "The Conference declares that the name of this Association shall be known as the Lutheran Free Church (not merged) unless changed by future action."[15]

Representatives of the LFC administration who were present at the conference immediately reported the decision to the headquarters in Minneapolis, and a telegram received from their legal counsel warned against the use of this name by the new association. The leaders of the new association believed that the addition of "not merged" should solve the problem and clearly distinguish them from their former affiliation. The LFC Board of Administration did not agree, and a temporary injunction was obtained that forbade the use of the name, Lutheran Free Church (not merged). The case eventually reached the Minnesota State Supreme Court, which ruled in favor of the plaintiffs. There was some confusion for several months about what to call the new fellowship, and some tried using "Free Lutheran Association" or the "Free Association of Lutheran Congregations." The name "Association of Free Lutheran Congregations" (AFLC) was semi-officially used by the time of the 1963 Annual Conference.

A second courtroom conflict, which challenged the legality of the merger itself, involved First Lutheran Church of Valley City, North Dakota, and its pastor, Rev. Fritjof B. Monseth, vice-president of the new association. The leadership of the LFC declared that congregations would be certified as members of The ALC unless they voted by a two-thirds majority to withdraw from the Lutheran Free Church, due to the fact that the 1962 Annual Conference had approved the merger of the two church bodies. Opponents of this procedure insisted that it was contrary to the principles (*Fundamental Principle 10*) of the LFC, which state that "Free and independent congregations have no right to demand that other congregations shall submit to their opinion, will, judgment, or decision; therefore all domination of a majority of congregations over a minority shall not be tolerated."[16]

Confusion was rampant in many congregations as people who voted to remain with the Lutheran Free Church were informed afterwards that this was a vote to merge with The ALC.

First Lutheran Church, which had consistently voted against merger, was divided on the issue, with a majority of the current church council in opposition to a majority of the congregation. When a vote was announced of ninety-nine to remain a Free Lutheran congregation versus ninety-one for merger with The ALC, Dr. John Stensvaag, president of the LFC, certified the congregation into the merged church, since it was not a resolution to withdraw from the Lutheran Free Church, which would have required a two-thirds majority. He apparently decided to make a test case of First Lutheran Church, perhaps due to the strength of the pro-merger minority, since a similar resolution from other congregations was not challenged.

On August 18, 1963, members of the church council padlocked the church doors to prevent the pastor from conducting worship services and took legal steps to evict him from the parsonage. Representatives of the majority challenged these actions, but the court ruled in favor of the pro-merger minority, declaring that the LFC had virtually become a synod over the years so that its conference decisions were binding on local congregations. Efforts to refer this decision to a higher court were abandoned, as a growing number of AFLC people were becoming uneasy about appealing to the courts for a settlement of church conflicts.

The Lutheran Free Church officially became part of The American Lutheran Church on February 1, 1963. Dr. Stensvaag reported that forty-one congregations "by proper congregational action" and fifteen pastors, including four who were retired and two in other church work or without call, elected to stay out of the merger. During a three-month grace period, eleven additional congregations withdrew and one rejoined. "Much of the feeling against merger," Stensvaag wrote, "has developed as a result of misunderstanding and misrepresentation," but he was hopeful many would reconsider their decision as a clearer picture emerged.[17] On the contrary, however, it was clear that the reorganized fellowship of Free Lutherans was already moving forward in growth and development of ministries.

The 41 congregations whose withdrawals were recognized by the LFC administration were:

Minnesota

Badger Creek	Greenbush, MN
Bethania	Greenbush, MN
Bethania	Newfolden, MN
Dovre	Winger, MN

Emmanuel	Greenbush, MN
Green Lake	Spicer, MN
Landstad	Shevlin, MN
Maple Bay	Winger, MN
Norland	Roseau, MN
Oiland	Greenbush, MN
Our Saviour's	Thief River Falls, MN
Reiner	Goodridge, MN
Rose	Roseau, MN
Sell Lake	Shevlin, MN
Spruce	Roseau, MN
Trinity	Henning, MN *(later reversed its vote)*
Trinity	Sacred Heart, MN
Trinity	Shevlin, MN
Union Lake	Winger, MN
Westaker	Newfolden, MN

North Dakota

Aspelund	Walhalla, ND
Beaver Creek	Tioga, ND
Bethany	Binford, ND
Lebanon	Brinsmade, ND
Lindahl	Tioga, ND
New Luther Valley	McVille, ND
Norman	Tioga, ND
St. Olaf	Tioga, ND
Temple	Tioga, ND
Zion	Alsen, ND
Zion	Tioga, ND
Zion	Valley City, ND
Zoar	Hatton, ND

South Dakota

Bethel	Faith, SD
Emmanuel	Faith, SD
Pukwana	Pukwana, SD
St. Olaf	Pukwana, SD

Washington
  First   Ferndale, WA
  Golgotha   Ferndale, WA

Wisconsin
  Running Valley   Colfax, WI

Saskatchewan, Canada
  Nordland   Stewart Valley, SK

The LFC clergymen not certified into the merged church were Carl Berg, Trygve Dahle, Einar Dreyer, Marius Haakenstad, Jonas Helland, Julius Hermunslie, Arvid Hokonson, Raynard Huglen, Fritjof Monseth, Carl Ostby, Harold Schafer, Richard Snipstead, Lars Stalsbroten, Karl Stendal, and John Strand.

Speaking for those who withdrew from the merger, Raynard Huglen wrote:

> We would not be honest if we said that we are satisfied with the way everything has been handled. We are not. But what *is done is done.* The Lutheran Free Church *is gone.* Things will not be the same for them or for us. We shall each face new doors of opportunity, and in this we shall find new blessings. Let us, in our fellowship, together with those who may join us, seek to work for free and living congregations in our time. This will challenge the best that is in us. So help us, God.[18]

Eugene Fevold stated in his 1969 history of the LFC that "by and large, a congregation tended to follow the leadership of its pastor in regard to the question of merger."[19] It is difficult to compare the lists of withdrawing congregations used by The ALC and the Free Lutheran Association, since there were apparently some congregations that did not immediately notify the church officials of their votes or their notification was disregarded. The picture that emerges, however, is certainly not a case of merely following pastoral leadership. Some parishes were without a pastor, and a few pastors remained neutral, yet only about fifty percent of the congregations that withdrew from the merger were served by anti-merger pastors. In one unique instance, Bethany Lutheran Church, Abercrombie, North Dakota, voted to continue as a Free Lutheran congregation in spite of the fact that it had been served as part of an ELC/TALC parish for many years. Also, the parishes of two of the original pastors who opted out of the merger chose to become part of The ALC.

There is another consequence of the merger even more difficult to measure, and that is the divisions that resulted. Some LFC people voted with their feet and found a home in congregations of other denominations. During the years 1963-64, approximately fifteen new congregations were established due to a division in some that merged, and a new Free Lutheran congregation in south Minneapolis included members from at least five former LFC churches.

The first annual conference of the new association was held June 12-16, 1963, in Fargo, North Dakota, which would serve as headquarters both officially and unofficially for almost two years. The theme was "An Open Door" (Revelation 3:8), and Rev. Raynard Huglen preached the keynote message. Registration included 435 lay people and 21 pastors, representing 65-70 congregations, an impressive attendance for the young association, even though not all of the above were formally affiliated with it yet. Rev. John Strand, who was re-elected president, noted in his report to the conference that, in spite of uncertainty and struggles, the work had come further than they had hoped. "Let us take what God would give us," he declared. "Let us be faithful in prayer. Let us love one another. Our future is in the hand of God."[20]

During the preceding months, however, major strides of development had taken place. A church magazine, *The Lutheran Ambassador*, was already in publication, edited by Rev. Raynard Huglen, marking the beginning of a ministry of publications and parish education that currently includes a complete Sunday school curriculum as well as other instructional and devotional materials. Mrs. David C. (Helen) Hanson became the "resource advisor" and later executive secretary for parish education in the AFLC, and together with Judith Wold, Mrs. William (Esther) Farrier, Mrs. Vernon (Betty) Nelson, and the editor of *The Lutheran Ambassador* organized a series of training workshops throughout the districts and provided helpful material through the pages of the church magazine.

The first issue of the new magazine, which immediately followed the last issue of the LFC's *The Lutheran Messenger*, featured an article entitled "Fear" by AFLC President Strand. He outlined several reasons to fear not, including the presence of God, the strength of the fellowship, the good will of many fellow Lutherans, and the task before us. His concluding words, addressed to former co-laborers who joined the merged church, reflected the spirit that the magazine sought to maintain:

> To our brethren who will not be with us in our church, we wish you well as you go into the new church. We are still brothers in Christ. To say less would be to be tragically sectarian. God bless you in your chosen vineyard. We will pray for you and we can covet your prayers. Brethren, contend earnestly for the faith![21]

The 1963 Fargo conference met in a recently acquired church and headquarters building (the current home of St. Paul's congregation) purchased for thirty thousand dollars. A brief financial drive led by area representatives raised the needed funds in less than one month, an achievement that seemed miraculous to the fledging association, and offices were established there in mid-May.

A winter Bible conference that was to become an annual event had been held in McVille, North Dakota, in February. A national women's auxiliary (the Women's Missionary Federation) was already functioning, led by a committee elected at the organizational conference in Thief River Falls, consisting of Mrs. Julius (Marit) Hermunslie, Mrs. Tarkel (Elaine) Ose, Mrs. Herbert (Dorothy) Presteng, Mrs. Richard (Leone) Snipstead, and Mrs. Ole K. (Alma) Ose, with the latter serving as president pro tem. This organization, which continues to be a vital arm of the fellowship, preserved a strong continuity with its Lutheran Free Church counterpart, in some instances retaining the same district officers.

Another significant development during these first months of the AFLC was the beginning of a mission outreach. Rev. John H. Abel, a veteran missionary to Brazil, had been troubled for several years by what he termed "an eroding away of our firm Lutheran position on inspiration, as well as an increasing worldliness in the church."[22] These concerns, together with a disturbing change of direction for the mission work in Brazil, led him to consider leaving missionary service completely. While on furlough, however, he read about the conference in Thief River Falls, discovering that others shared his concerns and were acting on them. He resigned from The ALC Board of Missions and accepted a call to serve as both home and world missions director for the new Free Lutheran Association, establishing headquarters in the newly purchased church building at Fargo, North Dakota.

Available funds were limited, but assistance was given to some newly organized or re-established parishes during the first years of the AFLC. St. Paul's Lutheran Church, Fargo, North Dakota, was the inaugural home mission project of the new fellowship, followed by the newly established Newfolden, Minnesota, and Hatton, North Dakota, parishes. Rev. Harold Schafer, pastor of an independent congregation in DeKalb, Illinois, served as chairman of the Mission Committee during the formative phase of development and worked closely with the mission director to provide leadership in this important area of ministry for the future of the fellowship. The first mission congregations usually consisted of those who withdrew from former LFC parishes.

With a vision for planting churches in the rapidly expanding frontier regions of Brazil, John and Ruby Abel returned to South America with their children in 1964, soon followed by Alvin and Frances Grothe and their family, to become the first world missionaries of the new association. A second mission outpost was adopted the same year when an independent

Lutheran congregation near the Mexican border in Nogales, Arizona, and its pastor, Rev. Lawrence Dynneson, joined the AFLC.

The year 1963 also witnessed the inauguration of three ventures especially aimed at youth and families. "The Ambassadors," a musical team of five young college students (Francis Monseth, Al Henrickson, Terry Simonson, Roger Strom, and Dave Johnson), traveled throughout the congregations for three months to present inspirational programs and to promote youth activities, the first of many summer youth gospel teams. Their ministry was a special source of encouragement to the fledgling church body, too, indicating that there would be young men preparing for future pastoral service.

Several young future pastors were recruited for parish service during the early years of the AFLC, due to the shortage of clergy. Gary Skramstad, Francis Monseth, Alan Hendrickson, Robert and John Rieth, Erling Aaserud, Oliver Urdahl, Connely Dyrud, Kenneth Moland, and this writer all served as "student pastors" during their college years on a part-time or full-time basis. This unusual window of opportunity created by the immediate need for more clergy provided these men with a unique head start in pastoral ministry.

Second, the first Family Bible Camp was held July 8-14 at Lake Geneva near Alexandria, Minnesota, the beginning of an almost unbroken series of summer family camps that have served to immeasurably strengthen the fellowship. A total of 455 women, men, and children registered by the weekend, with still others attending for only the Sunday services, an amazing enrollment for the new venture. The large number of children and teenagers in attendance was a special encouragement, since there were those who had predicted that the new association would primarily consist of older adults. The 1964 Family Bible Camp, which was expected to be smaller because it was held during harvest time in August, surprisingly surpassed the previous summer's enrollment by registering nearly 650 people. An important individual to this ministry during these busy years was Sheldon Mortrud, Thief River Falls, Minnesota, who served as the camp manager.

After the Lake Geneva site was no longer available, the AFLC sponsored family camps at Lake Bronson, Minnesota, and since 1980 at the Association Retreat Center (ARC), a former air force radar base near Osceola, Wisconsin, whose purchase was approved by the association the previous year. A unique "wilderness" camping program has also been developed near Lake Park, Minnesota, on property donated by Lawrence and Sylvia Dahlgren in 1975.

Former LFC congregations in three districts were able to retain control of their area Bible camp facilities: Bethany Bible Camp near Bemidji, Minnesota, operated by congregations of the North Central Minnesota District; Galilee Bible Camp, Lake Bronson, Minnesota, by the Northern Minnesota District; and Pickerel Lake Bible Camp, near Grenville, South Dakota, by AFLC congregations in South Dakota (still in cooperation with some former LFC congregations that merged into The ALC/ELCA). A continuity with the past district organization was also maintained by the Sheyenne Valley Bible Camp Association in eastern North Dakota. The ministry of Bible camps has been recognized as an important outreach of free and living congregations, providing an opportunity for some to be brought into fellowship with Christ and others to get to know Him better through the Word.

The third new church-wide program originating in 1963 was the Luther League Federation (LLF), which held its first post-merger convention November 8-10 in Fargo. Organized as a continuation of the LFC national youth ministry, the first officers (Rev. Richard Snipstead, president; Francis Monseth, first vice president; Bonnie Quam, second vice-president; Janet Aasness, secretary; JoAnn Broden, treasurer; and Karen Moe, devotional life secretary) were entrusted with the planning of biennial conventions, guided by a Youth Board that was elected by the annual conference. Early attempts were also made to provide resources for local youth ministries and to encourage district activities.

Free and living congregations need pastors who share the same vision, and the founders of the AFLC dared to dream that a theological seminary might be established.

The Association of Free Lutheran Congregations

Prayers were answered as the Lord provided a campus, faculty, and student body for the new school that opened its doors in the fall of 1964. The conference center of the Hauge Lutheran Innermission Federation was purchased, located on a spacious lakeside campus in suburban Minneapolis (Plymouth), and Dr. Uuras Saarnivaara, a noted Finnish Lutheran theologian, agreed to serve as the main instructor for the ten men who enrolled. The following year Dr. Iver B. Olson, a former Augsburg professor of theology, also joined the faculty, providing an important link to the past in the preparation of future pastors who would share the dream, too. Other instructors included Rev. Clair Jennings and AFLC President John P. Strand, who moved to the Twin Cities to serve as part-time president as well as dean of the school during the formative years. The first pastors to graduate from the seminary after completing a three-year program plus summer internships were: Richard Gunderson, Edwin Kjos, Howard Kjos, David Molstre, Francis Monseth, and Robert Rieth.

The first pastor to be ordained by the new church association was not a graduate of the seminary, but a licensed lay pastor, Mr. Jay G. Erickson, who served a two-point parish at Faith, South Dakota, and had received seminary instruction from the Church of the Lutheran Brethren. The need for clergy also led to the licensing of other non-seminary trained men for pastoral service, including Gene Sundby, Otto Saukerson, Roy Quanrud, Melvin Walla, and Sidney Swenson, and this practice continues in the AFLC today. Professor George Soberg, founding pastor of two Minneapolis area AFLC congregations, is an exceptional example of this calling, having completed seminary training while serving on the faculty of Augsburg College but never seeking ordination.

Free and living congregations need spiritually alive and equipped lay people. The Bible School movement had been a significant source of blessing to the Lutheran Free Church, primarily preparing Christian men and women for ministry within the local congregation, and from the beginning there were those who dreamed of an AFLC Bible School. This was fulfilled in the fall of 1966 when thirteen students enrolled for classes on the seminary campus in Minneapolis, commencing a program that would eventually multiply to become the largest Lutheran Bible school in the world.

A survey of growth in the number of congregations is also quite impressive. In 1966 there were 80 congregations affiliated with the association, and by 1973-74 there were 125. This grew to 138 by 1983-84 and then leaped forward to 186 in 1988-89 and 200 in 1989-90. The year of the greatest surge of growth was 1988, when thirty congregations were welcomed at the annual conference, most of them joining as a result of the ELCA merger. The editor of *The Lutheran Ambassador* commented on the "widened fellowship" as early as 1966, noting that those in attendance at the pastors' banquet represented eight Lutheran seminaries during the annual conference. "We find, therefore, that the Association in her early stages is a melting pot of various strains and heritages. It is a mixture, an amalgamation, in which there is a unifying agent, to be sure. That agent is a common attitude toward the Scriptures and the congregation."[23]

Our largest congregations reflect the mosaic-like spiritual heritage that has developed within the fellowship: Ruthfred, Bethel Park, Pennsylvania, established fifty years ago by the old ALC; Abiding Savior, Sioux Falls, South Dakota, planted by the AFLC ten years ago; Emmaus, Bloomington, Minnesota, a former LFC congregation that joined at the time of the ELCA merger; and St. Paul's, Cloquet, Minnesota, a century-old congregation with roots in the Suomi Synod. Representative of the whole association as well is the fact that each of these congregations has members only recently introduced to the AFLC and its principles. Concerned conservative Lutherans continue to look to the AFLC for a home, but most important of all, unsaved and unchurched people are being reached for Jesus Christ and His Kingdom, which makes our congregations genuine melting pots. Today, in the year 2002, with approximately 250 affiliated congregations, the AFLC is the fourth largest Lutheran denomination in the United States, and the prospect for further growth continues to be strong.

The dream that was born over a century ago for a fellowship of free and living Lutheran congregations still lives, and a new generation is committed to carrying it into a new millennium. Most of our members probably no longer trace their denominational roots to the former Lutheran Free Church, yet the words written a generation ago by Dr. B. M. Christensen, an LFC leader and long-time president of Augsburg College and Seminary, still ring true for the future of the Association of Free Lutheran Congregations:

> The Lutheran Free Church is a venture of faith. It is an attempt to build an effective and orderly Christian fellowship with a minimum of human organization. It is an experiment in extreme ecclesiastical democracy and decentralization. It is a searching test of faith in the power of the Spirit of God. . . .
>
> The Lutheran Free Church is a cooperative venture in building Lutheran congregations by means of a dominant emphasis neither upon organization nor upon the intricacies of doctrine but upon living and personal Christian experience. It is an attempt to carry out in everyday practice the Reformation principle of the universal priesthood of believers. It is a concrete expression of revolt against ritualism and formalism, and of the desire to nourish the spiritual life in utter simplicity upon the Word of God. It is an effort to provide orderly channels for the cultivation of the laity's personal witness for Christ, both in public and in private. Yet it cherishes the ordered ministry of consecrated and trained men, and the noble heritage of Christian worship, that its people may know themselves to be one with Christ of all the ages. . . .
>
> The Lutheran Free Church was born of a dream of spiritual power and vitality; yet it has been able to carry on even when its power and spiritual vitality seemed at lower ebb. It was launched under a great and inspiring leadership in a period of intense struggle; yet it has not perished when led through calmer seas and by spirits less flaming. It has been ridiculed as small, impractical, and visionary; yet those who know it best know that none of these words is a fatal indictment. It has been accused of "separatism;" yet it has throughout all of its history been earnestly in favor of full spiritual cooperation. Its dissolution has been long and often foretold; but it still lives. . . .

The Lutheran Free Church is sincerely grateful for the work of other Lutherans; yet it desires to have its own peculiar share in the mighty work and witness of the Lutheran Church. It does not seek to pass judgment on the relative contribution to Lutheranism of groups small or large; it earnestly seeks to be kept truly humble because of the imperfection of its achievements, and rightly proud because of the greatness of its heritage. Limited in numbers so that not even its name is known in many Lutheran circles of our country, and conscious that it will probably never be regarded as "successful" in the eyes of the world, it still believes in the continuing urgency of its message. Willing if necessary to find its success in seeming failure, the Lutheran Free Church is committed, together with others of like mind, to the struggle for true congregational life in the Lutheran Church, in America.[24]

NOTES

[1] Andreas Helland, *Georg Sverdrup: The Man and His Message 1848-1907* (Minneapolis: The Messenger Press, 1947), Epigraph.

[2] Bernhard M. Christensen, "What Is the Lutheran Free Church?" *The Lutheran Messenger* 24, no.12 (April 10, 1941): 5.

[3] The *Fundamental Principles* of the Lutheran Free Church were written in Norwegian in 1897 and originally entitled *Ledende Principer*. *Ledende* may be translated as "Guiding," "Leading," or "Fundamental." "Fundamental" is the word most commonly used in the AFLC today.

[4] Arnold L. Cook, *Historical Drift* (Camp Hill, Pennsylvania: Christian Publications, 2000), xiii.

[5] Eugene L. Fevold, *The Lutheran Free Church: A Fellowship of American Lutheran Congregations, 1897-1963* (Minneapolis: Augsburg Publishing House, 1969), 226.

[6] John Stensvaag, "Report of the (LFC) Committee on Relations with Other Lutheran Bodies," *1955 Annual Report of the Lutheran Free Church*, 117.

[7] Bernard M. Christensen, "Reflections on the Merger Meetings," *The Lutheran Messenger* 37, no. 22 (October 26, 1954): 5.

[8] Clarence J. Carlsen, "The Alternatives to Merger," *The Lutheran Messenger* Volume XC, no. 11 (May 21, 1957): 6.

[9] Note the use of *hypocrite* (*Fundamental Principle 4*) in Clarence J. Carlsen, *The Years of Our Church* (Minneapolis: The Lutheran Free Church Publishing Company, 1942), 44.

[10] E. Clifford Nelson, *Lutheranism in North America 1914-1970* (Minneapolis: Augsburg Publishing House, 1972), 164.

[11] Carl H. Chrislock, *From Fjord to Freeway: 100 Years–Augsburg College* (Minneapolis, 1969), 214.

[12] Gilbert Almquist, Hamar Benson, Carl Berg, Ernst Dahle, Trygve Dahle, Einar Dreyer, Clemmence Dyrud, Morris Eggen, Knut Gjesfjeld, Marius Haakenstad, Jonas Helland, Julius Hermunslie, Fritjof Monseth, Carl Ostby, Ernest Raaum, A. C. Rykken, Harold Schafer, Richard Snipstead, Lars Stalsbroten, Karl Stendal, John Strand. J. J. Pederson also agreed to sign the letter but died before it was published.

[13] "Journal," *1963 Annual Report of the Association of Free Lutheran Congregations*, 98. The minutes from the 1962 Organizational Meeting in Thief River Falls are recorded in the *1963 Annual Report*.

[14] "Journal," *1963 Annual Report of the Association of Free Lutheran Congregations*, 98.

[15] "Journal," *1963 Annual Report of the Association of Free Lutheran Congregations*, 100.

[16] Clarence J. Carlsen, *The Years of Our Church* (Minneapolis: The Lutheran Free Church Publishing Company, 1942), 49.

[17] John Stensvaag, Letter, February 11, 1963.

[18] Raynard O. J. Huglen, "There Was Something Different," *The Lutheran Ambassador* 1, no. 2 (February 26, 1963): 5.

[19] Fevold, *The Lutheran Free Church*, 295.

[20] John P. Strand, "President's Message," *1963 Annual Report of the Association of Free Lutheran Congregations*, 14.

[21] John P. Strand, "Fear," *The Lutheran Ambassador* 1, no. 1 (February 12, 1963): 8.

[22] John H. Abel, "An Open Letter to Friends," 1963.

[23] Raynard O. J. Huglen, "Widened Fellowship," *The Lutheran Ambassador* 4, no. 15 (July 26, 1966): 9.

[24] Christensen, "What Is the Lutheran Free Church?" 5.

In the desire to build God's kingdom, the Word of God must be the authority. . . . The Word of God must be the authority in all that pertains to the congregation and all church matters. It is with childlike faith we seek guidance from God's Word, not with worldly wisdom or critical analysis.

—John P. Strand

4

The Biblical Basis of Congregational Polity

The Freedom of the Congregation

Francis Wesley Monseth

The most definitive document outlining the biblical understanding of the Christian congregation in the Association of Free Lutheran Congregations is the *Fundamental* (or *Guiding*) *Principles*. Framed by the founders of the former Lutheran Free Church, these twelve statements succinctly set forth the congregation's marks, membership, and mission in the light of the New Testament. The deliberate and repeated reference point in these principles is the Word of God.

The first of these principles states, "According to the Word of God, the congregation is the right form of the Kingdom of God on earth." This statement witnesses to the authority of the Scriptures in matters related to the nature as well as to the form of the congregation. It is neither historic precedent nor contemporary expediency that informs and guides the Church concerning its polity. It is solely the Word of God. The Scriptures are the all-sufficient authority not only in matters of faith and life, but also in all the subjects they treat (II Timothy 3:16-17). This includes the structure of the Church. God has given an instructive model as well as guiding principles for the form the Church should take until the second advent of Christ. That standard is found in the inspired and inerrant Word of God.[1]

The principle above also recognizes the local congregation as "the right form of the Kingdom of God on earth." The only visible entity in the New Testament commissioned by God to implement and carry forward His great and gracious purposes is the local congregation. Wherever the Apostle Paul traveled on his missionary journeys, congregations were planted as people were converted to Christ. There were no hierarchical structures that imposed requirements or limitations on these new congregations. Though the New Testament churches were not exempt from trials and tribulations, the Kingdom of God advanced magnificently through the simple preaching of the dynamic Word of God.

Fundamental Principle 5 states the case for congregational polity even more specifically: "The congregation directs its own affairs, subject to the authority of the Word and the Spirit of God, and acknowledges no other ecclesiastical authority or government above itself."

This principle describes the congregation as autonomous. No leader or organization outside the congregation can exert authority or compulsion over the congregation legitimately. This does not mean a rejection of all authority on the part of the congregation. The congregation is bound by the highest authorities of all, the sacred Scriptures and the Spirit of God. Georg Sverdrup, a leading figure in crafting the *Fundamental Principles*, spoke of this authority as so absolute that "a congregation is no longer a congregation when it tears itself loose from it. And only so far is a congregation a true congregation as it subjects itself to this authority."[2] No wonder Sverdrup asks rhetorically, "Is it really wrong, then, when the days are evil and the night is approaching, to lift up our eyes and mind from the confused and dwarfed present, and to turn to the true, real picture of the congregation which the New Testament gives us?"[3]

What then is the "true, real picture of the congregation" as portrayed in the Word of God? The following discussion seeks to explore and summarize the New Testament record.

Early Development

The Church of the New Testament began with the coming of the Holy Spirit on the day of Pentecost. From 120 believers who constituted the "upper room" prayer group to thousands upon thousands of converts in a span of about thirty years, the growth was explosive and expansive. To be sure, conditions for growth were favorable with the Roman Empire's *Pax Romana* in effect. The political situation was stable because of Rome's enforcement of law and order throughout her empire. The relative calm and the state of peace combined to make the spread of the Gospel simpler and safer. In addition, a spirit of dissatisfaction as well as a spirit of inquiry characterized the populace because of the unwelcome and often harsh rule of the Romans. People were generally more open to those who professed to have answers for life's puzzling questions.

It is evident that formal organization was not undertaken at the founding of the first congregation in Jerusalem. It is equally clear that the apostles, whom Christ had personally equipped, empowered, and commissioned, were looked to for spiritual leadership. From the beginning, the believers met at given places, worshiping and fellowshipping together as members of one body under the ministry of the apostles. They were united by a common faith in Christ and joined with one another regularly and often to hear the preaching of the Word of God, to share commonly in the Lord's Supper, to fellowship together as brothers and sisters in Christ, and to pray with and for each other (Acts 2:42).

The infant congregation in Jerusalem is described as "of one heart and soul" (Acts 4:32, NASB). This inner spiritual life and unity was demonstrated in many ways: a dramatic increase in membership through conversions (Acts 2:46-47, 4:4, 5:14, *et al.*), an effective and fervent prayer fellowship (Acts 4:23-31), and a loving concern for one another manifesting itself to the extent of sacrificial sharing of their material blessings with one another (Acts 2:44-45, 4:32). No wonder Dr. Luke gives such an enthusiastic description of the Jerusalem congregation, "And with great power the apostles were giving witness to the resurrection of the Lord Jesus, and abundant grace was upon them all" (Acts 4:33).

Because of the rapid growth of the Jerusalem congregation as well as the formation of congregations elsewhere with mixed Jewish and Gentile membership, opportunities grew, and problems arose which were beyond the capacity of the apostles to meet personally. They needed people to assist them in ministry to the spiritual and physical needs. Thus, gradually as needs arose and circumstances warranted, special offices were created to perform various functions in the congregation under the direction and supervision of the apostles, but all under the Head of the Church, the Lord Jesus Christ.

The Role of the Apostles

It is of special interest to consider the role of the apostles in the New Testament in relationship to polity. Some interpret the exercise of authority by the apostles as a model for ongoing rule from the "top down" in some type of hierarchical structure over and above the local congregation. However, the uniqueness and the temporary nature of the apostolic office must be recognized in order to understand its role in the Early Church.

The original apostles were called and discipled by the Lord Jesus Christ Himself. Step by step, He had taught them by precept and by example. At last, He entrusted to them the great mission of extending the Gospel to the ends of the earth (Matthew 28:18-20; Mark 16:15-16; Luke 24:44-48; John 20:21; Acts 1:8; *et al.*). To the first apostles were added others. The indispensable qualification for apostleship was that each one had received his commission from the risen Lord.

When his apostleship was challenged, the Apostle Paul defended his position on the basis of having met Jesus Christ after His resurrection (I Corinthians 9:1-2). No doubt his personal encounter was on the Damascus Road where the murderous Saul became the transformed Paul in a dramatic conversion experience and subsequent call to preach the Gospel to the Gentiles (Acts 9:3-16).

The apostles occupied unique positions of authority over the local congregations as well as the Church at large in the opening moments of its New Testament existence. They were looked to for spiritual leadership and supervision under Christ, the Head of the Church. Indeed, it was His authority they exercised as His representatives in matters pertaining to preaching, teaching, and discipline. They were conscious that they were servants of Christ and exercised their authority as such. Claiming no ecclesiastical superiority, the Apostle Peter placed himself on a par with his "fellow-elder[s]" (I Peter 5:1-4). However, with the death of the last apostle, John, the gift and office of apostleship as defined by the New Testament ceased. There were no others after them who were to possess the unique qualifications of an apostle.

It is not coincidental that the canon of Scripture closed with the death of the Apostle John. As the writer of the final book of the New Testament, he had been the last of the apostles to write under the inspiration of the Holy Spirit. The severe judgment he pronounces upon anyone who would add to or subtract from what he had written underscores not only his apostolic authority but also the cessation of divine revelation (Revelation 22:18-19). With the last of the apostolic writings, the prophetic promise of Jesus to His apostles was fulfilled (John 16:12,15). The Holy Spirit had now led them into "all truth." All God intended to say through the prophets and the apostles had now been said. The Scriptures were at last completed. The perfect sufficiency of the Scriptures for salvation and life are affirmed in the statement that they make one "wise unto salvation" and equip for "every good work" (II Timothy 3:15-17).

With the cessation of the office of apostle, it is appropriate to ask whether this created a vacancy in terms of leadership in the New Testament congregations? Did the congregations collapse in disorder and confusion? Were others called by God to lead in the same way as the apostles had done? Had the apostles set a precedent for a continuing leadership structure in the churches? In light of the uniqueness and the temporary nature of the apostolic office, the answer to these questions must be in the negative. There were no others who could step forward and rightly claim the qualifications of an apostle.

Though the Church no longer is related to the persons of the apostles, she continues to benefit from the apostolic gift and to experience its blessed effects through the inspired writings of the apostles. Indeed, the Church was and is "built upon the foundation of the apostles and prophets, Christ Jesus Himself being the corner stone" (Ephesians 2:20). This enduring "foundation" is the apostolic and prophetic Word, the Scriptures, which continues to teach, reprove, correct, and instruct in righteousness (II Timothy 3:16).

The Scriptures are sufficient not only to nourish and guide individual believers but also to guide congregations. It may be said with assurance that the congregation is "thoroughly equipped for every good work." Certainly this all-encompassing statement includes the form the congregation should take as well as the ministry it should exercise (II Timothy 3:17). Although the apostles who exercised authority over the congregations are no longer present, the congregations are still subject to the authority of the apostolic office through the written Word.

The lesson we learn from the New Testament apostolic office is not that the congregation should have some kind of human authority over it, but that the congregation must be subject to the authority of the apostolic Word. Therefore, the *Fundamental Principles* declare that the local congregation is "subject to the authority of the Word and the Spirit of God" alone (*Fundamental Principle 5*).

The Organizational Model

As has been observed, the ministry of the Word and the administrative leadership in the New Testament Church at first devolved upon the apostles themselves. With the dramatic and rapid growth, however, it did not take long before the purely administrative functions of the Jerusalem congregation attained such proportions that the personal spiritual ministrations of the apostles were jeopardized.

The Selection of "Deacons"

Bringing the urgent need for an expanded ministry team to a head was a complaint that arose because of the apparent neglect of the Hellenistic widows in the daily distribution of physical necessities. These Greek-speaking Jews were sensitive to what seemed to them a purposeful slight. The apostles recognized their inability to fulfill adequately their main calling of devoting themselves to prayer and the ministry of the Word (Acts 6:4) if the situation should continue as it was. Therefore, they called the whole congregation together to address the problem. Instruction was given to the congregation to take the initiative in selecting qualified men who would assist in the ministry (Acts 6:3). Encouraged by this wise and timely provision, the congregation chose seven men whom the apostles recognized and affirmed with prayer and the laying on of hands (Acts 6:5-6). The congregation was recognized by the apostles as a self-governing body in this matter, choosing in a democratic manner these first "deacons"[4] out of their own company to serve the Lord and the congregation in the provision for the material needs of the congregation and thereby relieve the apostles of this responsibility.

There are particular terms in the passage under discussion (Acts 6:2-6) that are worthy of special attention. The expression translated from the Greek, "seek out from among you" (NKJV) or "select from among you" (NASB), means to look carefully, to inspect, or to pick out. The congregation is directed to proceed with careful deliberation in choosing these seven individuals from their own number. It is their freedom as well as their responsibility before God to do so. The word translated "appoint" (NKJV) or "put in charge" (NASB) has the connotation of constituting or setting in place. In this case, it is setting in place or installing men chosen by the congregation for the position to which they had been selected. This is precisely what took place when these men were set before the apostles by the Jerusalem congregation. The apostles proceeded to induct them into their office by prayer and the laying on of hands. It was the congregation that was given the initiative to select these leaders, and the apostles' role was one of recognition and affirmation of what had taken place.

In this initial step in the transitional development of New Testament church polity, it is evident that the principles of self-government and democratic process in the organizational functioning of the congregations were recognized and practiced. It will be observed that these principles were consistently adhered to in the ongoing development of church polity during the apostolic period—a self-governing polity, however, that was strictly under the authority of the Word of God and the Spirit of God.

The Sending of "Missionaries"

With the mounting persecution of the growing congregation in Jerusalem, the believers ultimately were forced to leave the city. In their departure, they were scattered throughout the regions of Judea and Samaria. Our Lord had commissioned them to go to those places among others (Acts 1:8); the persecution served to hasten the fulfillment of His mandate. As they fled the intense persecution in Jerusalem, however, they did not conceal their identities or their message. Wherever they went, they preached the Word of God (Acts 8:4). Since the apostles had remained in Jerusalem, it was a new generation of "preachers" that now had stepped forward. Underscored and illustrated in the ministry activity of these scattered believers is the precious truth of the priesthood of all believers. With the recognition of this common priesthood is an additional affirmation not only of the right of every believer to proclaim the Word of God as His commissioned witness but also the God-given competency of every believer to be entrusted with the sacred calling of the New Testament priesthood (I Peter 2:9).

Originating with the dramatic and decisive conversion of one of the most rabid and notorious persecutors of believers, Paul, and his subsequent commitment to world evangelization, there began a ministry of the Gospel to the uttermost boundary, "even to the remotest part of the earth" (Acts 1:8). In three successive missionary journeys, the Apostle Paul and his missionary party were used of God to plant and nurture many congregations throughout most regions of the Roman Empire.

It was while Paul was active in the ministry and fellowship of the congregation in Antioch that he and Barnabas were set apart as missionaries of the Gospel (Acts 13:1-6). To this local congregation, the Holy Spirit made known His will regarding the vocation of Paul and Barnabas, and in obedient recognition and affirmation of their call, the congregation sent them out.

The Antioch congregation was acting under the guidance of the Holy Spirit in sending Paul and Barnabas. *How important to remember that the autonomy of the congregation is an autonomy always to be exercised under the absolute authority of the Holy Spirit working through the Word of God!* The posture of the congregation is to be that of submission to the Holy Spirit and the Word. The freedom of the congregation can only be realized in biblical authenticity in obedience to the Holy Spirit. The Holy Spirit ministers through the congregation, but the congregation has no authority to act except by the guidance of the Holy Spirit through the Word of God. There is one Holy Spirit, and He calls all who are to serve in and through the Church.

How do we account for the definite leading of the Holy Spirit that the congregation at Antioch experienced in calling the first missionaries? The answer is found, first of all, in the ministry of the prophets and teachers in the congregation. The presence of such a ministry implies that the congregation was being enlightened and edified by the hearing of the Word of God. To be a true prophet is to be one who faithfully proclaims the Word; to be a true teacher is to be one who faithfully interprets and expounds the Word. The context in which a congregation can receive divine guidance is invariably where the Word of God is being taught faithfully and is being received in faith.

A further indication of how divine guidance is received by a congregation is the description of the Antioch congregation as "ministering to the Lord [worshiping] and fasting" (Acts 13:2).

The word translated "ministering" is instructive in this regard. It is the same word from which we derive the word, "liturgy." The congregation at Antioch was engaged in worship. "Ministering to the Lord" is the activity of a worshiping people. The outcome of Spirit-empowered worship, worship in "spirit and truth" (John 4:24), is always a readiness to respond in childlike trust in God and humble obedience to His Word. It is in the context of true worship that the Lord reveals Himself and His will through His Word to a congregation.

But not only did the congregation at Antioch minister to the Lord in worship; they fasted. Fasting indicates a voluntary and temporary abstention from regular mundane activities, such as eating, for the purpose of meditation upon the Word and extended time in prayer. God's purposes and plans will be revealed to a congregation guided by the ministry of the Word and devoted to seeking His will in prayer. There is no biblical warrant to expect that God guides a Christian congregation today in any other way than He has done in the past, by His Word and Spirit.

In summarizing the autonomous nature of the congregation at Antioch, it is evident that they possessed the God-given right and privilege to call and ordain individuals to proclaim the Gospel of Christ. No other extra-congregational authorities are in sight; it is simply *Antioch Christian Church* acting under the authority of the Word of God. The call and ordination of these early missionaries by an individual congregation was fully sufficient for validating their special mission of extending the Kingdom of God through Word and sacrament.

The Election of Elders

Though not without active and continual opposition, the first missionary journey of Paul and Barnabas was marked by multitudes of people in many places turning to Christ in repentance and faith. In every city and village, congregations were begun, composed of the new believers. In each new church, elders were appointed to oversee the spiritual welfare of the people and to provide a godly, Christ-like example in life and ministry. The instructions given in regard to the provision of spiritual leaders in these new congregations is not only informative but also instructive for Christian congregations until the second advent.

The procedure for providing spiritual leadership in the congregations is described as follows: "So when they had appointed elders in every church, and prayed with fasting, they commended them to the Lord in whom they had believed" (Acts 14:23, NKJV). The word translated "appointed" literally means to raise one's hand, that is, to vote by the raising of hands. This Greek word occurs only twice in the New Testament, here and in II Corinthians 8:19. In both instances, the New American Standard Version translates it with "appoint" while the King James Version translates it with "ordain" in the first passage (Acts 14:23) and "chosen" in the second (II Corinthians 8:19). The implication even in the first case is that elders were chosen by a vote of hands by the respective congregations, a choice which was confirmed by Paul and Barnabas. In the second case (II Corinthians 8:19), it is very evident that the companion of Titus was elected by the congregations ("chosen by the churches") rather than singularly put in place by the Apostle Paul. The sense is that Paul presided over the choice, but the congregations did the actual choosing or appointing.

With the congregation at Antioch exercising its God-given authority in calling and ordaining Paul and Barnabas, the transition from personal apostolic authority to the authority of the congregation under the written Word was complete. The principle of congregational autonomy emerged as the divine and enduring pattern of church polity. This was the case with the constituting of elders in the other congregations as well. It was the gathered assembly of believers rightly administering the Word and sacrament in any given place who were recognized as God's instrument in determining the course of action as they were guided by the Word and Spirit.

The Cooperation of Congregations

As the transition from direct apostolic authority to the exclusive authority of the prophetic and apostolic Word was completed, are there any exceptions to be found in regard to the principle of congregational autonomy? There are those who would point to the doctrinal discussion described in Acts 15 as such a case. The meeting described in this chapter has been referred to by some as "the first Christian Council of the Church of the New Testament." They would conclude that this "council" gives evidence of supra-congregational authority at work. This view obviously militates against the understanding that "the congregation is the right form of the Kingdom of God on earth."

It is important to examine the nature of the meeting

described in Acts 15. Was it really a "council" and, if so, what kind of a council was it? It is significant to observe that it was not a convention of delegates but rather a meeting of the congregation in Jerusalem with representatives from the congregation at Antioch. The purpose of the meeting was to discuss a matter of great importance to the burgeoning missionary enterprise. The main issue involved the insistence of some Jewish believers who had come to Antioch that unless the Gentile believers were circumcised, they could not be saved. The purpose of this "council" was to consider this problem together. It was not to learn what the leaders of the Jerusalem congregation had to say on this subject, accept it as the "last word," and then go back to Antioch. Rather, it is evident in Paul's account that it was an informal conference and that it was a lively meeting with differences freely and earnestly debated before agreement was reached. It is clear from Paul's description of this meeting that he did not look to the church leaders in Jerusalem as the final authorities in matters of faith and life (Galatians 2:1-10).

But what was the outcome? Was it merely a human decree that settled the matter for these earnest conferees? Was it James, the pastor at Jerusalem, who had the last word? Rather, the decision was framed this way: "For it seemed good to the Holy Spirit and to us" (Acts 15:28a). It was a decision under the guidance of the Holy Spirit who had prevailed over the entire assembly (v.25).

In summary, what we observe in the conference at Jerusalem is an independent congregation, faced with a problem of doctrine and practice, seeking to learn the will of the Holy Spirit in consultation with the congregational leaders in Jerusalem. The letter containing the unanimous decision was not only produced by the apostles but also by the elders and "the brethren." Again, what we see in this situation is one congregation (Jerusalem) seeking to help another congregation (Antioch) know the mind of the Holy Spirit and the Word in the issue they mutually considered.

Church Discipline

In our Lord's instructions regarding church discipline, He speaks of the congregation as the final arbiter. Outlining three steps to be followed, He says in Matthew 18:15-17 (NKJV),

> "Moreover if your brother sins against you, go and tell him his fault between you and him alone. If he hears you, you have gained your brother. But if he will not hear, take with you one or two more, that 'by the mouth of two or three witnesses every word may be established.' And if he refuses to hear them, tell it to the church. But if he refuses even to hear the church, let him be to you like a heathen and a tax collector."

In giving directions for the resolution of difficulties among believers, our Lord directs that the first step should be that the offended one meet with the offender in private for the purpose of reconciliation. If that effort fails, he is to take one or two more as witnesses. Again, the sole purpose of such a meeting would be the resolving of the problem. If that second attempt is futile, then the church is to be approached for intervention. However, if that is unsuccessful and the offender refuses to repent, the offender is to be considered in the same category as an unbeliever. The action of the church is final unless there is repentance and reconciliation. There is no ecclesiastical court of appeals that can overrule the action of the congregation. Neither Jesus nor His apostles ever mentioned any hierarchical structure, be it synod, assembly, conference, or convention that could supersede a congregation's authority under God. We must conclude that any extra-congregational entity that attempts to place itself as an authority over a Christian congregation is of human origin and lacks Scriptural sanction and Scriptural authority. Our Lord gives the local church the highest possible ecclesiastical authority as it is guided by the Word and the Spirit, the power of excommunication as well as restoration to the fellowship upon repentance. Its authority under God is recognized in heaven and is final.

The Congregation's Accountability

In our Lord's separate addresses to the seven congregations mentioned in Revelation 2 and 3, He offers counsel, warning, reproof, and commendation depending upon the particular situation in each church. He holds each congregation responsible for its faithfulness to the Word of God, its Christian conduct, as well as its exercise of church discipline. There is no hint of a wider constituency such as a "Church of Asia Minor" or a "Synod of Sardis." Each of the seven congregations is approached as an independent fellowship responsible only to Christ, the Head of the Church.

The Congregation's Rights and Responsibilities

The autonomy of the congregation carries with it the enjoyment of great privileges as well as the acceptance of great responsibilities. To claim freedom without accepting responsibility before God and His Word is lawlessness. The New Testament congregation is free to determine its own response toward plans and programs that are humanly devised; it is not free to determine its responsibilities to God when He has already spoken in His Word.

The congregation has the right and the responsibility to determine its doctrinal position according to the Scriptures and in obedience to the Spirit of God. It follows that it has the right and responsibility to apply its doctrinal standards in its policies and in its affiliations. It cannot do this unless it is free from external authority or coercion. It has the right and the responsibility to exclude from its pulpit those who preach "another gospel" contrary to the Word of God, regardless of their denominational affiliation or position in church circles. It has the right and the responsibility to use only those Christian education resources which are true to the congregation's doctrinal convictions. It has the right and the responsibility to choose its own objects of benevolence and to exclude from its consideration any cause which it discerns is untrue to the standards of the Word of God in faith and practice. It has the right and the responsibility to cooperate with "like-minded" congregations or movements in programs of evangelism and fellowship. It has the right and the responsibility to refuse fellowship with churches or movements which it considers unscriptural. It has the right and the responsibility to call its own pastor(s) as led by the Word and the Spirit of God; it has the right and the responsibility to dismiss its pastor(s) if he is found to be preaching contrary to the Word of God and/or living in moral failure or dereliction.

Unless the congregation has these rights under God, it is not truly a free congregation. Unless it prayerfully exercises these responsibilities in dependence upon God, its freedom is in extreme peril.

The freedom of the congregation is neither an arbitrary concept of church government nor an archaic segment of historical development in the Early Church of the New Testament. The free congregation is the "right form" of the Kingdom of God on earth. Freedom is fundamental to the spiritual growth and preservation of the Christian congregation. The congregation will function most effectively as it lives under the gracious authority of the Word of God and the Spirit of God, and under that authority alone. New Testament polity–congregational polity–is rooted deeply in the great truths of the Christian faith, truths that bring spiritual life and spiritual freedom in Christ. The congregation thrives when this precious freedom is exercised in dependence upon the Word and Spirit; it suffers when this freedom is diminished, surrendered, or lost.

NOTES

[1] The founders of the Lutheran Free Church were unique in American Lutheranism in that they did not consider church polity an "open question" or an *adiaphora* (an indifferent matter). They were united in the conviction that the New Testament sets forth an instructive model of congregational life that is to be emulated and applied ever after. This includes the structure of the congregation. Georg Sverdrup, one of the founders of the LFC, was a main spokesman for this view. One of the later presidents of the LFC described Sverdrup's position as follows: "His concepts were not built on human theo-

ries, but on a sound Biblicism. He held that God's Word was a final authority in regard to the nature of the congregation and church polity fully as much as in matters of doctrine." John Stensvaag, "The Living Congregation: Georg Sverdrup's Views on Lay Activity in the Church" (seminary thesis, Augsburg Theological Seminary, n.d.), 4.

[2] Clarence J. Carlsen, *The Years of Our Church* (Minneapolis: The Lutheran Free Church Publishing Company, 1942), 46.

[3] Andreas Helland, *Georg Sverdrup: The Man and His Message 1848-1907* (Minneapolis: The Messenger Press, 1947), Epigraph.

[4] Many believe that Acts 6:2-6 is describing the origins of the office of deacon in the New Testament church even though the title of deacon is not applied to the seven men chosen to assist the apostles. While it is possible that what we see here is a temporary measure to meet a particular need, most would affirm that the emergence of the role of deacon in other New Testament congregations is connected to the model presented in Acts 6 by action of the Jerusalem congregation.

In Paul's greeting to the church at Philippi (Philippians 1:1), he recognizes two main orders of ministry in the congregation, namely, overseers (bishops) and deacons. The qualifications for these two offices are presented in I Timothy 3:2-13. In Acts 20:17-28, the terms overseer and elder are used interchangeably in reference to the same leaders from the church in Ephesus. It seems that the office of pastor is also applied to the same individuals in Paul's charge to these elders/overseers: "shepherd (pastor) the church of God which He purchased with His own blood" (v.28).

The list of qualifications in Titus 1:5-9 for spiritual leadership are also applied to persons who are referred to in the same context as elders (v.5) and overseers (v.7). Again, the designations appear interchangeable, referring to the same office. It has been argued that if the role of elder/overseer is distinct from that of the pastoral office, it is strange indeed that there is such scant reference to the office of pastor in the New Testament (Ephesians 4:11) and that there are no qualifications mentioned. It would seem most consistent in dealing with the New Testament texts to recognize and affirm two offices of spiritual leadership: first, the role of elder/overseer/pastor, and second, the role of deacon. Again, these are the two offices addressed in Philippians 1:1.

Though it is not a New Testament office, many congregations include "trustees" as a part of the leadership of the congregation. This office originated when the incorporation of congregations was quite difficult. As a consequence, it became the custom to place the title of the church property in the name of designated members of the congregation who served as "trustees." Today in many congregations the office is exercised by individuals who are entrusted with the care and management of the church property as well as other matters related to the material well-being of the congregation.

Very little is written or taught of the Christian congregation in our day. There is much concern of Christian fellowship, evangelism, doctrines of God, the Father, Son, and Holy Spirit, missions, ecumenism, denominations, the Word, history, eschatology, Christian education, youth work, liturgy, stewardship, etc., but little real concern for the congregation as such. This seems strange for the Christian congregation is so central in the New Testament. It was for the sake of the congregation, Paul suffered and labored: it was to strengthen, lead and build up congregations, he wrote his epistles: it was the congregations that he expected to carry the Gospel, to be God's house on earth, the pillar and foundation of truth. It was the congregation he considered to be Christ's body, Christ's bride. We stand in awe as we consider Christ and the congregation. Should we not be more concerned with the congregation than we are? Truly much more attention needs to be given this great subject. Living congregations are the life giving stream for our society, for the world.

—John P. Strand

5

Freedom, Life, and the Local Congregation

Georg Sverdrup's Theology of the Congregation

Martin L. Horn

As Georg Sverdrup surveyed Lutheranism in the mid-nineteenth century, he saw congregations in ruins. In his homeland of Norway, the congregations were in bondage to the state, and in many congregations true spiritual life was buried under worldliness and spiritual sleepiness.

When he came to America, Sverdrup saw that few Norwegian Lutheran congregations fared better here. Though free from bondage to the state, many congregations were under the domination of clergy and synod. Some congregations allowed themselves to be put to sleep by trusting their pure doctrine. Others were buried under worldliness and spiritual death.

Georg Sverdrup had one overriding objective: to restore the congregation to its New Testament and apostolic form. Sverdrup sought to "raise up . . . from the rubble"[1] the broken and enslaved congregations and to restore them in all their God-given glory as "the body of Christ, the bride of Christ, God's living temple of living stones, God's people, and his abode in the Spirit."[2]

What did Sverdrup believe was the apostolic and biblical congregation? First, he believed the congregation, and the congregation alone, was the true kingdom of God on earth, ruled only by Christ and His Spirit, and as such deserving the highest honor and glory. Second, the congregation is living when its members are awakened from spiritual sleep and raised from spiritual death. Third, when the congregation is living, it is also free; free from domination by men, free from worldliness, free from bondage to sin, and subject only to the Spirit and the Word. A biblical congregation, Sverdrup believed, could be summed up in what became the rallying cry of the Lutheran Free Church: "a free and living congregation."

Georg Sverdrup's life was consumed with the question "What is the congregation?" As he sought to answer this question, he did not turn to tradition, human reason, or pragmatism but solely to the Word of God. Sverdrup sought a thoroughly biblical understanding of the congregation.

The Biblical Congregation

The following pages will explore what Sverdrup believed about the identity and marks of the biblical congregation.

Sverdrup believed that the congregation is the visible form of the Kingdom of God on earth, and as a corollary is identical to the Kingdom of God. This understanding of the congregation led Sverdrup to see that the congregation occupies a central position in New Testament theology.

Sverdrup's appreciation of the congregation was further developed as he studied the images of the Kingdom of God such as the Bride of Christ and the Body of Christ. These representations of the Kingdom, Sverdrup observed, apply directly to the congregation and thus reveal the true glory of the congregation as the Kingdom of God.

This understanding of the congregation led Sverdrup to the conclusion that the congregation alone is the biblical form of the church on earth. Organizations such as synods that tie congregations together are not the church in the biblical sense, but are of human origin. They are not to be an authority over the congregation, but at best they are to serve the congregation.

Finally, Sverdrup believed that the congregation is the creation of the Holy Spirit and is sustained solely by the Spirit. Therefore he believed that the ministry of the congregation is the ministry of the Spirit's chosen means of grace, the Word and sacrament.

The Congregation and the Kingdom of God

The heart of Sverdrup's understanding of the biblical congregation is expressed in *Fundamental Principle 1* of the Lutheran Free Church, of which he was the principle author: "The congregation is the right form of the kingdom of God on earth." This principle expresses the biblical relationship between the two "forms" of the church spoken of in Scripture–the Kingdom of God, or the universal church, and the local congregation.

The universal church is the body of all Christians throughout the world in whom the Holy Spirit has created a true faith in Jesus Christ. Jesus referred to this church when He said to Peter, "Upon this rock I will build My church" (Matthew 16:18, NASB). Paul also spoke of the universal church in his letter to the Ephesians: "And He put all things in subjection under His feet, and gave Him as head over all things to the church" (Ephesians 1:22). Faith in Christ is the single identifying mark of the universal church. This was true from the beginning of the Christian church as recorded in the book of Acts. Founded on the day of Pentecost, Luke records that the church was comprised of "believers." Membership in the universal church is not defined by denominational distinctives, nor by levels of piety, nor by any other mark, except by faith in Christ.

Though outwardly the Christian church appears to be divided by denominational differences, Sverdrup believed the universal church possesses a unity of faith that transcends denominational lines. He writes, "just as it is not within the power of men to divide Christ, so it is not within the power of men to bring to naught the unity of His body. Men can establish many churches, but the body remains one."[3] The existence of denominations does not destroy the inward unity of the true church. On the other hand, the outward merger of denominations and synods does little to produce unity in the body of Christ. Sverdrup also says, "Friends, let us not go so astray that we imagine that we, by [an] external political church organization, can produce the unity . . . of believers."[4] Human action cannot produce unity, because the body of Christ is already one.

Because it is of faith, the universal church is invisible; that is, it cannot be seen by human eyes. Only God knows the heart and who is truly part of this church. Therefore, the universal church and its true glory are hidden to the world.[5]

There is a common belief that the congregation, with all its warts and imperfections, does not possess the same glory or status as the universal church. Consider Francis Schaeffer writing in *The Mark of the Christian*: "In theological terms there are, to be sure, a visible church and an invisible church. The invisible Church is the real Church—in a way, the only church that has the right to be spelled with a capital."[6] Is this true? Is only the universal church the "real" church and the local congregation, though good and deserving of respect, somehow lesser? Sverdrup would strongly disagree.

His answer is found in *Fundamental Principle 1*: "The congregation is the right *form* [emphasis mine] of the kingdom of God on earth." He means that the local congregation is not something separate from the universal church. The congregation is the local and visible form that the universal and invisible church assumes as it is revealed in the world.

Sverdrup believed that the church is both invisible and visible.[7] As stated earlier, the universal church is of faith and cannot be seen. Yet, Scripture declares the church is revealed for all the world to see. The same church whose life is "hidden with Christ in God" (Colossians 3:3) is at the same time the "city set on a hill" which "cannot be hidden" (Matthew 5:14).

How is the invisible, universal church revealed? According to *Fundamental Principle 1*, the church is made visible in the form of the local congregation.[8]

Sverdrup spoke of the congregation being visible in two ways. First, the congregation is visible because of the presence of the visible signs of the regular preaching of the Word and the right administration of the sacraments.[9] In fact, the means of grace are essential to the identity of the congregation. Sverdrup writes,

> Therefore it is the use of the Word and Sacraments that constitute a congregation in the Biblical sense. The cri-

terion of a congregation and its members is this, that they use the Word, baptism, and the Lord's Supper for the salvation of themselves and others.[10]

The congregation is a visible gathering of believers around the means of the Word and the sacraments. Unbelievers and hypocrites may be associated with the congregation and may even hold offices in its outward organization.[11] But the congregation should never be identified as all (believers and unbelievers) gathered together in one place. The congregation consists only of the believers.

Sverdrup was deeply concerned about the witness of the congregation in the world. Therefore, he not only defined the the congregation as visible through the objective signs of Word and sacrament, he also stressed that the congregation is made visible through the outward and subjective sanctification of its members.[12] The church is the body of Christ, he writes, and the congregation's purpose is to visibly reveal Christ.[13] The Word and sacraments are the light that reveals Christ. But in a worldly and sleepy congregation, sin obscures this light and dulls the testimony of the congregation. The congregation itself is also the "light of the world." The lives of its members are to shine in such a way that the congregation is visibly the body of Christ. As Sverdrup says, the congregation is truly visible when there are within it "believing men and women who work with the Word and the Sacraments."[14]

Sverdrup believed that the congregation is visible as the lives of its members are "rich in the fruits of grace and mercy."[15] Though a matter of the heart and essentially invisible, faith reveals itself outwardly. Jesus said, "Let your light shine before men in such a way that they may see your good works, and glorify your Father who is in heaven" (Matthew 5:16). The congregation is visible as it manifests the fruit of the Spirit (Galatians 5:22-23). The congregation is visible as believers exercise their spiritual gifts in real ministry within the congregation and without. Though the love and good works of the congregation are never perfect,[16] they visibly demonstrate the presence of God's people in a sinful world.

The universal church and the local congregation are simply the church seen from two different perspectives. The universal church is the church as seen through the eyes of faith. By faith, one understands that the church is an assembly of men justified by grace through faith and is thus holy, righteous, and full of glory.[17] This glory, though real, is hidden and cannot be seen by human eye.

The local congregation, on the other hand, is the church as revealed in this world and as seen by human eyes. Seen through human eyes, the congregation is small and seemingly weak and tainted by sin. Yet, in the congregation, one can see the Christian faith revealed in very practical and visible ways as the believers love and serve one another and care for the poor and needy in the world.

Because he believed the congregation is simply the invisible church made visible, Sverdrup is able to say that they are "one." He writes, "The visible and the invisible church are the same church. . . . The Scripture does not know any more than one church."[18] In another place he writes, "Are they two different kinds of churches? Far from it, for then they could not be called by the same name. . . . That Scripture uses the same word everywhere is proof enough that it does not differentiate between the church and the congregation."[19] The reason the New Testament uses the same name *ecclesia* for both, Sverdrup believes, is because *they are one and the same.*

Why was it so important to Sverdrup that the universal church and the congregation are one? Why does he say the universal church "is not a more exalted kind of community than the congregation,"[20] or "that the congregation has everything that the church has and is everything that the church is"?[21] Why is this conviction such a crucial element of Sverdrup's theology of the congregation?

If one does not understand this unity, one will not treat the local congregation with respect and honor. If one accepts Schaeffer's view, which is a view held by many Christians (whether consciously or unconsciously), one tends to focus on the local congregation's imperfections and weaknesses. Sverdrup knew that outwardly the congregation was far from perfect. In fact, he says, "the visible congregation will often present a spectacle not only of weakness and insignificance, but also of the contamination of sin. Its glory is not only hidden, but, what is worse, it is often darkened by hideous blemishes."[22] Nevertheless, because the congregation is the true church made up of justified believers, it is the bride of Christ, it is "holy and blameless" and without "spot or wrinkle" (Ephesians 5:27).

Once this truth shapes the believer's heart, his attitude toward the congregation changes. Though he may realize his local congregation is not what it should be, he won't belittle it or write it off as unworthy. Instead, he will see it as holy, precious, and worthy of the deepest respect because it is "the Kingdom of God on earth."

The Congregation: Glorious and Holy

Sverdrup's perception of the congregation was greatly influenced by the metaphors and images of the congregation portrayed in the New Testament. These images express the congregation's glory as God's people.

The New Testament image Sverdrup referred to most often is the congregation as the "body of Christ." In I Corinthians 12:27 Paul writes, "Now you are Christ's body, and individually members of it." In one sense, Christ is no longer present to personally minister in this world, but in another sense He is. As the body of Christ, the congregation is the physical presence of Christ in this world, and its members are His hands and feet, His mouth and eyes. As members of the congregation serve each other and the world around them, it is Christ who is serving. As the congregation speaks the Word of Christ, it is Christ who is speaking. As the congregation feeds the hungry, it is Christ who feeds the hungry. The local congregation is nothing less than the physical presence of Christ in a needy world. The congregation, then, as the body of Christ is His chosen means of ministry in this world.

Another New Testament image Sverdrup often refers to is the congregation as the "bride of Christ." According to Ephesians 5, the death of Christ is presented as the ultimate act of a loving groom so that His intended bride be cleansed from all impurity. The Church is then sanctified through "the washing of water with the word" in baptism. Thus the Church, His chosen bride, is "holy and blameless," without "spot or wrinkle" (Ephesians 5:25-27). Though this passage directly refers to the universal church, according to Sverdrup, it applies as well to the congregation. As a groom delights in his bride, so Christ delights in His congregation no matter how deficient it may be. This reveals how a congregation should be seen, not through human eyes that see the sin and hypocrisy of its members but through the eyes of Christ that see it as His holy and pure bride.

Sverdrup also spoke of the congregation as the "temple of God." In I Corinthians 6:19, Paul refers to the individual Christian ["your body" singular] as the temple of God; however, in 3:16, Paul refers to the Corinthian congregation. Paul writes to the Corinthians, "Do you not know that you [plural] are a temple of God, and that the Spirit of God dwells in you?" (I Corinthians 3:16). As the temple of God, the congregation is the dwelling place of the Holy Spirit and therefore holy and inviolable. Thus Paul warns with chilling words those who would sow division in the congregation, "If any man destroys the temple of God, God will destroy him, for the temple of God is holy, and that is what you are" (I Corinthians 3:17).

Sverdrup's understanding of the congregation is not limited to those portions of the New Testament that directly refer to the congregation. He writes, "Everything that is said about the only holy church is also said about the individual churches in each place."[23] This means that all of the images of the church in the New Testament apply to the congregation, even when they are not directly attributed to the congregation. Of these images, some of the most significant are found in the Kingdom parables. The congregation is the "treasure hidden in a field" and the "pearl of great price" (Matthew 13:44-46, NKJV) for the sake of which a man would give up everything he possessed.

In light of these New Testament images, Sverdrup admonishes both pastors and members to revere and esteem their congregation:

> And, since it is an irreversible fact that the New Testament speaks with the deepest reverence and the most sacred earnestness concerning just these local congregations and calls them God's congregations and God's temple, the body of Christ and the bride of Christ, it behooves us also to speak with all reverence and respect of this divine institution among us and deem it very highly for the sake of Christ and God.[24]

The congregation is a "divine institution" to be honored and revered.

Sverdrup anticipated that some would ask, "How can the congregation be considered holy when it is so marked by sin and hypocrisy?" Sverdrup answered that the congregation is not holy because of the holiness of its members but because of the holiness of Christ present in the congregation.

> The congregation is holy, not by its own, but [by] God's holiness, which is present through the means of grace. It is a gathering of people who have dared to take up, for their and their fellow men's use, the only holy thing that is found on earth: the Lord's Word and sacraments. . . . It is He Himself that makes the house holy. He Himself is the only source of holiness and from Him holiness goes out by Word and sacraments to the congregation and its members.[25]

As the individual believer is not righteous in himself but possesses the righteousness of Christ by faith, so too the congregation is not righteous in itself but possesses the righteousness of Christ.[26]

Sverdrup believed that the failure to recognize the holiness of the congregation leads to a diminished view of the congregation and to unbiblical judgmentalism and strife. Because of dissatisfaction over the sin and unbelief within it, some treat the congregation with disdain. They either stand above and apart in judgment of their congregation or leave it altogether. Others are tempted to take matters into their own hands and seek to purify the congregation by human means. This judgmental spirit invariably ends with a congregation in discord.[27]

The Congregation and Christian Organizations

When Sverdrup says "the congregation is the right form of the Kingdom of God on earth," he is insisting that the congregation is not simply an outward form, it is the *sole* form of the Kingdom of God on earth. Some would say there are other valid forms of the church such as a synod, or a denomination, or an historic episcopate. In most cases these forms of the "church" are regarded as superior to and as having authority over the congregation.

Sverdrup would not agree. According to James Hamre in *Georg Sverdrup: Educator, Theologian, Churchman*, Sverdrup believes that the congregation is the "only divinely instituted form of the Kingdom of God on earth."[28] Sverdrup observed that no other ecclesiastical institution or organization is found in Scripture:

> We mean that in the New Testament nothing is said about an episcopate over or in more than one congregation; nothing is said about a papacy, church department, consistory, council, or synod. In every place where there are Christians there is a congregation. . . . According to the New Testament it is necessary for the Kingdom of God to have a congregation, but we cannot see that some other outer organization over the congregation is a necessary part of Christianity.[29]

Sverdrup concluded that since they are not found in Scripture, no other religious institution, whether the Roman Catholic papacy, the historic episcopate, presbytery, synod, or other denominational organization can rightly be called the Church. He states flatly: "there is no other church apart from the congregations in all the individual places."[30] All other ecclesiastical organizations are of human origin. Sverdrup believed that the congregation alone is sanctioned by Scripture and "the congregation is an adequate form for the kingdom of God, and that no other form is required from the time of the outpouring of the Spirit until Christ's return."[31]

Sverdrup, however, did not believe that congregations should necessarily be independent of each other. He believed that, according to Scripture, congregations can and do cooperate with one another in areas of mutual concern and ministry. Furthermore, congregations may form organizations expressly to facilitate their mutual work. But such organizations exist only to serve the local congregation and must not exercise any authority over the congregation or individual believer.

What about other Christian organizations–college "parachurch" ministries such as InterVarsity Fellowship and Campus Crusade, independent mission boards, and evangelistic associations? How can the congregation be the sole form of the Kingdom of God on earth when so much positive spiritual work is done through organizations such as these? Do they not accomplish just as significant work for the Kingdom of God as the local congregation, and in some cases even more?

The unique position the congregation occupies does not invalidate these spiritual enterprises. These may, indeed, be led by the Spirit and accomplish valid spiritual work. Nevertheless, the congregation occupies a position no other Christian organization can match.

Johan Rødvik, a Lutheran Free Church pastor in the 1920s, referred to the congregation as the "saving fellowship" and to other such groups as a Bible Society or an Inner Mission as a "fellowship of the saved."[32] By this he meant that the congregation alone possesses all the saving means of grace–the Word, baptism, and the Lord's Supper. Only in the congregation can the believer find all the means the Spirit uses to create, strengthen, and sustain a living faith. Therefore, for the sake of his own soul, the believer seeks to be a part of a local congregation. On the other hand, these other spiritual enterprises are a "fellowship of believers." That is, they are composed of individual believers, often from several different congregations, who freely come together for a specific purpose and work.

But no other human organization can offer the full measure of God's saving grace as the congregation as it preaches the saving Word, baptizes the lost, and strengthens the believer through the Lord's Supper. All other organizations are temporary and voluntary; only the congregation is essential.

The Congregation and the Spirit

Sverdrup believed passionately in the need for the work of the Holy Spirit in the congregation. He writes that "where the mighty power of the Spirit is not present . . . there is no congregation."[33] Sverdrup believed in what could be called the "Spirit-driven" congregation. The congregation is a creation of the Spirit and is dependent entirely upon the presence, work, and leading of the Holy Spirit. The presence and work of the Holy Spirit is far more important to the building of the congregation than any plan or program man can devise. Pastor Ludvig Pederson, speaking at a Bible conference on "The Congregation," said, "The power and cleverness of men cannot yield spiritual profit. The work of a congregation depends on God's Spirit. We must pray that the Holy Spirit will lead us."[34] Therefore, pastor and laymen together must prayerfully seek the Spirit of God to direct their congregation.

How does the Holy Spirit direct the congregation? The Holy Spirit gathers and sustains the local congregation through the means of grace–the Word and the sacraments.

The Spirit-driven congregation is centered on the preaching of the Word. Sverdrup declares "that the congregation must be gathered by means of God's Word."[35] He goes on to say that "The invitation, persuasion, and compulsion of the Word are the only means to be used to bring people into the congregation."[36]

Sverdrup also reminds us that Word-centered preaching is preaching that is focused on Christ.

> Jesus Christ is the truth. Only by means of a true preaching of Christ will there come to be a congregation. Let that sound forth, and the congregation will be built, will grow, and will be strengthened. Put something else

in its place, no matter how popular it may be, and the congregation will stagnate . . . and will lose more and more of its nature and strength.[37]

It is apparent that pastor and congregation must resist the latest popular trends if these trends crowd out the message of Christ from the central position in the congregation.

The Spirit-driven congregation holds the sacraments of baptism and the Lord's Supper as vital, for they convey the same promise and the same gospel as the Word. It is the same Word that is attached to the visible signs.

Sverdrup urges the congregation to use the means of grace, then, for the sake of her spiritual life.

> The congregation, which from the beginning is born of the Spirit, can live only by the Spirit. Thus, the Spirit's means, the word and sacraments, are the means whereby the life of the congregation is transmitted and preserved. Only baptism, the word, and the Lord's supper, when used properly, can bring forth and sustain a living congregation.[38]

> The Word and the Sacraments must be used, and they must be used according to the ordinance of God. They must be used to bring about conversion and faith both within the congregation and outside of it. They must be used to preserve, strengthen, nourish, and sustain the faith and life in the congregation.[39]

The ultimate program of the congregation is to employ the Word and the sacraments so that the Holy Spirit has the greatest opportunity to bring life. All the Spirit's means necessary for spiritual life are found in the congregation.

It is contrary to Scripture to say a person can call oneself a Christian and deliberately live apart from a congregation. To deliberately separate oneself from the congregation is to deliberately separate oneself from the Kingdom of God and the work of the Holy Spirit. For according to Sverdrup, "The congregation is the right form of the Kingdom of God on earth." The congregation *is* the Kingdom of God. It is the body of Christ, the bride of Christ, and the temple of God. It is where the Holy Spirit reveals Himself through the means of grace. The congregation is where the believer finds the full wealth of God's salvation in Christ.

The Living Congregation

Sverdrup believed that, above all, the congregation should be alive. The congregation is the body of Christ, he noted, but the only difference between a body and a corpse is life.[40] Therefore, spiritual life is a fundamental necessity of a congregation. Without spiritual life, the congregation ceases to exist.

Sverdrup's concern for life in the congregation began in Norway, where as a young man he saw so many lifeless congregations. Church membership was compulsory. Many people belonged to the church, but few were converted. In many congregations, spiritual life was at low ebb, and what little life they had was buried under apathy, sin, and spiritual deadness.

Sverdrup saw this again when he came to America. Numerous Lutheran congregations were being established in Norwegian communities, and thousands were gathered into the congregations. Unfortunately, many members were brought in without any apparent concern over their spiritual condition. They were gathered, not by the Spirit and the Word, but by "habit and custom."[41] Sverdrup was not satisfied. The goal of the Spirit is not large organizations, but "living congregations."[42]

The Congregation and Spiritual Life

What did Sverdrup mean by the "living congregation"? Simply put, a living congregation is one where the Holy Spirit has produced life through the Word and sacraments in its members, and these "living" members are the norm and not the exception. By contrast, in a "dead congregation," the spiritually alive are the exception and not the rule. In a "dead congregation," true spiritual life may be all but buried beneath sin and hypocrisy.

Some questioned Sverdrup's distinction between "living" and "dead" congregations. "Are not all congregations alive?" they asked. "Didn't Jesus say that 'where two or three have gathered together in My name, there I am in their midst'? If Christ is present in the congregation, is it not a true congregation, and thus living?"

Sverdrup defended his distinction between "living" and "dead" congregations as biblical by drawing attention to Revelation 3:1-6 and the church of Sardis.[43] The congregation in Sardis was certainly a true congregation. In verse one, Christ Himself calls it a church and later affirms that there were a few who had not "soiled their garments," who still had a heart of faith. In spite of its deplorable spiritual condition, the Sardis congregation did not cease to be a congregation.

But the congregation in Sardis was dead. Verse one reads, "He who has the seven Spirits of God, and the seven stars, says this: 'I know your deeds, that you have a name that you are alive, and you are dead.'" The congregation had a reputation for life, but it was dead. Believers were few, and what little life there was, was buried under sin and unbelief.

Christ did not reject the Sardis congregation. It was still His body and His holy bride. It was still precious to Him. Therefore, He warned them, "'Wake up, and strengthen the things that remain, which were about to die'" (v.2). He encouraged them to remember what they had received and "keep it, and repent" (v.3). Clearly, from Scripture, a true congregation may have unbelievers in its midst, but as C. J. Carlsen says in *The Years of Our Church*, "it is equally clear from the Scriptures that the congregations were not to be content with this state of affairs; they were to seek to win the unbelieving church members to the new life in God."[44] Christ was not content with spiritual deadness then. Neither is He now. The Lord desires "living congregations."

Sverdrup saw that believers have a biblical responsibility to seek life in the congregation. He writes, "So then, because the New Testament will have life and unceasingly works against death, therefore we believe that it is a holy calling and duty to work for 'living congregations.'"[45] Some were willing to be content with a spiritually dead congregation. "The word is preached, the Spirit has worked what it will," they said, "and who are we to question the outcome?" Sverdrup would have nothing to do with this fatalism. True, the Spirit "blows where it will." But Sverdrup believed the Spirit also gives believers a deep concern and zeal for the lost. He himself prayed and worked and longed for revival in the congregation.

However, Sverdrup also believed that those working to bring about a living congregation must proceed carefully. He observed that some pastors, in their zeal for spiritual life, treated their congregations as "mission fields."[46] True, the congregation is a mission in the sense that unbelievers are to be evangelized. But some took this to its extreme. These pastors did not take seriously the fact that their congregation was still a congregation and that there were still believers there, though hidden under sin and unbelief. In their zeal to convert the unbelievers, they often confused those who were already believers and caused some to stumble.

Some people believe that the congregation should guard against spiritual deadness by allowing only true Christians into membership. These people believe the congregation should judge the hearts of men by separating believers from unbelievers.

There are several objections to this. First, the congregation cannot infallibly discern the heart. Only God can do so. The Church can only consider the outward signs of faith and exclude "the openly sinful and perverse."[47] Second, even if a congregation were formed with a "pure" membership, its purity would not last long. Sin can easily snare some, others may fall asleep, and the congregation would no longer be pure. Finally, purifying the outward membership is a human solution to a spiritual problem. Man cannot purify the congregation and make it living. Only the Holy Spirit can create a living congregation through the Word and sacraments. The Spirit creates life where there is none and strengthens what life there is.

What is the work for a "living congregation"? Sverdrup outlined the congregation's work in an article entitled "Congregations Made Alive," published in 1898.[48]

Sverdrup believed that a major and foundational part of the work toward a living congregation is infant baptism. He writes, "The right work for a living congregation has its starting point in infant baptism. It is impossible to have the right practice in a Lutheran congregation if we do not make a good stand there."[49] Sverdrup firmly held to the Lutheran teaching that baptism is a means of grace, and through baptism the Spirit of God creates spiritual life in the infant.[50] Life in the congregation begins here, and the work for a congregation begins here. In contrast to some who minimized infant baptism in their quest for spiritual life, Sverdrup prized it as essential for the "living congregation."

Sverdrup did not believe the work for a "living congregation" ends in infant baptism. That is, in practical terms he did not believe that infant baptism was a *de facto* form of eternal security. The baptized can and often do fall away from their baptismal faith. Tragically, many Lutheran congregations are "spiritually dead" as their pews have become filled with the "baptized lost."

Sverdrup, therefore, taught that the work for a living congregation continues as the spiritual life granted in baptism must be nourished so none of these little children will be lost:

> But as our children receive with baptism life in God, spiritual life, so that they become living members of Jesus' living body, so it is clear that baptism brings the high and holy obligation, that life be nourished and preserved by the Word of life in and through the congregation. . . . If the little ones shall not be starved to death spiritually, nor either be torn away from Christ's body by force and power or by Satan's cunning and deceiving ways, or by the cunning power of the world, so must all the members of the congregation both know their responsibility and be on guard and accomplish the work in the right time and the right way.
>
> This is the place, where above all things, it is neces-

sary to redeem the opportune time and begin early and continue until late, yes, "without letup." This is the work from generation to generation across the fading times.[51]

The work to strengthen children's faith is a ministry of the Word, and this work requires all the resources of the congregation: parents, pastors, teachers, men and women. All are obligated to labor together for the sake of the children's spiritual life.

The work for a living congregation does not end with the children. Sverdrup believed if the adults themselves are not spiritually alive, the work for the sake of the children of the congregation becomes nothing more than an exercise in "the blind leading the blind."[52]

The work for a living congregation also includes evangelization of the lost in the congregation, including the "baptized lost." The congregation cannot grow complacent about unbelievers in the congregation. Instead, Sverdrup writes that the congregation "must awaken to a serious concern for the salvation of souls and life in the congregation."[53] John Strand, the first president of the AFLC, strongly agreed. He writes in one of the early issues of *The Lutheran Ambassador*,

> we must not consider all our people Christians. . . . While we believe in baptismal regeneration, because many are not taught God's Word in home and church as they ought to be, because many reject God's claims on them through the Word, they lose their faith and their souls. They need to be brought back. There ought to be a great burden on our hearts for the unsaved.[54]

Both men unreservedly advocated evangelism in Lutheran congregations.

In his theology of the "living congregation," Sverdrup demonstrated a true evangelical Lutheran understanding of the relationship between infant baptism and the spiritual life of the adult. Sverdrup was not a "sacramentalist." He did not believe that all who participate in the sacraments are necessarily

Christians. Some of those baptized as infants fall from grace. Some receive the Lord's Supper with indifferent and unbelieving hearts.

But neither was Sverdrup a "sacramentarian," that is, he did not minimize the sacraments of baptism and the Lord's Supper, as some do who treat them as unnecessary or even dangerous to true spiritual life in the congregation.

Like a man driving on an icy road, Sverdrup strove to "drive straight," without sliding into the ditch of sacramentalism on one side or the ditch of sacramentarianism on the other. His goal was life in the congregation.

Sverdrup firmly believed that infant baptism is a true means of grace whereby the Lord creates faith and life in the heart of the infant. The child, by the work of the Holy Spirit, is able to remain in this saving faith all his life, and many do. Sverdrup also knew that the believer is capable of falling away from faith, and many do. He passionately believed that evangelism in the congregation is absolutely necessary. The Word must be preached that the lost be saved. The Holy Spirit must call through the Gospel. The lost must be converted. This must continue to be the conviction of the AFLC–to drive straight ahead, avoiding the ditches on either side, with the goal of living congregations clearly in mind.

The Congregation and Spiritual Gifts

Sverdrup believed that a living congregation is an active congregation. A dead body is inactive, but life is revealed through activity. For Sverdrup, this had a specific meaning in the congregation. A living congregation is not necessarily a busy congregation with a full calendar of events. A living congregation is one where the members exercise their spiritual gifts in real ministry and service to those within and without the congregation under the direction of the Spirit.

Like the members of the physical body, each member of the congregation has been given by God a specific role and purpose. In order that the believer may effectively exercise his role in the body of Christ, God has granted him spiritual gifts.

Thus, Scripture teaches that every member of the congregation is necessary to the congregation. Paul writes to the Corinthian congregation, "But to each one is given the manifestation of the Spirit for the common good" (I Corinthians 12:7). Note Paul's phrase "each one." Spiritual gifts are not reserved for a few in the congregation. Each believer is equipped; each one has a role and a work to do in the congregation. No one should think he is unimportant and without a purpose in the ministry of the congregation (I Corinthians 12:15-16).

Further, a Christian should not see that he is a part of his congregation by accident. In I Corinthians 12:18 Paul writes, "But now God has placed the members, each one of them, in the body, just as He desired." Believers are placed in the congregation by the will and wisdom of God.

A Christian should never despise his congregation, or his place in the congregation. If God in His wisdom has placed him in that congregation, he is where God wills him to be, both for his own sake and for the sake of his brothers and sisters in Christ. Because of this, Sverdrup encouraged believers to stay in their congregation even if it seemed spiritually dead and worldly. Sverdrup said that such a believer must remember that even though sin is present in the congregation, Christ and the Spirit are still there, and he should pray "that he himself might be worthy for the calling by which he is called" in that congregation.[55] Andreas Helland summed up Sverdrup's response to those who were considering leaving their congregation because of worldliness and sin: "Remain where you are and work and suffer, rather than choosing the easier way, to go out."[56]

One must be careful here. Sverdrup is not addressing the issue of leaving a church that is teaching false doctrine. He is only addressing the situation where a member feels his congregation is not as "holy" or "spiritual" as he thinks it should be. It is sometimes true that there is need for the painful step of leaving a congregation when efforts to address false teaching have failed.

Sverdrup also believed that in a living congregation all the gifts must be exercised. A physical body functions best when all the members work together in harmony. The body may be able to function if some of its members are missing or inactive, but not to the full extent that God intends for it. In the same way, the congregation functions as it should when all the members exercise their spiritual gifts in harmony. Sverdrup writes,

> The gifts and powers of the Spirit are all to be used. None ought to lie unused, no talent should be hidden in the ground. . . . All are considered to be important. Men, women, and children, young and old–all are to join in, for that is the demand of freedom and the Spirit.[57]

When only a few are actively using their spiritual gifts in the congregation, the body of Christ is crippled and impoverished.

This is especially true when the pastor alone ministers in the congregation. The pastor is the leader of the congregation in the work of ministry, but as Sverdrup writes, he is not their substitute.

> many members of congregations would gladly have the pastor do their living and working for them; this is easier for them. . . . [But] Scripture describes individual Christians as alive and working, witnessing and prophesying, and these tasks simply cannot be done vicariously for the members by a salaried pastor.[58]

Far from being their substitute, Sverdrup believed the pastor has the significant role of encouraging the members in the use of their spiritual gifts.[59] Sverdrup's comparison of the pastor to a choir director is instructive,

> The congregation is not organized, unless there is work for all. It is not for a congregation to hire a preacher to work for it, so they themselves can escape their duty. No, the congregation in this way is likened to a choir [which] has to have a song leader to instruct and lead. Shall the instructor sing alone? Shall not all join in? Such is the congregation; it is a gathering of God's servants who

work for God's kingdom, for Christ's cause. The leader is not superfluous, but is the more necessary so that they may sing in unison.⁶⁰

The pastor not only encourages but also strengthens the members for the work the Lord gives them. Sverdrup writes of the layman's work: "The work ought to be difficult enough for flesh and blood so that there will be a real cross to bear in the footsteps of Jesus."⁶¹ The pastor's work is not to make the work easy for the members of the congregation, but to equip the saints for the work of service (Ephesians 4:11-12).

Sverdrup's understanding of the biblical form of the congregation was far different from what he saw around him. The work of the congregation is not accomplished by religious professionals as they spoon feed a passive laity. In a living congregation, pastor and lay people join together in a common work that requires the cooperation and the gifts of all.

The Free Congregation

"Where the Spirit of the Lord is, there is freedom" (II Corinthians 3:17, RSV). In this verse, Sverdrup shows that as the congregation is the work of the Holy Spirit and as the Spirit creates life within it, the true congregation is in essence free. He writes, "The Gospel produces the freest of all free, a child of God. It also produces the free fellowship, the congregation."⁶² Sverdrup prized freedom as one of the Spirit's greatest gifts to the congregation.

But Sverdrup saw that a large number of congregations were not free. Many forces conspired to rob the congregations of their freedom—well-meaning but overly-zealous pastors, spiritual laziness, and outright worldliness. Therefore, as Sverdrup sought to restore life to the congregation, he sought to set the congregation free.

The freedom of the congregation is a dominant theme in Sverdrup's writings. As he writes, Sverdrup addresses two different aspects of congregational freedom. First, congregational freedom is freedom from domination by human authority, freedom that gives the Spirit of God the most room in which to work. Second, congregational freedom is true inner spiritual freedom, the freedom from sin and worldliness that is the result of spiritual life.

Freedom from Human Authority

In the 1800s the Lutheran church was the established religion of Norway.[63] The nation was officially Lutheran. The church was a department of state, and pastors were royal officials.

As a young man growing up in Norway, Sverdrup was critical of the state church. He was sympathetic to the Church Reform movement, which sought to correct problems caused by the control the state had over the church. He felt the root problem was that the state church hindered spiritual life in the congregations.

Sverdrup was deeply concerned that the state discouraged spiritual activity among the laymen. Lay preaching and testimony were in many instances prohibited. Laymen had no responsibility for either the temporal or spiritual welfare of the congregation.[64] Laymen were not even permitted to take an offering for missions in their own congregations until legislation was passed specifically permitting them to do so.[65]

On the other hand, the state church benevolently cared for all the needs of the church such as training pastors, building and keeping up the churches, and paying the pastors' salaries.[66] The state was responsible for the religious education of the young, and confirmation was compulsory. Some saw these as great benefits that the church should not give up. But Sverdrup saw such care by the state as nothing less than spiritual bondage.[67] True freedom is not freedom from responsibility but freedom to be servants of the Lord. Such dependency on the state kept believers from spiritual maturity by not allowing them to shoulder responsibility for their own congregation.[68] The state church had a devastating effect on the congregation. The state church, Andreas Helland writes, "impaired the will to work and had thus retarded spiritual progress"[69] in the congregation.

Sverdrup advocated that the congregation be freed from the authority of the state. Responsibility for the affairs of the congregation should be placed in the hands of the laymen in order to encourage spiritual maturity. He admitted that by becoming independent of the state the congregation would lose much "in the way of ease and external advantages."[70] But this loss would be more than offset by what the congregation would gain. Sverdrup observed that shouldering responsibility for one's own congregation requires, "a little bit of the renunciation of flesh and blood in order to belong to a congregation; and even though this is just a small cross, it has already brought about considerable good effects."[71] As believers take up their cross and follow Jesus, even in a small way, they are on the path of spiritual maturity, and the congregation itself becomes strengthened.

When Sverdrup accepted a call to Augsburg Seminary in 1874, he saw America as a God-given opportunity to restore the congregation to its true apostolic form as found in the New Testament.[72] He sought to establish free congregations and believed it could best be done in a country where religion was completely free from the authority of the state.

However, Sverdrup was careful to point out that freedom from the state does not mean that the congregation is necessarily free. If this were true, he said, the Catholic Church would be a free church.[73] The Catholic Church is free of the state, but it is still bound under human authority in the form of an ecclesiastical hierarchy that stifles the spiritual life of the congregation.

Therefore, Sverdrup believed the congregation must not only be free from the state but also free from any ecclesiastical authority. When Sverdrup came to America, he saw that many Norwegian Lutheran congregations were not truly free. They merely traded subjection to the state for subjection to a synod.

New Testament congregations, Sverdrup saw, were free from any form of ecclesiastical authority over them. He saw synods and other church organizations that were over the congregation as non-biblical and unnecessary.[74] But more than that, any such organization, no matter how benevolent, serves to bind and stifle the congregation. Sverdrup believed that ecclesiastical authority is a greater threat to the freedom of the congregation than the secular power of the state.[75]

The congregation must also be free from domination by the pastor. Sverdrup wrote that pastors can become the masters of their congregations from both base and noble motives.[76] Some pastors dominate the congregation from a desire for power. Others dominate the congregation out of a zeal for holiness. Both can enslave the congregation.

Even when the congregation is free of ecclesiastical authority and domination by the clergy, Sverdrup made it very clear that this does not guarantee that the congregation is truly free. The only true freedom is the freedom of the Spirit as He sets men free from sin. A congregation may be "free" outwardly but not possess true freedom. Sverdrup writes, "we have only a travesty of a free congregation, as long as genuine worldliness and death are not only found, but even rule in the congregation as it does in so many places."[77] In 1918 at a Bible conference on "The Congregation," Elias Harbo warned that there still was spiritual sleepiness and death and slavery to sin in many congregations of the Lutheran Free Church, and one should not assume that one's congregation is a true free church.[78]

If outward freedom does not guarantee true spiritual freedom, why did Sverdrup insist on it? Because any form of human authority, no matter how benevolent it appears, may be detrimental to the congregation.

Only the Spirit and the Word produce life. Any other power or authority over the congregation has a deadening effect as the leading of man replaces the leading of the Holy Spirit. Thus, such human authority hinders the work of the Holy Spirit in the congregation. A congregation, Sverdrup says, is free, "but not so free that it can give away freedom without . . . suffering harm."[79] Sverdrup believed that freedom gives the Spirit "more room to work" and provides the best "seed-bed" for life. Therefore, the freedom of the congregation must be fiercely guarded.

Freedom from Spiritual Bondage

Sverdrup believed emphatically that freedom is ultimately spiritual freedom. He often appealed to John 8:36: "If therefore the Son shall make you free, you shall be free indeed." Freedom from external bondage is necessary, but the congregation is truly free when the hearts of its members are set free by Christ.

What is spiritual freedom? Andreas Helland, in "The Lutheran Free Church," writes,

> true Christian liberty is fundamentally freedom from the bondage of sin. . . . For this reason the congregation can not be truly free, except the Son of God make it free. Consequently there is no freedom, except there be life, spiritual life born of true faith in Jesus Christ. Only in so far as the congregation is a living congregation, is it a free congregation. For freedom is the fruit, not the root of life.[80]

The truly free congregation is not only free from human authority but also free from an even greater bondage, the bondage of sin.

"Now the Lord is the Spirit; and where the Spirit of the Lord is, there is freedom" (II Corinthians 3:17, RSV). Because Sverdrup and others believed this verse demonstrated true Christian freedom, it was used as a theme verse for the LFC and has continued as such in the AFLC. True freedom is freedom brought by the Holy Spirit. True freedom is therefore not primarily outward, organizational freedom but inward, spiritual freedom. James Hamre writes that Sverdrup believed, "Genuine freedom is a spiritual reality, a gift of the Spirit who works through word and sacraments in the free and living congregations. It is a release from the bondage of sin made possible by Jesus Christ."[81] This is the freedom spoken of by Paul in Romans 8:2, "For the law of the Spirit of life in Christ Jesus has set you free from the law of sin and of death." The bonds of sin are broken in Christ.

Christian freedom is not license or freedom to do what one

wants. Paul instructs the Galatian congregations, "For you were called to freedom, brethren; only do not turn your freedom into an opportunity for the flesh, but through love serve one another" (Galatians 5:13). Andreas Helland, commenting on Sverdrup's understanding of Christian freedom, writes, "It is liberty, not license. It is to be in harmony with the will of God, not to yield to one's own selfishness. It is freedom from the bondage of sin, from worldliness, from one's own sinful lusts and desires."[82]

Sverdrup did not believe in "sinless perfection." Spiritual freedom was not freedom from sin, but freedom from bondage or slavery to sin. Romans 6:14 reads, "For sin shall not be master over you, for you are not under law, but under grace." The believer is not without sin. He still has his old nature. But sin no longer reigns over him and enslaves him.

Sverdrup also understood that freedom is the freedom to serve. He writes, "Where the Spirit of the Lord is, there is freedom–freedom to work, freedom to suffer, freedom to live for a cause, freedom even to die for a cause."[83] One can see that the most humble servant of the Lord is the most truly free.

Sverdrup further understood that service to God is ultimately expressed in service to one's local congregation. He encourages with these words, "This, then, is freedom, that each man and each woman who loves the Lord may have the permission and opportunity to serve Him in the congregation."[84] And again, he writes of the Apostle Paul, "Paul's blessed exultation is that one serves God by serving God's congregation, fighting for it, suffering for it, loving it, and sacrificing for it."[85] In fact, Sverdrup pointed to Paul as the example of sacrificial service to God and the congregation.

> It was for the congregation Paul offered a life full of the greatest exertion and the most painful suffering; it was in order to build up the congregation that he traveled and preached; it was to strengthen, secure, inform, and build up the congregation that he wrote his precious letters.[86]

Here is the genius of freedom through the eyes of Sverdrup. He saw the free congregation. But this freedom is not the freedom of the flesh, the freedom to do what one wants. This freedom is the freedom of the Spirit, the freedom to be what God intends one to be–a servant of God. Thus a truly free congregation is a congregation of servants, and when the members of the congregation are nothing more than servants of God by His Spirit, the congregation has achieved the highest form of freedom.

Conclusion

Sverdrup sought one thing–to recover the New Testament congregation. What did he find? The bride of Christ, sanctified and made holy by His blood. A holy temple, filled with the Spirit of God. The congregation is a living body, animated by the Spirit, active in ministry both within and without, and finally, free men enjoying the greatest freedom possible–selfless service to God and their own congregation.

Do we dare seek the same in our time? Do we dare set aside our own understanding and our own wisdom and pursue the true congregation? May these words by Sverdrup apply to us also:

> And this cause is for these times our people's and our churches' greatest task, that the congregation can win its right form among us. If that happens, then these sufferings that come over us will be nothing compared to the blessings which will flow from generation to generation from congregations truly made free. If the city on the hill is built truly solid and fast and high, lighting up wide around with God's Word and the love of Jesus Christ, so shall truly the light carry blessing with itself to the souls both near and far, both at home and in the heathen land. And down through the long ages will the fruit show itself of that work the Lord did also in our days, that He led His congregation to the freedom of Spirit and faith, of life and love.[87]

NOTES

[1] Georg Sverdrup, "A Visible Congregation," in *Veiledning i Den Lutherske Frikirkes Principer*, ed. John Evjen; trans. Martin Horn (Minneapolis: The Free Church Book Concern, 1914), 38.

[2] Georg Sverdrup, "Members of the Congregation," (*Professor Georg Sverdrups Samlede skrifter i udvalg*, ed. Andreas Helland 3:268-272) in James S. Hamre, "Georg Sverdrup's Concept of the Role and Calling of the Norwegian-American Lutherans: An Annotated Translation of Selected Writings" (Ph. D. diss., University of Iowa,1967), 215.

[3] Andreas Helland, *Georg Sverdrup: The Man and His Message* (Minneapolis: Messenger Press, 1947), 212.

[4] Sverdrup, "The Unity of Believers," in *Samlede skrifter*, trans. Bernhard Nelson, 2:376.

[5] Sverdrup, "The Free Church Fellowship," in *Samlede skrifter*, trans. Martin Bjornson, 2:55.

[6] Francis Schaeffer, *The Mark of the Christian* (Downers Grove: InterVarsity Press, 1980), 20.

[7] Sverdrup, "The Free Church Fellowship," in *Samlede skrifter*, trans. Martin Bjornson, 2:55.

[8] Georg Sverdrup, "What Is the Congregation?" (*Samlede skrifter* 2:8-12) *The Lutheran Ambassador* 3, no. 18 (September 21, 1965): 3.

[9] C. F. W. Walther, a Missouri Synod theologian and an early contemporary of Sverdrup wrote, "While the one holy Christian church as a spiritual temple cannot be seen, but only be believed, there are nevertheless infallible outward marks by which its presence can be known. These marks are the unadulterated preaching of the divine Word and the uncorrupted administration of the holy sacraments." C. F. W. Walther, *The True Visible Church and The Form of a Christian Congregation*, Concordia Heritage Series (St. Louis: Concordia Publishing House, 1961), 8.

[10] Sverdrup, "What Is the Congregation?" (*Samlede skrifter* 2:8-12) *The Lutheran Ambassador* 3, no. 18 (September 21, 1965): 3. Note *Fundamental Principle 2*: "The congregation consists of believers who, by using the means of grace and the spiritual gifts as directed by the Word of God, seek salvation and eternal blessedness for themselves and for their fellow men."

[11] "Members of the organized congregation are not, in every instance, believers, and such hypocrites often derive false hope from their external connection with the congregation" (*Fundamental Principle 4*).

[12] C. F. W. Walther, by contrast, only defined the visible congregation objectively through the visible means of grace, as seen above. When he spoke

further of the visible congregation, he only spoke of the congregation in the "improper" sense, the visible congregation as the aggregate of all, believers and unbelievers, gathered around the means of grace. "In an improper sense Scripture calls also those visible communions 'churches' which, though consisting not only of believers as are sanctified by faith, but having also hypocrites and wicked persons, nevertheless teach the Gospel in its purity and administer the holy sacraments according to the Gospel." Walther, *The True Visible Church*, 12.

[13] Sverdrup, "A Visible Congregation," in *Veiledning*, 37.

[14] Sverdrup, "A Visible Congregation," in *Veiledning*, 38.

[15] Melvin Helland, trans., *The Heritage of Faith: Selections from the Writings of Georg Sverdrup* (Minneapolis: Augsburg Publishing House, 1969), 38.

[16] Melvin Helland, trans., *The Heritage of Faith*, 38.

[17] Sverdrup, "The Free Church Fellowship," *Samlede skrifter*, 2:55.

[18] Sverdrup, "Living Congregations," *Samlede skrifter*, trans. Martin Horn, 2:28.

[19] Melvin Helland, trans., *The Heritage of Faith*, 39.

[20] Melvin Helland, trans., *The Heritage of Faith*, 39.

[21] Sverdrup, "Members of the Congregation," (*Samlede skrifter* 3:268-272) in Hamre, "Georg Sverdrup's Concept of the Role and Calling," 215.

[22] Sverdrup, "The Free Church Fellowship," in *Samlede skrifter*, trans. Martin Bjornson, 2:56.

[23] Melvin Helland, trans., *The Heritage of Faith*, 39.

[24] Sverdrup, "What Is the Congregation?" (*Samlede skrifter* 2:8-12) *The Lutheran Ambassador* 3, no. 18 (September 21, 1965): 3.

[25] Sverdrup, "On the Congregation's Holiness," in *Samlede skrifter*, trans. John Horn, 2:15.

[26] K. L. Schmidt writes "agiotes (holiness) is ascribed to the ekklesia. . . . In other words, a true conception of the Church, the community, the assembly of God in Christ, stands or falls with a true conception of justification." K. L. Schmidt, "ekklesia," in *Theological Dictionary of the New Testament*, ed. Gerhard Kittel (Grand Rapids: Eerdmans, 1965), 3:512.

[27] Sverdrup, "On the Congregation's Holiness," in *Samlede skrifter*, trans. John Horn, 2:13-14.

[28] Hamre, *Georg Sverdrup: Educator, Theologian, Churchman* (Northfield, MN: The Norwegian-American Historical Association, 1986), 137.

[29] Sverdrup, "The Congregation," (*Samlede skrifter* 3:265-268) in Hamre,

"Georg Sverdrup's Concept of the Role and Calling," 208-209.

[30] Georg Sverdrup, "Is It Possible for Norwegian Lutherans to Build a Christian Free Church in America?" (*Samlede skrifter* 2:101-119) in Hamre, "Georg Sverdrup's Concept of the Role and Calling," 49.

[31] Sverdrup, "The Congregation," (*Samlede skrifter* 3:265-268) in Hamre "Georg Sverdrup's Concept of the Role and Calling," 209.

[32] Johan Rødvik, *Legems- og Hustankerne hos Paulus* (Minneapolis: The Lutheran Free Church Publishing Company, n.d.), 51.

[33] Sverdrup, "Members of the Congregation," (*Samlede skrifter* 3:268-272) in Hamre, "Georg Sverdrup's Concept of the Role and Calling," 213.

[34] Ludvig Pederson, "The Congregation's Origin, Makeup, and Format," in *Menigheten Foredrag holdt under bibelkonferansen i Eagle Lake Menighet, Willmar, Minnesota 19de til 21de Mars, 1918,* trans. Martin Horn (Willmar, Minnesota: Folkebladets Trykkeri, n.d.), 24.

[35] Melvin Helland, trans., *The Heritage of Faith*, 42.

[36] Melvin Helland, trans., *The Heritage of Faith*, 42.

[37] Sverdrup, "The Congregations Call to Cleanse Itself," (*Samlede skrifter* 3:276-280) in Hamre, "Georg Sverdrup's Concept of the Role and Calling," 227.

[38] Sverdrup, "The Congregation's Organization," (*Samlede skrifter* 3:272-276) in Hamre, "Georg Sverdrup's Concept of the Role and Calling," 218.

[39] Sverdrup, "What Is the Congregation?" *The Lutheran Ambassador* 3, no. 18 (September 21, 1965): 4. According to Paul, the unity of the congregation arises out of the sacraments. See I Corinthians 10:16-17, "Is not the cup of blessing which we bless a sharing in the blood of Christ? Is not the bread which we break a sharing in the body of Christ? Since there is one bread, we who are many are one body; for we all partake of the one bread." See also I Corinthians 12:13: "For by one Spirit we are all baptized into one body, whether Jews or Greeks, whether slaves or free."

[40] Sverdrup, "Congregations Made Alive," *Samlede skrifter*, trans. John Horn, 2:27.

[41] Sverdrup, "The Freedom of the Congregation," *Samlede skrifter*, trans. John Horn, 2:19.

[42] Sverdrup, "Congregations Made Alive," *Samlede skrifter*, trans. John Horn, 2:26.

[43] Sverdrup, "Congregations Made Alive," *Samlede skrifter*, trans. John Horn, 2:27.

[44] Clarence Carlsen, *The Years of Our Church* (Minneapolis: The Lutheran Free Church Publishing Company, 1942), 45.

⁴⁵ Sverdrup, "Congregations Made Alive," *Samlede skrifter*, trans. John Horn, 2:28.

⁴⁶ Sverdrup, "On the Congregation's Holiness," *Samlede skrifter*, trans. John Horn, 2:14.

⁴⁷ *Fundamental Principle 4* says: "Members of the organized congregation are not, in every instance believers." C. J. Carlsen wrote concerning those who sought "pure" churches, "The Lutheran Free Church took issue very decidedly with the proponents of this movement, seeing in it a judging of the hearts of others which was foreign to the Scriptures." Carlsen, *The Years of Our Church*, 58.

⁴⁸ Sverdrup, "Congregations Made Alive," *Samlede skrifter*, trans. John Horn, 2:26-36.

⁴⁹ Sverdrup, "Congregations Made Alive," *Samlede skrifter*, trans. John Horn, 2:34.

⁵⁰ In an article on Sverdrup, John Evjen wrote, "He [Sverdrup] taught that the baptism of children was not identical with regeneration." John Evjen, "Georg Sverdrup," in *Augsburg Seminary and the Lutheran Free Church*, ed. Lars Lillehei (Minneapolis, 1928), 12. If Evjen means that Sverdrup did not believe that baptism was a means of grace through which the Holy Spirit conveys spiritual life, then this writer disagrees. Sverdrup certainly taught that infant baptism was a means of regeneration and conveyed the gift of spiritual life. He writes, "our children receive with baptism life in God, spiritual life so that they will be living members of Jesus' living body." Sverdrup, "Congregations Made Alive," in *Samlede skrifter*, trans. John Horn, 2:34. Sverdrup writes elsewhere that even if the congregation is dead and full of worldliness, a true congregation still exists, even if it consists of nothing but the baptized babies. Sverdrup, "Visible Congregation," in *Veiledning*, 36. Baptismal regeneration was strongly held by others in the early LFC. Pastor Ludvig Pederson, in an address given at a Bible Conference on "The Congregation" writes, "Baptism is . . . the beginning, the entry into God's Church. Baptism is a means of grace, whereby God creates the new life. To take away the power of rebirth [regeneration] in baptism and make it a symbol is to lessen this means of grace." Pederson, "The Congregation's Origin, Makeup, and Format," in *Menigheten Foredrag holdt under bibelkonferansen i Eagle Lake Menighet*, trans. unknown, 25.

⁵¹ Sverdrup, "Congregations Made Alive," *Samlede skrifter*, trans. John Horn, 2:34.

⁵² Sverdrup, "Congregations Made Alive," *Samlede skrifter*, trans. John Horn, 2:35.

⁵³ Sverdrup, "Congregations Made Alive," *Samlede skrifter*, trans. John Horn, 2:35.

54 John Strand, "What Do We Want?" *The Lutheran Ambassador* 1, no. 17 (September 24, 1963): 3.

55 Sverdrup, "On the Congregation's Holiness," *Samlede skrifter*, trans. John Horn, 2:16.

56 Andreas Helland, *Georg Sverdrup*, 168. Helland states that Sverdrup believed not only should individuals remain in their congregation even when it appears to be worldly, but congregations should also stay in their church bodies. But this writer believes evidence suggests otherwise. In Georg Sverdrup's "On Withdrawal from a Church Body," Sverdrup responded to a letter urging that the congregations of the Friends of Augsburg stay in the United Church. The author of the letter gave several reasons for the congregation to stay. For instance, the author said God desires unity in the body of Christ, but to leave the body destroys this unity; the task of the congregation is to "build up" the body, not abandon it; believers are called to bear up under others' faults. Sverdrup responded that the author's arguments against leaving applied very well to the individual leaving his congregation but not to the congregation leaving its church body. The congregation is not under the same constraints as the individual Christian. Georg Sverdrup, "On Withdrawal from a Church Body," in *Veiledning,* 148-151. In another place, Sven Oftedal writes, "As a congregation freely decides to join a church body . . . so is its indisputable right . . . to step out of such a church-body whenever it finds useful." Sven Oftedal, "The Concept of the Church Body and the Union in 1890," in *Veiledning*, trans. Martin Horn, 9.

57 Sverdrup, "The Freedom of the Congregation," (*Samlede skrifter* 2:138-143) in Hamre, "Georg Sverdrup's Concept of the Role and Calling," 94.

58 Melvin Helland, trans., *The Heritage of Faith*, 50.

59 Sverdrup, "Is It Possible for Norwegian Lutherans to Build a Christian Free Church in America?" (*Samlede skrifter* 2:101-119) in Hamre, "Georg Sverdrup's Concept of the Role and Calling," 56.

60 Sverdrup, "The Congregation's Call to Cleanse Itself," in *Samlede skrifter*, trans. John Horn, 3:279.

61 Sverdrup, "The Congregation's Call to Cleanse Itself," (*Samlede skrifter* 3:276-280) in Hamre, "Georg Sverdrup's Concept of the Role and Calling," 228.

62 Georg Sverdrup, "The Principles of Augsburg," in *Samlede skrifter*, trans. Martin Horn, 111:19.

63 The following are the relevant articles from the Norwegian constitution of 1814 that established the Lutheran Church as the state church of Norway. Article 2: "The Evangelical Lutheran religion shall remain the public religion of the state. Such inhabitants as profess this religion are required to educate their children therein." Article 4: "The king shall always profess,

maintain, and defend the Evangelical Lutheran religion." Article 16: "The King shall regulate all public religious and church service, all meetings and assemblies relating to religious matters, and shall see that the public teachers of religion follow the rules prescribed for their guidance." Hamre, *Georg Sverdrup*, 13.

64 Hamre, *Georg Sverdrup*, 17.

65 Andreas Helland, *Georg Sverdrup*, 27.

66 Carlsen, *The Years of our Church*, 12.

67 Andreas Helland, *Georg Sverdrup*, 250-251.

68 Hamre, *Georg Sverdrup*, 96.

69 Andreas Helland, *Georg Sverdrup*, 251.

70 Sverdrup, "Is It Possible for Norwegian Lutherans to Build a Christian Free Church in America?" (*Samlede skrifter* 2:101-119) in Hamre, "Georg Sverdrup's Concept of the Role and Calling," 40.

71 Sverdrup, "Is It Possible for Norwegian Lutherans to Build a Christian Free Church in America?" (*Samlede skrifter* 2:101-119) in Hamre, "Georg Sverdrup's Concept of the Role and Calling," 40.

72 James Hamre, "Georg Sverdrup's 'Errand into the Wilderness': Building the 'Free and Living' Congregation," *Concordia Historical Institute Quarterly* 53 (Spring 1980): 40. See also, James Hamre, "Georg Sverdrup's Expression of A Lutheran Restorationism in America," *Lutheran Quarterly* 14 (Spring 2000): 53-78.

73 Sverdrup, "The Lutheran Free Church," in *Samlede skrifter,* 3:261.

74 Sverdrup, "The Congregation," (*Samlede skrifter* 3:265-268) in Hamre, "Georg Sverdrup's Concept of the Role and Calling," 209.

75 Sverdrup, "The Lutheran Free Church," in *Veiledning*, 40.

76 Melvin Helland, trans., *The Heritage of Faith*, 46.

77 Sverdrup, "The Lutheran Free Church," in *Veiledning*, trans. unknown, 40.

78 Elias Harbo, "The Lutheran Free Church's Exceptional Position, Its Call and Task," in *Menigheten Foredrag holdt under bibelkonferansen i Eagle Lake Menighet*, 61.

79 Sverdrup, "The Free Church and the Congregation," in *Veiledning*, trans. unknown, 34.

80 Andreas Helland, "The Lutheran Free Church," *The Lutheran Quarterly* 57 (July 1927), 379. Sverdrup writes, "First, when the congregations are liberated from the yoke of worldliness, they are [truly] free." Sverdrup, "The Lutheran Free Church," in *Veiledning*, 41.

[81] Hamre, "Georg Sverdrup's Concept of the Role and Calling," 21.

[82] Andreas Helland, *Georg Sverdrup*, 250.

[83] Sverdrup, "Mutual Assistance," (*Samlede skrifter* 3:284-287) in Hamre, "Georg Sverdrup's Concept of the Role and Calling," 239.

[84] Sverdrup, "Is It Possible for Norwegian Lutherans to Build a Christian Free Church in America?" (*Samlede skrifter* 2:101-119) in Hamre, "Georg Sverdrup's Concept of the Role and Calling," 56.

[85] Sverdrup, "Is It Possible for Norwegian Lutherans to Build a Christian Free Church in America?" (*Samlede skrifter* 2:101-119) in Hamre, "Georg Sverdrup's Concept of the Role and Calling," 48.

[86] Sverdrup, "The Central Question in the Free Church," in *Samlede skrifter*, trans. John Horn, 2:5-6.

[87] Sverdrup, "The Freedom of the Congregation," in *Samlede skrifter*, trans. John Horn, 2:24-25.

The pastors are not to be directors, but shepherds who lead. They are responsible to the congregations, not the congregations to them....

There is an authority over the congregation, but not an earthly authority. The only authority over itself that the Christian congregation ought to recognize is the Word and Spirit of God.

—John P. Strand

6

The Pastor

Servant of the Congregation

Bruce J. Dalager

The role of the pastor in a free church is unique. In reality it is no different from the role which the pastor should fulfill in any church and which is indeed carried out in many other churches. However, in a free church, the congregation is under no other protection than that provided by the Word and Spirit of God. Because the pastor is ordinarily the one primarily responsible for the preaching of the Word and administering the sacraments, it is imperative that the pastor serve as God has intended if the congregation is to remain free and living. Where the purpose of the congregation has become something other than bringing spiritual life to lost souls and nurturing them in the faith, the pastor may serve in a capacity that differs from what God's Word directs. For instance, where a congregation has become a business primarily concerned with larger attendance and a larger budget, the pastor may serve as a business manager or a chief executive officer. Another congregation's choice of direction may call for the pastor to be a kind of cheerleader or public relations man. But where the congregation's purpose is the salvation of souls and the nurturing of believers in the faith through the faithful use of the means of grace, there the pastor serves in a singular capacity.

Since the congregation's existence as free and living is dependent not on good business practices or the most recently developed program for "success" but is rather dependent on the Word and Spirit of God, it follows that the pastor's role in such a congregation is unique. He must work as the entire Christian congregation works, according to Professor Georg Sverdrup, "for the upkeep and preservation of life."[1]

Thus in our thoughts regarding the role of the pastor in the free church, we will not give attention to how the pastor can make a church large or busy, traits which in our society are taken as marks of a successful church. We will focus instead on the role the pastor fills as he is used by God in nurturing the freedom and life of the Christian and the congregation. For unless the congregation remains in the life and freedom that are given by the Spirit of God, it has lost its purpose for existence, for it then has ceased to be a part of the Kingdom of God.

The Pastor as Teacher – A Gift of God to the Church

It is the Lord Jesus Christ who gave the church pastors (Ephesians 4:11). Pastors are listed along with apostles, prophets, evangelists, and others as gifts given to the church. Jesus, in His infinite love and wisdom, knowing what the church would need, gave pastors. The position of pastor in the church was not a human idea, established because people thought it was a good idea or filled a need. No, none other than Jesus, the Head of the Church, established the position. For that reason, the position should be highly esteemed.

Christ's purpose in giving pastors was "for the equipping of the saints for the work of service to the building up of the body of Christ; until we all attain to the unity of the faith, and of the knowledge of the Son of God, to a mature man, to the measure of the stature which belongs to the fullness of Christ. . . . to grow up in all aspects into Him, who is the head, even Christ" (Ephesians 4:12-15, NASB). The pastor is serving Christ while he carries out Christ's purpose. The matter of how he carries out that purpose and the tools he uses will be considered later. For now, the pastor should be assured that by serving the congregation he serves Christ.

The pastor is part of the congregation. In writing about the Norwegian-Danish Conference from which Augsburg Seminary and the Lutheran Free Church arose, Georg Sverdrup, one of the chief founders of the Lutheran Free Church, discusses the Conference's understanding of the relationship between the congregation and the pastor:

> The pastoral office they looked upon as one of the functions of the congregation, and they stressed very strongly that the pastor is not mainly the liturgist performing the sacramental ceremonies, nor the teacher instructing his ignorant hearers, but the organ of the congregation proclaiming the Word of God.[2]

The pastoral office should not be looked upon as one individual carrying out his role. Instead, the position should be viewed as the congregation doing its preaching and teaching through this one arm of the congregation. That is his function as a part of the body.

With this role for the pastor in mind, the forerunners of the LFC asked for a seminary that did "not lift the pastors above and out of the congregation by means of humanistic learning, but which conducted the future pastors into the deep springs of the congregations."[3] Sverdrup emphasized that the pastor is to "enter into a Christian congregation in order to be a co-worker."[4] His seminary training is to enable him "to enter into the nature and the spirit of the congregation, so that when he as minister returned to the congregation he then might know and understand the people, and they might accept him. He does not then come as a sort of royal official but as a minister of the Gospel, who in the mind and spirit of Christ is willing to suffer and work in order that the congregation might be made both living and free."[5] In his training and in his function, the pastor is not to be separated from the congregation. Instead his training is to prepare him for a function that will be carried on within the congregation.

Now when we see that Jesus gave pastors to the church, it follows that the church existed before the pastor. The pastor was given to the church, not the church to the pastor. He belongs to the congregation; the congregation does not belong to him. The true pastor then will want to conduct himself in such a way that he is indeed God's gift to the congregation. He is not that in himself. He is that because he has been made that in Christ. In himself he is not worthy to be called a child of God, much less a pastor in the body of Christ. But in Christ, filled with the Spirit of God, called and equipped, he is a gift.

There are times when the pastoral position is taken by one not sent by Jesus. Jesus' teaching in Matthew 23:2-3 applies to this situation: "The scribes and the Pharisees have seated themselves in the chair of Moses; therefore all that they tell you, do and observe, but do not do according to their deeds." The office established by God is to be respected and, to the extent that the person in the office preaches and teaches the Word of God, he is to be heeded. As Jesus warned people of His day to beware of the teaching of the Pharisees and Sadducees, so He has warned people down through the ages to beware of the teaching of any pastor who has assumed his position without the call of God. However, even when the man in the position is not worthy of it, the office should be honored, for it is Christ's creation.

The true pastor will humbly remember his place. The congregation existed before him and will exist after him unless he causes its death. By death we do not mean the official closing of the church but rather the spiritual death that would result if the pastor through his teaching and example led the congregation away from faith in Jesus Christ. The pastor who is surrendered to the will of God will recognize that he is not the head of the congregation. He will not seek to lead the congregation into fulfilling some agenda of his own creation. He will seek to lead the congregation into the Word of God.

A study of the etymology of the Greek words that have been translated "pastor" in the New Testament we leave to others. We do point out the fact, however, that a number of titles appear to be closely related and when taken together give us an idea of what the role of pastor includes. In Ephesians 4:11, the Greek word usually translated "pastor" means "shepherd." This harmonizes with the statement made by Jesus in John 21:15 where Peter was commanded to both "pasture" and "shepherd"

Christ's sheep. In Acts 20:28, those who were told to shepherd the church are called "overseers," and in 11:30, the overseers of the church are called "elders." In I Timothy 3:2, the word translated "overseer" is the Greek word from which the English word "episcopal" (and from this "bishop") is derived. It appears that "overseer" and "elder" are titles for the same officeholder. In any case, Paul's list of qualifications for an overseer in I Timothy 3 includes the ability to teach. This is significant since Paul in the list of gifts to the church (Ephesians 4) appears to combine pastors and teachers as one gift. We may rightly call this gift to the church a shepherd/teacher. So the pastor has the dual role of shepherding and teaching the flock of God.

In our modern, more urban society, the implications of the shepherd's role in the life of sheep are no longer obvious. However, Scripture clearly points out the role of a shepherd, and we have in the Good Shepherd the pattern for all under-shepherds to follow (see John 10:1-18). What a blessing that pastor is to his congregation who faithfully leads the people to the Good Shepherd! On the other hand, the pastor is warned of the judgment that is his if he proves to be unfaithful. Scripture contains warnings and judgments pronounced by God to the unfaithful shepherds of Israel (Ezekiel 34, Isaiah 56:9-12) that serve to warn and direct pastors in their role as shepherds of God's flock.

The Pastor – His Call

The LFC and AFLC have understood the call of the pastor to be twofold: there is an inner call and an outer call. The inner call, which a man senses from God, must be confirmed by an outer call received from a congregation. If the man experiences the first but that call is not confirmed by a call from a congregation, he is to take that as an indication that congregational ministry is not his calling. Sverdrup maintained, "The pastor receives his capacity and authority from God, if he has any; he receives his place of service, his external office, by means of the congregation's call."[6] For this reason also the congregation is over the pastor. He submits to her call or lack thereof.

The fact that the congregation existed before the pastor has an application here as well. It is the congregation's call that validates him as pastor. While the congregation is not dependent on him for validation, the pastor's call to congregational ministry is dependent on the congregation that can either confirm or deny the inner call. God has given the congregation great responsibility and power here. For that reason, only a congregation that is freed and quickened by the Holy Spirit is capable of carrying out the will of God in this regard. Sverdrup maintained, "According to the Scripture the congregation has the duty of recognizing who is 'full of the Spirit and of wisdom,' if it is really to be a free and self-governing congregation."[7]

The criteria a congregation uses when it is in the process of calling a pastor is critical to the future of the congregation. Unless the congregation is directed by the Holy Spirit in the decision of confirming or denying a pastor's inner call, it will make the mistake of confirming those who are not called by God or denying those whom God has called. Then wolves may be brought in among the flock. The results can be disastrous; though at the same time God's sovereign purpose is accomplished. God brings chastening upon a disobedient people by giving them what they want so that, having suffered the foolishness of their choice, they may return and surrender to His will. While that does serve to chasten the disobedient in the congregation, it at the same time brings upon the true members of God's flock strong temptation and sore testing. When the people in the congregation of Israel became dissatisfied with God's provision of manna in the wilderness and wanted things their way, God gave them such an abundance of what they wanted that they soon loathed it. Many other examples of this could be cited from both the Old and New Testaments as well as from church history. How unfortunate that congregation is that so strongly desires a man of its own liking that it fails to seek or follow the will of God in the matter.

The pastor is called to work among people. To do that, he must know human nature. In that regard, Sverdrup wrote, "Therefore, the congregation must demand of those who are to be pastors that they have insight into the passions which tear asunder the hearts and lives of men and that they understand how these passions bear inexpressible misery as a consequence."[8] He added regarding the pastor: "He must, if possible and as far as possible, know thoroughly the depths of the human heart, of the heart of God, and of Satan."[9] In addition to having a knowledge of these deviations from the will and plan of God, he must know God's plan for man's salvation. This knowledge does not come naturally. In order to acquire it, the pastor must be "thoroughly acquainted with God's word and the mystery of the Gospel not only in an external, literal, carnal manner, but . . . with the proper hunger of the soul and in a sincere poverty of spirit."[10]

Awesome responsibility, therefore, rests on the congregation when it considers candidates for the ministry. It must act in the power and life of Christ. For, as Sverdrup maintained, when the congregation through negligence or disobedience "opposes God's word there ceases to be a free congregation."[11] Thus, according to Sverdrup's understanding, the congregation ceases to be free not only when a negligent pastor through his influence brings death to the congregation but also when the congregation disobediently calls a pastor whom God has not called.

Above All – Given to Serve

The pastor "first and foremost must learn to walk in the lowly footsteps of Jesus."[12] If the lead Shepherd walked in humble servanthood, so should the shepherds under Him. Jesus told his disciples, "Now that I, your Lord and teacher, have washed your feet, you also should wash one another's feet. I have set you an example that you should do as I have done for you. I tell you the truth, no servant is greater than his master, nor is a messenger greater than the one who sent him. Now that you know these things, you will be blessed if you do them" (John 13:14-17).

In his treatise on *Christian Liberty*, Martin Luther wrote of what is true for every Christian. The pastor of a free church should accept these seemingly contradictory theses as applying to him as well: "A Christian is a perfectly free lord of all, subject to none. A Christian is a perfectly dutiful servant of all, subject to all."[13] A clear understanding of how these truths are to be applied to the inner and outer man will help the pastor understand his role as a servant. Because of what he has graciously received from his Father's hand, he should think as Luther wrote:

> Why should I not therefore freely, joyfully, with all my heart, and with an eager will do all things which I know are pleasing and acceptable to such a Father who has overwhelmed me with his inestimable riches? I will therefore give myself as a Christ to my neighbor, just as Christ offered himself to me; I will do nothing in this life except what I see is necessary, profitable, and salutary to my neighbor, since through faith I have an abundance of all good things in Christ.
>
> Behold from faith thus flow forth love and joy in the Lord and from love a joyful, willing, and free mind that serves one's neighbor willingly and takes no account of gratitude or ingratitude, of praise or blame, of gain or loss. For a man does not serve that he may put men under obligations. He does not distinguish between friends and enemies or anticipate their thankfulness or unthankfulness, but he most freely and most willingly spends himself and all that he has, whether he wastes all on the thankless or whether he gains a reward. As his Father does, distributing all things to all men richly and freely, making "his sun rise on the evil and on the good" (Matthew 5:45), so also the son does all things and suffers all things with that freely bestowing joy which is his delight when through Christ he sees it in God, the dispenser of such great benefits.[14]

It is essential, then, that the pastor be a servant of the congregation.

As a servant of the congregation, the pastor has no authority over the congregation. The Word of God that he preaches and teaches does. His leadership is none other than that which the Word of God exerts as he the shepherd/teacher preaches it and teaches it. According to Sverdrup, "The pastor has a leading position because he is the one who serves the congregation with God's word in self-sacrificing love, having occasion to devote all of his time to this."[15]

According to Sverdrup, as the pastor spends time with God's Word, he "does not grow out of and over the congregation by conceited knowledge, but rather increases in love even as he increases in understanding, developing more of Jesus' humble mind of a servant the deeper he sinks down into the depth of God's mercy."[16]

As shepherds/teachers,

> The pastors should, if it were possible, be the leaders in work, leaders in suffering, wisest in counsel, quickest in action–when it concerns the cause of the kingdom of God, examples of the flock, and servants of the souls for their eternal salvation. . . . Their calling is to proclaim the gospel of Christ to the souls and to urge, lead and strengthen the congregation of God in its work and its struggle.[17]

The congregation is not to be dominated by the pastor; neither is it to assign its responsibilities to the pastor. Sverdrup strongly maintained that "to delegate its rights and authority to the pastor is far from the freedom of the congregation. That is directly opposed to such freedom and directly opposed to God's word."[18] It is not the pastor's role to pick or choose who are to serve in the various positions in the congregation. A free and living congregation is capable of doing that itself. If the pastor feels he must be the one to determine who will be the leaders in the congregation, what does that say about his understanding of the freedom of the congregation? What does it say about his confidence in the Word of God to equip the congregation and make it living?

Sverdrup points out two ways in which pastors dominate

churches. He believes that pastors without a proper understanding of the nature of the congregation seek power in the congregation from both the basest and the most noble motives. Though pastors would agree that the ministerial office comes from God, some may see in that conception the opportunity for personal, secular gain, while others bring an even more insidious domination, according to Sverdrup:

> They are eager for living congregations but cut their pattern of a living Christian according to their own experience and measure others by this standard. When the uniform does not fit, the pastor becomes the more zealous to make the congregation conform to his standard. . . . He works, indeed, for Christian life as he understands it, but he destroys the life of the congregation with his smothering uniformity. . . .
>
> Both agree that the will of the pastor should be the law of the congregation. They both agree, moreover, but for different reasons, that all spiritual activity which is not under their control is extremely dangerous. Thus they both make ropes to bind their congregations. For they only attain their goal by cutting off the congregation's true relationship to God.[19]

In 1965, Rev. John Strand wrote an article saying that pastors are not to be directors but shepherds. Rev. Raynard Huglen concurs in an editorial: "A pastor must guard against the temptation to want everything his own way and to feel that he always has the clearer insight into what the will of God is."[20] Later on that same year, Huglen writes on the same subject: "A pastor should be glad when he is sometimes rebuffed. Then he at least knows that he isn't serving a congregation of stooges."[21]

When the congregation calls a pastor, it does not relieve the people of their responsibilities as believers. The pastor is not their substitute. But as their shepherd, he is to encourage and welcome the use of every gift the Lord has given His church. "His work and that of the laymen must go hand in hand, and . . . they are to be as brothers among brothers, not as superiors lording it over the congregation of God."[22] He is given by God and called by the congregation to be the congregation's shepherd-leader. That he must be.

The Pastor – Serving as a Man of Faith

Living pastors are essential for the well-being of living congregations. Sverdrup explains:

> By living pastor we simply mean men who are the true disciples of Jesus and who follow Him, especially at this point that they live, labor, suffer, and wrestle for the salvation of the souls of men, in faithfulness even unto death, men of Spirit, men with love, men who are fearless proclaimers of the truth, men of complete and full self-dedication.[23]

While the pastor is only one arm of the congregation, because he is the regular preacher and teacher of the Word, he carries a heavy weight of responsibility. If the congregation is to remain living, a condition that exists only as it is led continually into life in Christ, it must have a pastor who knows that same life by personal experience. If the pastor lacks repentance and faith with its accompanying gifts, he is not fit to lead the flock to green pastures or protect it against the attacks of the devil. The real fitness of the preacher, in Sverdrup's opinion, depends "on the personal experience of the saving power of the Gospel and the thorough knowledge of God's revelation and the need of the human heart."[24] The pastor must be able to preach what he has experienced, not merely what he has learned. Sverdrup held that "no one can be a true pastor such as a pastor should be unless he has both a true faith and the Spirit's gift of grace for the proclamation of God's word."[25]

In his message on the Twenty-Fifth Anniversary of Augsburg Seminary in 1894, Georg Sverdrup stated:

> The principle of Augsburg is this that he who is to be a witness concerning the salvation of the Lord must

have experienced it in his own heart. Only through a living experience can one gain the living conviction which gives a true and cordial ring and tone. And we do not fear that such a scribe shall become monotonous and tiresome in his preaching, unable to "entertain" his hearers. Or has anyone heard that the daily bread becomes tiresome for one who is hungry? Indeed, if the congregation of God is to be fed and the souls refreshed, it is not possible in any other way than by the gospel of Jesus Christ, the foolishness of His cross.[26]

We acknowledge that the life from God comes through the Word and sacraments and that these means of grace are effective even though they may be administered by unbelieving men. But the question arises: Can a pastor who has not himself experienced the life that comes through the means of grace rightly preach the Word of God or administer the sacraments according to the will of Christ? Luther believed that the world's greatest evil was a false preacher, for he "dominates men in God's name, puts them to death, and leads them into the abyss of hell through his false preaching."[27] And again Luther writes, "but a false sermon, nay a word that comes flying along in God's name clips off such a multitude of souls that a whole city and land may subsequently fall."[28] In the preface to the *Large Catechism*, Luther writes of pastors who are lax in the duty and dishonoring to the office: "Shameful gluttons occupied with their own appetites! They would make better herders of swine and keepers of dogs than watchers for souls and pastors of Christian people."[29]

Georg Sverdrup expressed similar thoughts:

> As long as the church of God has existed no one has ever seen a congregation born, develop, and grow under the guidance of a dead pastor. Show us a single example.
>
> It is impossible to find words that will adequately express the curse which a spiritually dead pastor is, both to the converted and unconverted among those who hear him. We are not now speaking about the unconverted

pastor's offensive life and the damaging effect of it. All can see that. We are talking about the damage which is caused by their public preaching and the administering of the sacraments. Those who are sleeping are confirmed in their false hope of heaven; those who are awake are lulled to sleep; the Christian warriors lose their courage and clarity of vision; and the suffering Christians become despondent in tribulations. All these are weak expressions for the frightful results of a diluted, abbreviated, dull, and empty proclamation by an unconverted pastor.[30]

Living congregations not only *need* living pastors; they will *call* living pastors. "If the congregation is to elect its pastors and officers in a proper and scriptural manner, it must try to elect those whom God has made fit, not some others."[31] A truly living congregation lacks neither the ability nor the authority to do that. Sverdrup had such high regard for the free and living congregation's ability to discern that he maintained "it is not the Lutheranism of the congregations which is to be judged by the Synod pastors, but the Lutheranism of the pastors which is to be judged by the congregations."[32] In the free church, the congregation has both the obligation and the right to judge the pastor to determine whether his teaching conforms with the Word of God. With that principle understood, the true pastor will not be reluctant to be judged by the congregation. At the same time he will, with the true interests of the free congregation at heart, be careful and diligent in his preaching and teaching so that what he passes on to the flock has the stamp of "Thus says the Lord!"

The pastor must also be a man of faith in regard to his understanding of the Christian congregation. Peter wrote, "But you are a chosen race, a royal priesthood, a holy nation, a people for God's own possession, that you may proclaim the excellencies of Him who has called you out of darkness into His marvelous light" (I Peter 2:9). The pastor is called to work among a holy nation. That is not to say that all members of the congregation he serves are believers. But most certainly it means that not all the members of the congregation are unsaved and need to be "won to the Lord."

We believe in the Holy Christian Church. The issue is one of faith, not of sight. The Christian congregation has a holiness that is from God. The pastor who does not recognize this but believes the congregation's holiness comes from the holiness of the members will tend to place himself above and outside the congregation as he judges and evaluates its holiness. He will discover that there are none righteous and will look upon his congregation as only a mission field. In an article written in 1889, Sverdrup maintained that

> the pastor that does not see his congregation as a mission field is a poor pastor; but on the other hand, if he only sees the congregation in this light, then he does not nourish the respect for its holiness and zealousness for God's house, which alone can give him the right starting point for the activity in his congregation.[33]

Andreas Helland says, "The Christian congregation as visualized by Professor Sverdrup is not a mission field for the pastor to work in; it is itself a missionary, a working unit for the advancement of the Kingdom of God."[34] The spiritual life possessed by the believing members of the congregation is a powerful force that moves them to be active in the service of the Lord. That spiritual activity should not only be tolerated by the pastor, but it should also be encouraged. Sverdrup was passionate in encouraging all Christians to carry on the work entrusted to them by God, a work also for which God had equipped them. So the pastor, trusting in the power of God's Word and relying on the Spirit of God to move God's people, will strive in his preaching and ministry to equip the saints for the work of service (Ephesians 4:12).

The Pastor – Serving in the Community

Paul's list of qualifications for an overseer in I Timothy 3 includes that an overseer must have a good reputation with those outside the church. We need not point out what grievous hurt has been caused the church through the outward and scandalous behavior of church leaders whose reputations have become tarnished. Satan is all too bold in broadcasting such falls in his attempt to destroy the Kingdom of God and discredit God's messengers. Only by the grace of God can the pastor be kept so that he is above reproach. By God's grace he should not be ashamed to say with the Apostle Paul, "Be imitators of me, just as I also am of Christ" (I Corinthians 11:1). The pastor must keep in mind that he is still a pastor even when he is not occupied with his official pastoral duties. He is not only the congregation's pastor from 8:00 to 4:00 with Mondays off. He is always God's representative, not unlike any other Christian. But he is more closely observed than most and, because of his calling, is capable of causing greater harm if he falls.

Even though the pastor is called to serve a congregation, it is not difficult for him to become involved in numerous community and religious affairs, many of which are good. Because of his role as pastor, he may be looked upon as one who can and should be active in other capacities.

There may also be cooperative efforts with other churches that call for his involvement. But since the pastor is under the congregation, the initiative for him to be involved in extra-congregational affairs should come from the congregation. Most certainly, before he becomes involved in activities that will compete for his time, the pastor must consult with the congregation, so it can determine whether such involvement on his part would have a detrimental effect on his ministry. The pastor with a servant heart will gladly submit to the congregation's will in this. If, while serving a congregation, he feels called to other ministry or service, he should, as a man of integrity, inform the congregation of his resignation from its call so that the congregation can begin the process of calling another pastor. To do otherwise, trying to fulfill two callings, does damage to the cause of Christ.

The Pastor – Serving as a Man of the Word

Life for the congregation comes from Christ, not from the pastor. Jesus said, "the words that I have spoken to you are spirit and are life" (John 6:63). It is thus the life of Christ revealed in the Word that must be constantly brought to the congregation. The pastor must be willing to die daily lest he lead his congregation to seek him rather than Christ and take glory for himself that belongs to Christ alone. He cannot serve by exalting himself or promoting his opinions. Sverdrup believed "To depend on human wisdom in pastoral work is, after all, only to make flesh one's arm and God's work is not furthered thereby."[35]

The congregation can exist without the pastor, but it cannot exist without the Word. Thus it is the sacred duty of the pastor in the free church to occupy himself with a right teaching and preaching of the Word and a correct administration of the sacraments. "Only by word and sacraments is the congregation God's congregation,"[36] Sverdrup asserted. Thus in spirit and conduct the pastor must show what John the Baptist said regarding his relationship with Jesus, "He must increase and I must decrease (John 3:30)."

In order to faithfully carry out his calling as a shepherd of the flock, the pastor's primary interest must be the Word of God. Since the congregation's life and freedom are dependent on the Word and Spirit of God, the pastor who does not give adequate time and attention to a personal reading and studying of the Word of God will be slowly starving both himself and the congregation to death. While it is true that the members of the congregation are to give themselves to reading and studying the Word of God, the pastor, because he should be freed from the duty of making a living, should have the time to give himself completely to that study. By virtue of his calling to shepherd the flock of God, the pastor must be so occupied with God's Word that he is not only controlled by it himself but can also make appropriate reference to it in his dealings with members of the congregation. Then the life that is in the Word also finds its way into them.

Because of the varied needs that are brought to the pastor, he may feel pressed to get training in psychology, financial advising, law, medicine, mechanics, or any number of other disciplines. In addition to that, he may have a definite interest in one or more of these. But the Scriptures must be his primary interest. According to Sverdrup, the needs of the congregation are served

> when the one who is to become a pastor becomes thoroughly acquainted with God's word and the mystery of the Gospel not only in an external, literal, carnal manner, but does so with the proper hunger of the soul and in a sincere poverty of spirit. For the congregation has "all its well-springs" in the word, and the more the one who is to be a shepherd knows these well-springs of Israel, the better suited will he be to refresh the thirsty with the water of life.[37]

The pastor must be faithful to his calling. He must let nothing be given preference over the Word of God. It is that Word alone which creates and sustains life in God in the congregation.

The true pastor is not weak. He has received from God both the command and authority to preach the Word of God without apology. That Word is "living and active and sharper than any two-edged sword, . . . and able to judge the thoughts and intentions of the heart" (Hebrews 4:12). He knows with Paul that "the weapons of our warfare are not of the flesh, but divinely powerful for the destruction of fortresses" (II Corinthians 10:4). He carries out his ministry with God-confidence. "Not that we are adequate [competent] in ourselves to consider anything as coming from ourselves, but our adequacy is from God, who also made us adequate as servants of a new covenant" (II Corinthians 3:5-6).

The Pastor – Serving in Prayer

The pastor is called to a divine task. Only God is able to rescue the lost and bring them into His Kingdom. Only God can preserve His children in the Christian faith. Though the pastor may be above average in talents and have a dynamic personality that impresses people, it is not by his power or ability that the Kingdom of God grows. "Unless the Lord builds the house, they labor in vain who build it" (Psalm 127:1). God does not build on human ability or potential but rather removes it so that the work accomplished may be credited solely to Him. Gideon's ability was removed so that God's ability might be praised. David denounced human ability (Saul's armor) when it was suggested he needed it to defeat Goliath. Throughout history, God has never relied on human ability or potential. It never aids His cause. It always gets in the way. God chooses the foolish to shame the wise, the weak to shame the strong, the lowly, despised, and even the things that are not to nullify the things that are, so that our only boast might be in the Lord (see I Corinthains 1:26-29). The pastor who is truly living knows that in himself there is no life. In himself, there is no potential for good. In himself is lack and need and deadness. He is not filled with self-confidence.

The awareness of his own weaknesses makes him a man of prayer. He needs daily forgiveness of his sin. Each day he faces challenges that are beyond his ability. Only by God's grace will he be of any benefit in ministering to the needs of his congregation. He must pray for the Spirit of God to work in him and through him those spiritual workings that would otherwise never be done. Sverdrup wrote that "the Christian life is absolutely dependent upon the daily acknowledgment of imperfection and the daily prayer for the divine Spirit, grace, power, and wisdom."[38] The true pastor prays that God's will would be done in him as it is in heaven. All that he does must be bathed in prayer.

The concerned pastor will pray for those under his spiritual care. He prays for them because he knows that only the Lord can provide what they need. Through contact with them, he will be aware of their needs and will bring those needs to the throne of grace both while visiting them and while in his private prayer chamber. He will be careful not to include in public prayers those things that have been shared with him in private, unless, of course, a request for such inclusion has been made by the person in need.

He will be a pattern in prayer for those in his congregation, and his prayer life should be worthy of imitation. As such, he must show God the honor due Him and let God be his God. In his teaching of the subject of prayer as well as by example, he must teach prayer as it was taught by our Lord. His example will show a humble dependence on God, an assurance that in all things God works for the good of those who love him, and a confident surrender to God's will in all things.

The Pastor – Serving the Lambs

Every letter of call or church constitution this writer has seen has in some way directed the pastor to promote the education of the children of the church in the Christian faith. Many of us have experimented with one course of instruction after another in an attempt to find the one that best does the job. Sverdrup would have rebuked such a search, for he says, "we stress the catechism because it fills congregational freedom with spirit and life."[39] He added, "The congregation is able to stand fast only when the Catechism is its foundation."[40]

Exuberant in his praise of the catechism, Sverdrup wrote:

> Catechism, which has been a mother's milk for all of us and which our dear church has nourished us with from the time we learned to stammer the Lord's Prayer over our small, folded hands, is something we cannot value too highly. Wherever our heart has been and wherever our cradle has had its rocker, in whatever valley or along whatever shore we played in the happy years of childhood, whether our parents' house was large or small, rich or poor, whether piety or impiety ruled in our homes–this simple childhood instruction has been the same for all of us. Like a father's voice when it is a matter of a child's eternal welfare, it has spoken the same simple language so intimately and yet so seriously to the hearts of children.

Was it wrong to esteem it highly? Even now, when we are scattered and separated in this great and glorious land, it speaks to us with the same import! Even now, when we are cast out into the motley life of the world, it has a message for us all from home, telling us to center our thoughts and minds on repentance and sincere amendment of life.[41]

The pastor's goal of nurturing freedom and life in the congregation is well served as he faithfully and consistently teaches the truths of the catechism to the children in the congregation and makes frequent reference to it in his ministry to the adults.

The Pastor – Serving the Sheep Through the Word

"The first and most important work of God's congregation is the proclamation of God's Word, and all other work and life in the congregation is dependent upon this."[42] As the spiritual leader of the congregation, the pastor's only tool is the Word of God. Other organizations have other means by which they govern, carry on their affairs and grow, but the Christian congregation is governed, is sustained, and grows only by the Spirit and Word of God. Nothing more than the Word of God is needed. Nothing less than the Word of God will do. It follows then that the pastor entrusted with the care of souls must use the Word of God.

The Word of God is sufficient for meeting the needs of the unsaved as well as believers' needs. In the congregation there will be those who are not Christians. Such people will in varying degrees have an effect on the life of the congregation. The role they may serve in the congregation is an issue to be addressed elsewhere, but how the pastor and congregation ought to deal with them fits the subject at hand. According to *Fundamental Principle 4* of the LFC and later the AFLC, "it is . . . the sacred obligation of the congregation to purify itself by the quickening preaching of the Word of God, by earnest admonition and exhortation, and by expelling the openly sinful and perverse." The congregation is purified by the preaching of the Word of God.

The pastor's duty is to preach the Word of God. To Sverdrup, "this was the heart of the pastor's work, in his public preaching and his private soul care."[43] The preaching of the Word is "quickening" or "life-giving." While it is never the pastor who is life-giving, he, through a right proclamation of the Word of God, holds the key to life. The pastor is not responsible for giving the Word power to produce life; it *has* that power. He may attempt to give life to his preaching through dynamic oratory, catchy anecdotes, or humorous stories, but the ability of his preaching to give life is not found in these. Such efforts may give a kind of liveliness to his preaching and may have a place in illustrating a text, but they do not produce life. It is most certainly not the pastor's calling to entertain. This is not to say that there is no place for story telling, anecdotes, or even humor, for even the preaching of the apostles included such. It does mean, however, that in order for his preaching to be life-giving, he must preach the Word of God. The dynamic for imparting spiritual life is in that Word.

The perception of many contemporary pastors regarding their role has in these days been affected by a contagious spirit of pragmatism[44] that sets aside the preaching of the Word. The Word is no longer considered the effective means for saving the lost. Instead, pastors turn from one promising program to another, explaining that "times change." While many would deny that this is evidence of an erosion of trust in the power of God's Word to do God's work, the fact remains that the straightforward, undecorated proclamation of the Word of God is increasingly looked upon as irrelevant and ineffective. One wonders how the Apostle Paul himself would be received today, he who preached without eloquence or wise and persuasive words lest the cross of Christ be emptied of its power and men's faith rest on men's wisdom rather than God's power (see I Corinthians 1:17, 2:1-5). "God [is] well-pleased through the foolishness of the message preached to save those who believe" (I Corinthians 1:21). The Word of God can be trusted to give and sustain life. Nothing else can. If the unsaved in the congregation would be won to faith in Christ, it will not be by giving them what they think they need but by proclaiming the Word of God.

The tendency to depart from a clear and unadulterated declaration of the Word of God is nothing new. Sverdrup addressed a similar situation in his day:

> For in America there has to be a lot of people, or a thing is not any good. And so by an unfortunate misunderstanding it is easy for the task of the pastor to become that of gathering many people by carnal eloquence instead of by God's living and saving Gospel. Thus, the sermon is to be entertaining in one matter or another so that many can be attracted to the pleasing or exciting or shocking "entertainment." So the preaching is about social and political questions and the sermon is made as sensational as possible. In that way there will be a large gathering and "many people."
>
> But that is *altogether worldliness* [emphasis mine]. For if the object throughout the entire proclamation is not to seek the one lost sheep so as to save it in order that daily and steadily there can be added "to the congregation those who are saved," then eternity, heaven, and salvation are no longer the object of the sermon.
>
> Let us be on guard! It is the old saving Gospel which is to be preached.[45]

Sverdrup further explained the result of such preaching: "It is no secret to any of us that there are thousands of congregations in America that scarcely deserve the honorable name of congregation any more because a secularized proclamation has dulled and blunted the sting of the Word until it no longer is able to accomplish its God-given task."[46]

In addition to changing the message in order to attract crowds, the pastor may be tempted to think that spiritual life is accomplished through changing long-held practices of the congregation. Tradition and form are often looked upon as hindrances to the working of the Spirit of God. New forms or new rituals are subscribed to as if these were the means by which spiritual life is fanned into being. This also is nothing new. Pastor and historian, Rev. Clarence Carlsen, wrote regarding the report of LFC President Harbo to the 1899 LFC Convention held in Dalton, Minnesota:

> The aim of the Lutheran Free Church, he went on to say, was to work for living and Spirit-filled congregations. The means to be employed in seeking to attain this objective were the Word of God and the Sacraments. Church customs and ceremonies were not the means. Nor would altering or abolishing church usages accomplish the desired result. President Harbo took particular pains to point out that great care should be exercised in changing the ritual and the customs of the churches. Such changes would not produce spiritual life, he warned. Only the diligent use of the Word and Sacrament will bring spiritual life. This life will thereupon find its proper forms.[47]

It is true that certain rituals or traditions may become a hindrance to the work of the Spirit of God, but to simply exchange them for new rituals or traditions will not of itself bring about spiritual life. Our society's obsession with the novel is often the motivation for changing long-held practices. The change is not always for the better.

When he has preached the Word of God, the pastor need not wonder about the results. Still, as one who himself possesses the fallen nature, he will be tempted to "produce" through his own persuading or effort the results which he thinks should follow. Such effort is capable of producing results, but any such results cannot be relied upon as having been produced by the Word of God. Lacking that foundation, they cannot stand before God. God's Word alone produces the fruit God desires. Sverdrup wrote, "this living Word of God is mighty and powerful to give the Spirit and grace, faith and love, hope and cheer to those who deal properly with it, so that they are able both to find and walk in this way themselves and to point to it for others by both word and example."[48]

The Apostle Paul acknowledged this danger and wrote: "And my message and my preaching were not in persuasive words of wisdom, . . . that your faith should not rest on the wisdom of men, but on the power of God" (I Corinthians 2:4-5). He went so far as to say that preaching with words of human wisdom ("cleverness") emptied the cross of its power (see I Corinthians 1:17).

Sverdrup emphasized the Word of God. "Hold up the light and rest assured that there will never be too much light in the church."[49] In another article, Sverdrup refers to the Word as the truth. "This is and remains the main concern in the church: light, light, and more light. It will never be too light or light enough. . . . Let the truth sound forth in all its fullness and there will be both contrition and opposition, faith and hardening of the heart, love and hatred."[50]

Having faithfully preached or taught the Word of God, the pastor must rest in the assurance that he has done his part. He has planted and watered; God will give the growth. The Spirit of God will bring about the results God desires. The pastor who proclaims God's Word has this assurance from God:

> For as the rain and the snow come down from heaven, and do not return there without watering the earth, and making it bear and sprout, and furnishing seed to the sower and bread to the eater; so shall My word be which goes forth from My mouth; it shall not return to Me empty, without accomplishing what I desire, and without succeeding in the matter for which I sent it (Isaiah 55:10-11).

When the congregation finds it necessary to purify itself through earnest admonition and exhortation or through expelling the openly sinful and perverse, it is the Word of God that must rule. When Paul told Timothy that he must "correct, rebuke and encourage" (II Timothy 4:2), Paul prefaced it all by writing, "preach the word." In addition, he ended the admonition by emphasizing that this be done "with great patience and careful instruction." The pastor is to be sure that the correcting and rebuking that occurs has its origin and substance in the Word of God. If it comes from him rather than the Word, the process of correcting becomes a battle of the wills, and the one being corrected then feels that he has as much right to determine his behavior as anyone else. Granted, such a person may also reject correction that comes from the Word of God, but in that case his battle is with the Spirit of God. Nevertheless, there is a power in the word of rebuke that Scripture gives that is not found in a scolding that originates in and is delivered by the pastor alone. The pastor must be content to let the Word correct and rebuke. Only the Word of God can bring about godly contrition and work true repentance. Even in this area the pastor comes as a servant, to serve God, the church, and the sinner.

Sverdrup's answer to the issue of spiritually unresponsive people in the church is recorded by Andreas Helland:

> Let the Word of God be preached in all its heart-searching power, and let the spiritual members in the congregation work the more intensely for the Kingdom, and the result will be that those who are asleep will either be awakened, or the pace will be too much for their carnal minds so that they will withdraw from the fellowship. He favored tolerating such members in the congregation as long as possible, even if they were far from measuring up to the ideal of a true Christian, rather than to expel them.[51]

It is not the pastor's job to purify the church. The congregation purifies itself. The congregation admonishes and exhorts. When necessary, the congregation expels. All these must be done by means of the Word of God so that human personalities and human frailties do not dominate in the situation. A right preaching of the Word of God will go a long way in preventing an atmosphere where public admonition of a sinner or expulsion from the congregation is necessary. Through the quickening preaching of the Word of God, the congregation will be purifying itself.

The Pastor – Rightly Dividing God's Word

The pastor whose resource is the Bible will grow in his understanding of the purpose and function of the Law and Gospel. The pastor whose desire is to work toward a free and living congregation will be careful to clearly distinguish between these two elements of God's Word.

In proclaiming the Law, the pastor is a bearer of bad news. The primary purpose of the Ten Commandments is to reveal sin. The right preaching/teaching of God's Law does not encourage or build up, give hope or bring life. Rather, it breaks, tears down, brings despair, and produces death. The Law, capable of this by itself, needs only to be proclaimed. Thus a right preaching of the Law of God leaves people with nothing in themselves to stand on, to work for, or even to promise. It silences every mouth. Its demand, a perfect holiness, leaves people destitute in their sins.

The true pastor, in his preaching and teaching, is always anxious for his people to see Christ.

Because of this, the pastor is also a bearer of good news. His preaching is not to leave people in death but to deliver them from death. As mentioned earlier, a true preaching of the Word of God is life-giving, life-giving because in addition to Law it contains the Gospel of God's grace in Jesus Christ our Savior. The Gospel "is the power of God for salvation to every one who believes" (Romans 1:16). Gospel should dominate the pastor's preaching.

It was in the power of the Gospel of Christ to make congregations free and living that Sverdrup rested. He wrote,

> Jesus Christ is the truth. Only by means of a true preaching of Christ will there come to be a congregation. Let that sound forth, and the congregation will be built, will grow, and will be strengthened. Put something else in its place, no matter how popular it may be, and the congregation will stagnate, will be damaged, and will lose more and more of its true nature and strength.
>
> This is the struggle for life in the congregation which

must be continued all the time as long as the congregation is here below.⁵²

Only the gospel of the cross and the cross of the gospel can preserve the congregation from becoming a disgraceful caricature of the body and bride of Christ.⁵³

Agreeing wholeheartedly with this need for Gospel emphasis, Rev. John Strand, who served as president of the AFLC for its first sixteen years, often exhorted young pastors on the day of their installation: "Pastor, don't be telling the people what they need to do. Tell them what Jesus has done for them and to rest in that."

The Pastor – Resting in God's Provision

The pastor needs the congregation. Sverdrup believed, "The sources of life are there, and he who is to become a true pastor must be 'born there.'"⁵⁴ He is not separate from the congregation. He is one member of it, gifted, but "he is not the only one who has received a gift of grace."⁵⁵ There he will be fed while other parts of the body minister to him, "since it is the congregation which possesses all the treasures of wisdom and knowledge hidden in Christ who is its head."⁵⁶ Furthermore, "the congregation has 'all its well-springs' in the word, and the more the one who is to be a shepherd knows these well-springs of Israel, the better suited will he be to refresh the thirsty with the water of life."⁵⁷

The challenges that come upon the pastor both from within himself and from without are not so great that God cannot give victory through His Word. The Word of God will lead the congregation. The Word of God will lead where God wants the congregation to go. The Word of God will lead to the glory of Christ.

NOTES

¹ Georg Sverdrup, "Congregations Made Alive," *Professor Georg Sverdrups samlede skrifter i udvalg*, ed. Andreas Helland; trans. John Horn (Minneapolis, 1909-1912), 2:33.

² Georg Sverdrup, "The Norwegian-Lutheran Churches in America," in *"Augsburg Seminary and The Lutheran Free Church*, ed. Lars Lillehei (Minneapolis, 1928), 69.

³ Sverdrup, "The Norwegian-Lutheran Churches in America," 69.

⁴ Georg Sverdrup, "A Few Words About the Difference," (*Samlede skrifter* 3:238-240) in James S. Hamre, "Georg Sverdrup's Concept of the Role and Calling of the Norwegian-American Lutherans: An Annotated Translation of Selected Writings" (Ph. D. diss., University of Iowa, 1967), 178.

⁵ E. E. Gynild, "The Position of the Lutheran Free Church" in *Augsburg Seminary and The Lutheran Free Church*, ed. Lars Lillehei (Minneapolis, 1928), 60-61.

⁶ Sverdrup, "The Freedom of the Congregation," (*Samlede skrifter* 2:138-143) in Hamre, "Georg Sverdrup's Concept of the Role and Calling," 95.

⁷ Sverdrup, "Congregational Self-Government and the Use of the Gifts of Grace," (*Samlede skrifter* 3:280-284) in Hamre, "Georg Sverdrup's Concept of the Role and Calling," 232.

⁸ Sverdrup, "Ministerial Education in Conformity With The Congregation," (Samlede skrifter 3:280-284) in Hamre, "Georg Sverdrup's Concept of the Role and Calling," 162.

⁹ Sverdrup, "Ministerial Education in Conformity With The Congregation," (Samlede skrifter 3:226-231) in Hamre, "Georg Sverdrup's Concept of the Role and Calling," 159.

¹⁰ Sverdrup, "Free Churchly Ministerial Education," (*Samlede skrifter* 3:234-236) in Hamre, "Georg Sverdrup's Concept of the Role and Calling," 172.

¹¹ Sverdrup, "Is It Possible for Norwegian Lutherans to Build a Christian Free Church in America?" (*Samlede skrifter* 2:101-119) in Hamre, "Georg Sverdrup's Concept of the Role and Calling," 50.

¹² Sverdrup, "Humanism's Lack of Feeling for the People," (*Samlede skrifter* 3:222-225) in Hamre, "Georg Sverdrup's Concept of the Role and Calling," 155.

¹³ Martin Luther, *Christian Liberty*, trans. W. A. Lambert, revised by Harold Grimm (Philadelphia: Fortress Press, 1957), 7.

¹⁴ Luther, *Christian Liberty*, 30.

¹⁵ Sverdrup, "A Few Words About the Difference," (*Samlede skrifter*

3:238-240) in Hamre, "Georg Sverdrup's Concept of the Role and Calling," 178-179.

[16] Sverdrup, "A Few Words About the Principles," (*Samlede skrifter* 3:231-234) in Hamre, "Georg Sverdrup's Concept of the Role and Calling," 168.

[17] Andreas Helland, *Georg Sverdrup: The Man and His Message* (Minneapolis: The Messenger Press, 1947), 259.

[18] Sverdrup, "The Freedom of the Congregation," (*Samlede skrifter* 2:138-143) in Hamre, "Georg Sverdrup's Concept of the Role and Calling," 95.

[19] Melvin Helland, trans. *The Heritage of Faith: Selections from the Writings of Georg Sverdrup* (Minneapolis: Augsburg Publishing House, 1969), 46-47.

[20] Raynard O. J. Huglen, "Shepherds Who Lead," *The Lutheran Ambassador* 3, no. 2 (January 26, 1965): 10.

[21] Raynard O. J. Huglen, "The Pastor As Servant," *The Lutheran Ambassador* 3, no. 20 (October 19, 1965): 10.

[22] Andreas Helland, *Georg Sverdrup*, 250.

[23] Sverdrup, "Living Pastors," (*Samlede skrifter* 2:238-241) in *Morning Glory*, unknown trans., (n.d.): 10.

[24] Sverdrup, "A Few Words About the Difference," (*Samlede skrifter* 3:238-240) in Hamre, "Georg Sverdrup's Concept of the Role and Calling," 178.

[25] Sverdrup, "Congregational Self-Government and the Use of the Gifts of Grace," (*Samlede skrifter* 3:280-284) in Hamre, "Georg Sverdrup's Concept of the Role and Calling," 230-231.

[26] Andreas Helland, *Georg Sverdrup*, 260.

[27] Ewald M. Plass, *What Luther Says: A Practical In-Home Anthology for the Active Christian* (St. Louis: Concordia Publishing House, 1959), 1124.

[28] Plass, *What Luther Says*, 1125.

[29] J. N. Lenker, trans., *Dr. Martin Luther's Large Catechism* (Minneapolis: Augsburg Publishing House, 1935), 35.

[30] Sverdrup, "Living Pastors," (*Samlede skrifter* 2:238-241) in *Morning Glory*, unknown trans., (n.d.): 10.

[31] Sverdrup, "Congregational Self-Government and the Use of the Gifts of Grace," (*Samlede skrifter* 3:280-284) in Hamre, "Georg Sverdrup's Concept of the Role and Calling," 231.

[32] Sverdrup, "The Union Movement," (*Samlede skrifter* 2:133-138) in Hamre, "Georg Sverdrup's Concept of the Role and Calling," 86.

[33] Sverdrup, "The Congregation's Holiness," trans. John Horn, *Samlede skrifter* 2:14.

[35] Andreas Helland, *Georg Sverdrup*, 260.

[36] Sverdrup, "Is It Possible for Norwegian Lutherans to Build a Christian Free Church in America?" (*Samlede skrifter* 2:101-119) in Hamre, "Georg Sverdrup's Concept of the Role and Calling," 50.

[37] Sverdrup, "Free Churchly Ministerial Education," (*Samlede skrifter* 3:234-236) in Hamre, "Georg Sverdrup's Concept of the Role and Calling," 172.

[38] Sverdrup, "A Few Words About the Difference," (*Samlede skrifter* 3:238-240) in Hamre, "Georg Sverdrup's Concept of the Role and Calling," 179.

[39] Sverdrup, "The Catechism," (*Samlede skrifter* 2:128-133) in Hamre, "Georg Sverdrup's Concept of the Role and Calling," 77.

[40] Sverdrup, "The Catechism," (*Samlede skrifter* 2:128-133) in Hamre, "Georg Sverdrup's Concept of the Role and Calling," 80.

[41] Sverdrup, "The Catechism," (*Samlede skrifter* 2:128-133) in Hamre, "Georg Sverdrup's Concept of the Role and Calling," 76-77.

[42] Sverdrup, "America And The Congregation," (*Samlede skrifter* 4:370-376) in Hamre, "Georg Sverdrup's Concept of the Role and Calling," 262-263.

[43] Andreas Helland, *Georg Sverdrup*, 174.

[44] By "spirit of pragmatism" I mean the attitude that man can know to what end the preaching of the Word is leading and that anything that appears to facilitate that end can and should be put to use. The errors of this philosophy are twofold: 1) Man cannot know specifically the mind of God regarding the goal of His Word. When man assumes to know the goal and pushes toward it, he may in fact be pushing where the Holy Spirit is pulling. 2) The Word of God alone is sufficient to do what God wants done. Anything man adds can only and will only get in the way, hindering what God wants to do.

A. W. Tozer writes: "The nervous compulsion to get things done is found everywhere among us. We are affected by a kind of religious tic, a deep inner necessity to accomplish something that can be seen and photographed and evaluated in terms of size, numbers, speed and distance. . . . [Pragmatic philosophy] asks no embarrassing questions about the wisdom of what we are doing or even about the morality of it. It accepts our chosen ends as right and good and casts about for efficient means and ways to get them accomplished. When it discovers something that works, it soon finds a text to justify it, 'consecrates' it to the Lord and plunges ahead. Next a magazine article is written about it, then a book, and finally the inventor is granted an honorary degree. After that any question about the scripturalness of things or even the moral validity of them is completely swept away. You cannot argue with success. The method works; *ergo*, it must be good." A. W. Tozer, *God Tells the Man Who Cares* (Camp Hill, Pennsylvania: Christian Publications, 1992), 82-83.

45 Sverdrup, "America And The Congregation," (*Samlede skrifter* 4:370-376) in Hamre, "Georg Sverdrup's Concept of the Role and Calling," 263-264.

46 Sverdrup, "America And The Congregation," (*Samlede skrifter* 4:370-376) in Hamre, "Georg Sverdrup's Concept of the Role and Calling," 263.

47 Clarence J. Carlsen, *The Years of Our Church* (Minneapolis: The Lutheran Free Church Publishing Company, 1942), 56.

48 Sverdrup, "Free Churchly Ministerial Education," (*Samlede skrifter* 3:234-272) in Hamre, "Georg Sverdrup's Concept of the Role and Calling," 172.

49 Sverdrup, "Members of the Congregation," (*Samlede skrifter* 3:268-272) in Hamre, "Georg Sverdrup's Concept of the Role and Calling," 214.

50 Sverdrup, "The Congregation's Call to Cleanse Itself," (*Samlede skrifter* 3:276-280) in Hamre, "Georg Sverdrup's Concept of the Role and Calling," 227.

51 Andreas Helland, *Georg Sverdrup*, 252.

52 Sverdrup, "The Congregation's Call to Cleanse Itself," (*Samlede skrifter* 3:276-280) in Hamre, "Georg Sverdrup's Concept of the Role and Calling," 227.

53 Sverdrup, "Congregational Self-Government and the Use of the Gifts of Grace," (*Samlede skrifter* 3:280-284) in Hamre, "Georg Sverdrup's Concept of the Role a6rrnd Calling," 229.

54 Sverdrup, "A Few Words About the Principles," (*Samlede skrifter* 3:231-234) in Hamre, "Georg Sverdrup's Concept of the Role and Calling," 165-166.

55 Sverdrup, "Congregationl Self-Government and the Use of the Gifts of Grace," (*Samlede skrifter* 3:280-284) in Hamre, "Georg Sverdrup's Concept of the Role and Calling," 231.

56 Sverdrup, "Ministerial Education In Conformity With the Congregation," (*Samlede skrifter* 3:226-231) in Hamre, "Georg Sverdrup's Concept of the Role and Calling," 159-160.

57 Sverdrup, "Free Churchly Ministerial Education," (*Samlede skrifter* 3:234-236) in Hamre, "Georg Sverdrup's Concept of the Role and Calling," 172.

As a congregation becomes living, it serves. It has a concern that the lost be saved, and the Gospel be preached. This concern is to be had by all, not only the clergy. Laymen too have the responsibility to proclaim the Gospel. They are encouraged to work, using all the gifts God gives them, for the salvation of souls, for the edification of the church.

—John P. Strand

7

THE LAITY

Serving in the Congregation

Keith D. Quanbeck

Dr. John Stensvaag, President of the Lutheran Free Church from 1958-1963, describes Georg Sverdrup's greatness as the ability to develop a vision and the skill to communicate its application:

> Few men are able to keep clearly in mind both a great ideal and its multitudinous practical implications. There is much truth in the saying that this or that individual is an impractical idealist. He is not able to translate his dream into everyday life. It is equally true that many a man cannot see the forest for the trees. His work is aimless and ineffective because he can only see the many details—a part here and there, but never the whole. He lacks perspective. He lacks a unifying element in his own life—the touchstone by which all the parts are to be tried.
>
> But only those who are able to grasp both these concepts simultaneously are great men. They are the leaders of our race. Such a man was Georg Sverdrup. Not only did he see a great vision, but he saw its practical implications as well.[1]

Sverdrup's vision was for free and living congregations. One of its practical implications involved lay activity. Sverdrup maintained that in practice no congregation could be considered truly alive unless it had an active laity.

It is not for the pastor alone to demonstrate a living faith, but for the whole congregation. At the heart of a free congregation is its laity actively using their gifts in the service of Christ. Thus the congregation is to become a fellowship of believers in which every gift of grace is encouraged and given the fullest possible chance for expression.

It was this belief that led Sverdrup to compare the congregation to a choir in which everyone sings:

> The congregation lives and exists for work. It is a gathering of workers. The congregation is not organized unless there is work for all. It is not a congregation where a group of people hires a minister to do the work for them so that they themselves may go free. No, the congregation may well be compared to a choir and its director. Shall the director sing alone? Shall they not all be along? So too in the congregation; it is a fellowship of God's servants who work for God's kingdom. The leader does not become superfluous but all the more necessary in such a group.[2]

Sverdrup also likened the congregation to an army with every man at his post.

> The pastor should be as a general in the army. The general certainly would not think it advantageous for himself to fight the enemy alone while the army slept. There is more than enough work in the congregation for all the children of God. . . .
>
> The wise pastor will make use of all the gifts of grace for the building up of the kingdom of God.[3]

Sverdrup always viewed the layman as having a vital part in a living and active congregation. He believed that Christ's work would be done most effectively if it also involved the laity. Though a graduate of the theology department of the University of Oslo in Oslo, Norway, and professor of Old

Testament at Augsburg Seminary in Minneapolis, Dr. Georg Sverdrup was never ordained and would frequently address his audience as "we lay people."[4]

Sverdrup's Formative Years

Sverdrup's passion for a vital role for the layman in the life of a congregation was instilled at an early age. In fact, concerns for the common man are seen in the work of his family as well.

Georg Sverdrup was born on December 16, 1848, at Balestrand, near Bergen, Norway. The Sverdrup family was a well-known family, active in Norway's political reform movements at the time. In 1814, Sverdrup's great uncle was a leader in the first Norwegian *Storting* (Congress), which gave Norway its independence. His father, Harald Ulrik Sverdrup, was a pastor at Balestrand and also served as a member of the *Storting*. An uncle, Johan Sverdup, was Prime Minister of Norway from 1884 to 1889, and a brother also served in the *Storting*.[5]

Even with a family heritage instrumental in bringing about reform measures, it was his father's assistant, Pastor Fredrik Schiorn, whom Sverdrup credits with awakening in him a concern for the congregation and the role of the layman. Sverdrup's early opposition to the state church with its concept of the elevated clergy and the diminished laity can be attributed to this mentor, Pastor Schiorn. Sverdup wrote in 1886 that he recalled Schiorn's agony over the state church's operation in Norway. "'It was for him' as Sverdrup continued, 'a daily torture of his conscience to be a pastor in the State Church whenever he thought how little it corresponded to the picture of the church found in God's Word.'"[6]

The Haugean Revival that spread across Norway in the first half of the nineteenth century was no doubt a major influence on Sverdrup and his family. This spiritual awakening named for the lay-evangelist Hans Nielsen Hauge was marked by its emphasis on lay preaching in congregations, adherence to Lutheran doctrine, and a pietistic life. Sverdrup felt very close to the Haugean Revival and spoke of it as a "true Christian awakening."[7]

Hauge, the son of a peasant farmer, preached in small gatherings, usually homes, throughout Norway for a period of eight years (1796-1804) until he was arrested and jailed. He spent most of the next ten years in prison because Norway's "Conventicle Act" forbade religious gatherings of a private nature. Hauge had no theological training. Yet, his intention was to preach and "to convict his hearers of sin and to awaken personal faith; his message was repentance and conversion."[8] The results were not only a revival of the spirit of the people but also a revival of the desire for laymen to participate actively in the life of their church. Hauge's followers did not believe in starting a separate church, but rather worked for spiritual renewal within the existing state church through prayer meetings and lay preaching.

Another strong influence on Sverdrup was Gisle Johnson, a theological professor at the University of Oslo. He was used by God in a second revival that took place in the 1850s that became known as "the Johnsonian Awakening."[9]

The Church Reform Movement, though not as far-reaching as the Hauge and Johnson revivals, influenced Sverdrup's view of "polity" (how a church body organizes itself) and as a result played a major influence on how he structured the Lutheran Free Church.[10] Among Reformist goals were that each local congregation should be allowed to establish its own church council and the laity should "have a more active part in their own congregational affairs, including participation in the selection of their pastor."[11]

It was from this background that Georg Sverdrup came to America in 1874 to accept a position at Augsburg Seminary. Sverdrup was convinced that the primary goal of the Norwegian Lutheran people in America was to model the congregation after the New Testament. He believed that the true congregation and the true work of the layman within the congregation had been lost within the structure of the state church. He looked to America as a place to re-establish what Christ had intended and what Luther had envisioned for the believer. Sverdrup devoted himself, along with his fellow Augsburg Seminary professors Sven Oftedal and Sven Gunnersen, to the promotion of congregational freedom and the development of spiritual life among the lay people. These Augsburg professors adopted the slogan: "A free church in a free state."[12]

The Gifts of the Spirit

In 1897, Georg Sverdrup, along with Sven Oftedal and others, wrote the *Fundamental Principles* for the Lutheran Free Church. *Principle 6* specifically champions lay activities: "A free congregation esteems and cherishes all the spiritual gifts which the Lord gives for its edification, and seeks to stimulate and encourage their use." Sverdrup believed that each member had been equipped by God with a special gift to be used to build up the congregation. Eugene Fevold in *The Lutheran Free Church: A Fellowship of American Lutheran Congregations, 1897-1963* quotes Sverdrup as saying:

> "For all believers, big and little, young and old, men and women, are to be workers in the vineyard." A "living" congregation is one in which the lay forces are mobilized and utilized. It is a fellowship of "believing, praying and working people, who have been equipped by the Lord with all that they need for their responsibilities. . ." as servants.[13]

Sverdrup believed that all lay members of the congregation must be actively involved. However, they are not all to do the same work. God gives different gifts to each member.

> For it is in the diversity and correct use of the gifts of grace that the freedom of the Spirit celebrates its genuine triumph. . . . Here there is room for the work and help of everyone, provided only that they allow love to rule and the Spirit to govern in order that everything may be for edification. There are gifts of speaking publicly and gifts of speaking in private; there are gifts for prayer and gifts for admonition; there are gifts for visiting the sick, comforting the afflicted, helping the dis-

turbed; there are gifts for clothing the naked, feeding the hungry, restoring the suffering; there are gifts for planning and conducting worship and building churches, gathering money, and keeping everything in proper order. Only one thing is needed and that is that everything take place in the right spirit.[14]

According to James Hamre, Sverdrup's theme was

that in the building of free and living congregations in a free church it was more important to put the emphasis upon Christian life than on correct doctrine. The latter, he felt, tended towards a passive laity and clerical domination while a stress on "life" made possible the full utilization of all the gifts of the Spirit.[15]

John Stensvaag translated several sections of Sverdrup's work and wrote often about Sverdrup's views of lay activity in the congregation. Sverdrup, he says, believed that "All Christians must practice lay activity, but not all in the same manner; it is determined and limited by abilities and gifts."[16] The problem with most congregations, however, is that rather than having too much lay activity there is too little:

But if one never seeks for the gifts of grace, one will surely not find them; yea, this neglect is the reason at times why they almost have to push themselves forward. As a result many gifts are in part lost and in part misdirected. We cannot afford this. The congregation should seek after the gifts as after precious, costly gold.[17]

Always, the congregation must seek to discover the gifts of grace among its members. And though the congregation should in a spirit of brotherliness freely discuss the work and encourage its workers, the responsibility for directing this work does lie with the pastor, for he, as Sverdrup liked to say, is the "choir director."

Lay Activity in the Congregation

Stensvaag in one of his early writings discusses Sverdrup's views on these important lay activities: prayer and witnessing (personal evangelism, testimonial meetings, and lay preaching).

Prayer

All lay activity should begin in earnest prayer for the guidance and power of the Holy Spirit. In too many congregations, prayer for the Holy Spirit's guidance is insincere. How different we are from the first Christians who came together as a group and prayed earnestly (Acts 2:14,42). Too often we pray without expecting anything. In some cases, we pray for God to send us a good pastor and to send others into the work so we don't have to get involved. Instead, we should pray: "Lord, send us! Lord, by thy Holy Spirit make us true workers in thy Kingdom!"[18]

According to Sverdrup, the fundamental necessity for lay activity to be effective is fervent prayer: "Pray, pray men and women! Pray in solitude and pray in groups, pray everyone for himself and everyone for his neighbor. Pray with the definite purpose that you will not shrink from the answer."[19] If more Christians spent as much time in prayer as they spend in criticism of each other, how much more effective the work would be. Prayer for each other in a congregation is important, but "Above all, there should be constant prayer for the pastor. 'The congregation should live in daily concern and prayer for the pastor, even as he for the congregation.'"[20]

Sverdrup believed there should be regular prayer meetings in the church as well as daily devotions in the home. "'And as long as there have been Christians on earth, they have always thought it necessary to keep holy a certain time each day by God's Word and prayer.'"[21] Daily meditation in God's Word and prayer are privileges of all believers that must not be neglected, for a daily devotional life is a vital part of nurturing spiritual life and growth.

Witnessing

One of the most basic forms of lay activity for Sverdrup was witnessing, and he and Oftedal address witnessing in *Fundamental Principle 12:*

> Every free congregation, as well as every individual believer, is constrained by the Spirit of God and by the privileges of Christian love to do good and to work for the salvation of souls and the quickening of spiritual life, as far as its abilities and power permit. Such free spiritual activity is limited neither by parish nor by synodical bounds.

Witnessing is not something the Christian should take lightly, for Sverdrup says, "It is necessary for the saved man to testify about the Saviour."[22] Though a Christian is a witness by his life and conduct, it is important for him to confess his Savior in words as well. Romans 10:9-10 says, "that if you confess with your mouth Jesus as Lord, and believe in your heart that God raised Him from the dead, you shall be saved; for with the heart man believes, resulting in righteousness, and with the mouth he confesses, resulting in salvation." Christ has called every Christian to witness to unbelievers.

Personal evangelism is an essential activity of an obedient Christian. Witnessing to others is an expression of the joy that comes from knowing Christ. It is sharing the freedom of living in the light with those who are living in darkness. It is the earnest desire that others experience the deliverance and joys of the Christian.

Personal evangelism begins in the home. Christian parents have a great privilege and responsibility to bring their children to Christ and to nurture their faith in Christ. This is not the primary responsibility of the pastor. Sverdrup says, "'The godly [parent] who leads [his or] her small children to Jesus is often the greatest worker of the 'living congregation.'"[23]

But witnessing should go beyond the home. It is further expected that a Christian would personally speak about Christ to friends, neighbors, and colleagues at work. "The activity which seems to be the most blessed, and which both could and ought to be the most common," according to Sverdrup, "is the individual's work with the individual soul."[24]

Testimonial meetings were considered essential by Sverdrup in order that the congregation might make use of all its powers and gifts. Besides the private testimony of one individual to another, Sverdrup believed the Christian should witness for his Savior in testimonial meetings and fellowship gatherings in the congregation.

> We must certainly be happy for every congregation where such fellowship meetings are held, and we must sorrow over every gathering of people that calls itself a congregation, and yet have not any spiritual gifts which it can use in this manner for its own edification.[25]

Even though a layman may feel he does not have the gift of witnessing, there should be people in every congregation who with the power of the Holy Spirit give testimony of their faith for the edification of fellow believers and for a testimony to the unbeliever. The congregation is built up through this activity. Sverdrup believed that regular fellowship meetings with all Christians participating with testimonies was the ideal for a living congregation.[26]

Lay preaching is a special gift given to some Christians for building up the kingdom. Though all Christians are to be workers in the congregation, God gives the gift of lay preaching to a few. Sverdrup defines a lay preacher as follows:

> A lay preacher is a man who has a message from God to bring to his fellow men, and who would be unfaithful if he kept silent with this message. Therefore he speaks God's message both in conversations with the individual, and in larger or smaller gatherings of one kind or another. But he continues to be a layman while he thus preaches and does not earn his living by preaching.[27]

If a layman believes he is called by God to preach, he must preach. He looks for every opportunity to share the Gospel. If he is truly called by God, other members of the congregation will affirm this gift, but he is never to quit his regular job. If he travels around as an evangelist full time, even if he were not ordained, Sverdrup believes he would then cease to be a lay preacher. Stensvaag adds that "when our fathers spoke of lay activity they had in mind primarily the work of lay witnessing and lay preaching. Where these two aspects fail to receive encouragement and opportunity for expression, there is no lay activity in the deepest sense of the word."[28]

Sverdrup's strong encouragement of lay preaching was not widely held among other Lutherans. Lay preaching was generally frowned upon and was to be used only when no pastor could be found. Because of this, many believed lay preaching should always be under the control of the clergy. Sverdrup, on the other hand, believed lay preaching "ought to be free, that is to say, prompted by the Spirit of God. Otherwise it cannot thrive, and no one can hope to promote it by bonds, compulsion, and control, but only by God's Spirit–by His freedom and love."[29] Nevertheless, Sverdrup believed there were some unscrupulous laymen who abused their role. "There is also danger from laymen who, because of laziness, pride, or desire for gain, travel about leading revival meetings when they should be working with their hands."[30]

The great value of lay preaching is that it is a gift from God and that the Spirit guides it. Where there are living congregations, gifts like these will be encouraged, and where there are living congregations, there will be opportunities to use these gifts.[31]

Financial Support

It is an obvious fact that financial support for the local congregation as well as for missions and other ministries must come from the laity. During Sverdrup's time, many synods had begun assessing individuals in the congregation a set amount that included an assessment for synodical operations as well.

Sverdrup opposed this because it infringed upon congregational independence. He believed that where the Spirit of God reigns, Christians become responsible givers. Stensvaag says,

> Accordingly he [Sverdrup] taught that where there is Spirit and freedom in the congregation, so that the all-important concern is the salvation of self and others, then the reign of covetousness and self-indulgence in the soul is broken. Men no longer live for money or the pleasure bought with money, but for God and his congregation. They seek rather to earn money in order to have something to give to the cause of Christ. "In this is freedom, when everything is of the Lord, and I only receive what he gives, and give only what I have received of him." In other words, Georg Sverdrup believed in the miracle of conversion—in a new, Spirit-led man. Such men live and act in a way quite incomprehensible to the world.[32]

The Office of Deacon: The Laity Working with the Pastor

There are pastors who would prefer to work alone in the congregation. They feel it is easier to do the work themselves or that it is their duty to minister alone. At the same time, there are parishioners who readily would have their pastor do all the work of ministry. Neither approach is biblical. Sverdrup wrote,

> All Christians are priests and witnesses, and yet the congregation as a whole must have its pastor who is to perform the congregation's duty of witnessing as a whole. Likewise, all Christians are to be servants or deacons in the footsteps of Jesus Christ, and yet the congregation as a whole will only be able to perform its duty of service through special deacons elected for that purpose.[33]

According to Sverdrup, deacons duly elected from the congregation can be of great benefit to the congregation and the pastor. They can ease the pastor's ministering load, they can point out people in need that he may have missed, they can befriend and encourage him in the time of personal challenges, and they can support him by praying with him as well as for him.

> The office of deacon is an indispensable support for the pastoral office in our congregations. . . . They can visit the sick when the pastor is unable to do so. They can assist with devotional meetings, and conduct services when the pastor is hindered from doing so. They can pray with him and give advice and help where one person would be both perplexed and helpless. It is at once apparent that it is the same now as in the apostolic times. If the pastor is to hold all offices and perform all the work in the congregation then his principal work will be neglected. He will have so many duties that the one will hinder the other. Such a condition is equally unsound for congregation and for pastor. Unfortunately, there are congregations in many places that want it that way. Many are true and well-informed pastors who recognize that the liberty and life of the congregation and the ministry's own grave responsibility demand a division of work.[34]

Sverdrup's attitude toward the work of laity is not merely one of respect. He believes their involvement is vital to the spiritual life of the congregation. Working together, they form a vital partnership with the pastor. Through the gifts of the Spirit, the congregation is edified. And though God has given each member a gift, it is the congregation's responsibility to provide expression for it. To this end, it should be the desire of every congregation to have an active, Spirit-led laity.

Yet, as we look upon our AFLC congregations today, we cannot help but reflect upon the words John Stensvaag used in his address celebrating Sverdrup and the founders during Augsburg's Diamond Anniversary. How committed really are we to an active laity?

> there is an ever-present tendency to fix a gulf between pastors and people. This gulf is evidenced in the notion that all public preaching, praying, and witnessing ought to be done by the pastors. Our founders were ridiculed and denounced because they rejected this view and taught that **all** believers were to be witnesses of Christ and workers in His vineyard. They insisted that all the gifts of grace, including the gift of lay preaching, must be ferreted out and put to use. Are we of the same spirit? Or have we permitted the old gulf to arise once more, in practice confining the spiritual work of the congregation to the pastor? Do we frown upon testimony meetings and give no room for lay preaching? Do we limit lay activity to the barest minimum instead of encouraging it to the greatest extent? Then we are not the true sons of our founders, and the honor we show them today is but empty lip service.[35]

NOTES

[1] John Stensvaag, "The Living Congregation: Georg Sverdrup's Views on Lay Activity in the Church," (seminary thesis, Augsburg Theological Seminary, n.d.), 11.

[2] Georg Sverdrup, *Professor Georg Sverdrups Samlede skrifter i udvalg*, ed. Andreas Helland; trans. John Stensvaag (Minneapolis, 1909-1912), 3:279.

[3] Sverdrup, *Samlede skrifter*, ed. Andreas Helland; trans. unknown, 2:302-303.

[4] Andreas Helland, *Georg Sverdrup: The Man and His Message* (Minneapolis: Messenger Press, 1947), 193.

[5] Francis W. Monseth, *Georg Sverdrup: Champion of the Free Congregation* (Minneapolis, 1997), 3-4.

[6] John O. Evjen, "Georg Sverdrup," in *Augsburg Seminary and The Lutheran Free Church*, ed. Lars Lillehei (Minneapolis, 1928), 6.

[7] James S. Hamre, "Georg Sverdrup's Concept of the Role and Calling of the Norwegian-American Lutherans: An Annotated Translation of Selected

Writings" (Ph. D. diss., University of Iowa, 1967), 12.

[8] Eugene L. Fevold, *The Lutheran Free Church: A Fellowship of American Lutheran Congregations, 1897-1963* (Minneapolis: Augsburg Publishing House, 1969), 7.

[9] Fevold, *The Lutheran Free Church*, 10.

[10] Fevold, *The Lutheran Free Church*, 14.

[11] Fevold, *The Lutheran Free Church*, 10.

[12] Fevold, *The Lutheran Free Church*, 17.

[13] Fevold, *The Lutheran Free Church*, 104.

[14] Sverdrup, "Is It Possible For Norwegian Lutherans To Build A Christian Free Church In America?" (*Samlede skrifter* 2:101-119) in Hamre, "Georg Sverdrup's Concept of the Role and Calling," 55.

[15] Sverdrup, "Is It Possible For Norwegian Lutherans To Build A Christian Free Church In America?" (*Samlede skrifter* 2:101-119) in Hamre, "Georg Sverdrup's Concept of the Role and Calling," (in footnote), 55.

[16] Sverdrup, "Lay Work According to Ability and Gifts," (*Samlede skrifter* 2:304) in Stensvaag, "The Living Congregation," 10.

[17] Sverdrup, "The Local Congregation and the Use of the Gifts of Grace," (*Samlede skrifter* 3:283) in Stensvaag, "The Living Congregation," 10.

[18] Stensvaag, "The Living Congregation," 11.

[19] Sverdrup, "Opening Sermon at the Meeting of 'The Friends of Augsburg,' June 26, 1895" (*Samlede skrifter* 6:297) in Stensvaag, "The Living Congregation," 11.

[20] Sverdrup, "Is Christian Faith the Responsibility of the Pastor?" (*Samlede skrifter* 3:251) in Stensvaag, "The Living Congregation," 11.

[21] Sverdrup, "The Norwegian Synod and the Norwegian Children's Teaching,"(*Samlede skrifter* 1:305) in Stensvaag, "The Living Congregation," 12.

[22] Sverdrup, "Work for the Congregation" (*Samlede skrifter* 2:261) in Stensvaag, "The Living Congregation," 12.

[23] Sverdrup, "What Is the Best Work for the Living and Free Congregation?" (*Samlede skrifter* 2:275) in Stensvaag, "The Living Congregation," 13.

[24] Sverdrup, "What Is the Best Work for the Living and Free Congregation?" (*Samlede skrifter* 2:276) in Stensvaag, "The Living Congregation," 13.

[25] Sverdrup, "Living Congregations" (*Samlede skrifter* 2:28) in

Stensvaag, "The Living Congregation," 13.

[26] Stensvaag, "The Living Congregation," 13.

[27] Sverdrup, "The Congregation and the Laymen's Work" (*Samlede skrifter* 2:317) in Stensvaag, "The Living Congregation," 14.

[28] Stensvaag, "The Living Congregation," 14.

[29] Sverdrup, "The Willmar Meeting and the Work of the Layman" (*Samlede skrifter* 2:294) in Stensvaag, "The Living Congregation," 14.

[30] Melvin Helland, trans. *The Heritage of Faith: Selections from the Writings of Georg Sverdrup* (Minneapolis: Augsburg Publishing House, 1969), 52.

[31] Stensvaag, "The Living Congregation," 15.

[32] Stensvaag, "The Living Congregation," 17.

[33] Sverdrup, "The Office of the Deacon in the Congregation," trans. Martin Bjornson, *Samlede skrifter* 2:80.

[34] Sverdrup, "The Office of the Deacon in the Congregation," trans. Martin Bjornson *Samlede skrifter* 2:84.

[35] John Stensvaag, "Are We Hypocrites?" in *Freedom and Christian Education*, ed. John A. Houkom (Minneapolis: Board of Trustees, 1945), 57.

GEORG SVERDRUP (1848-1907)

Born in 1848, Georg Sverdrup came from a distinguished Norwegian family that had produced prime ministers, professors, and pastors. His father, parish pastor H. U. Sverdrup, revised Pontoppidan's *Truth Unto Godliness* into what we know today as *Luther's Small Catechism Explained*. This text is still used for confirmation in many AFLC congregations. He was called to Augsburg Seminary as Old Testament professor in 1874, and with his close friend, Sven Oftedal, founded the Lutheran Free Church in 1897. At the relatively young age of fifty-eight, he died of heart failure. In 1930, Dr. John O. Evjen referred to him as the greatest Lutheran theologian that America has ever had. After his death, Augsburg Professor Andreas Helland assembled and edited his writing into a six-volume set under the title *Professor Georg Sverdrups samlede skrifter i udvalg*. Some years later, John Evjen published more of Dr. Sverdrup's work under the title *Veiledning i Den Lutherske Frikirkes Principer*.

Courtesy Augsburg College Archives

Courtesy Augsburg College Archives

SVEN OFTEDAL (1844-1911)

Born in Norway in 1844, Sven Oftedal studied at the University of Oslo where he was a close friend of Georg Sverdrup. Called to Augsburg Seminary as the New Testament professor in 1873, he was instrumental in persuading his classmate, Sverdrup, to come to America and build "A Free Church in a Free Land." A more flamboyant, colorful man than his colleague, Oftedal was noted for his speaking eloquence, organizational skills, linguistic gifts, and leadership qualities. At the time of his death in 1911, he was President of Augsburg Seminary, having assumed that position after the death of Sverdrup. He and Sverdrup were the primary writers of the *Fundamental Principles* and *Rules for Work* that continue to guide the AFLC today.

The Powers Hotel—Fargo, ND

"If we had our way, there would be some memorial in the Association of Free Lutheran Congregations bearing the name 'Powers.' For if any one place was strategic in her history, this was.

"Reel off the names of significance: Fergus Falls, Thief River Falls, Pelican Rapids, Willmar, Valley City, Minneapolis. None compares with Fargo and notably the Powers Hotel. For it was there that committee work prepared for the Thief River conference held in October, 1962, and that the committees that conference named did much of their ensuing work.

"Who of those who took part will forget the prayer sessions, the hours of discussion (the light moments and the tense ones), the meals together, the coffee breaks? It was secular ground, to be sure, but it was also a haven, for work such as ours was not welcome everywhere.

"The Powers was a link to the past also. It was a logical hostelry during Annual Conferences of the Lutheran Free Church. It was the meeting place for pastoral advisors of the Luther League Federation.

"Then for almost two years it was the 'headquarters' for the fledgling Association."

Raynard Hugle
The Lutheran Ambassador
January 12, 196

St. Paul's Free Lutheran Church—Fargo, ND

St. Paul's was purchased by the AFLC in 1963 to serve as the Mission Center. Rev. John Abel served as the Mission Director until he left for Brazil in 1964 to open the first AFLC Foreign Mission Field. St. Paul's congregation was organized in 1963 and was the host congregation for the first AFLC Annual Conference that same year.

Rev. John and Mildred Strand

Pastor Strand served as the first President of the AFLC (1962-1978), the first Dean of the Seminary (1964-1966), and the first Dean of the Bible School (1966-1968). When he declined re-election for the AFLC presidency in 1978, he accepted a call to serve St. Paul's Free Lutheran in Fargo, ND. There he served until his retirement in 1982.

Association of Free Lutheran Congregations

Rev. John P. Strand
President 1962-78

Rev. Richard Snipstead
President 1978-92

Rev. Robert L. Lee
President 1992-

The AFLC Administration Building was completed in 1992 and overlooks Medicine Lake in suburban Minneapolis. The building houses the office of the President of the AFLC and the offices for the Directors of Foreign Missions, Home Missions, Evangelism, Parish Education, and Youth. The lower level includes a bookstore as well as other offices.

Free Lutheran Theological Seminary

Rev. John P. Strand
Dean 1964-66

Dr. Iver Olson
Dean 1966-71

Rev. Amos Dyrud
Dean 1971-81

Dr. Francis Monseth
Dean 1981-

FLC Schools Administration Building Overlooking Medicine Lake in suburban Minneapolis, MN, this building houses the Association Free Lutheran Theological Seminary, Bible School, Chapel, and offices. Built in 1960 by the Lauge Lutheran Innermission Federation, the building with twenty-one acres of land was purchased by the AFLC in 1964. Until 1992, the administrative offices of the AFLC were located here as well.

First Seminary Graduating Class (1967) Howard Kjos, Bob Reith, Richard Gunderson, Edwin Kjos, David Molstre; not pictured: Francis Monseth

First Seminary Class (1964-65) Seated l to r: Francis Monseth, James Jacobson, Reuben Evenson, Edwin Kjos, David Molstre, Richard Gunderson, Robert Reith, Howard Kjos, Raymond Peterson; not pictured: Arlie Kuhl
Faculty, standing: Rev. John Strand, Dr. Uuras Saarnivaara, Rev. Clair Jenning

WMF Officers Elected at the First Annual Conference in 1963
Mrs. O. K. Ose, Mrs. Herbert Presteng, Mrs. Julius Hermunslie, Mrs. Raymond Jacobson, Mrs. Albert Moen

WMF Gathering at the 1963 Conference
St. Paul's Free Lutheran, Fargo, ND

Rev. Raynard Huglen
First Editor of
The Lutheran Ambassador

Rev. John and Ruby Abel
First Mission Director
and First Missionaries to Brazil

Rev. Herbert Franz
Home Missions and Evangelism

Rev. Trygve Dahle
Stewardship

Rev. Karl Stendal
Early Organizer of Congregations

Miss Judith Wold
First Full-Time Parish
Education Director

Rev. Julius Hermunslie
First Chairman of
the Coordinating Committee

Rev. Ernest Langness
Schools Board of Trustees

First Association Free Lutheran Bible School Class (1967-68)
1st row l to r: Maureen Hartsoch, Jean Presteng, Rosemary Hanson, Annita Haugen, Janette Hove, Connie Broden, Bonnie Ferguson. 2nd row l to r: Norma Ness, Richard Aasness, Joseph Miller, Louie Falk, Ralph Peterson, Richard Anderson

First AFLBS Choir (1967-68) 1st row l to r: Director Esther Farrier, Annita Haugen, Jean Presteng, Maureen Hartsoch. 2nd row l to r: Rosemary Hanson, Norma Ness, Bonnie Ferguson, Janette Hove, Connie Broden. 3rd row l to r: Joseph Miller, Paul Haugen (seminarian), Louie Falk, Richard Anderson, Ralph Peterson.

Early Lay Leaders in the AFLC

Paul Bjornstad　　Morris Borstad　　Russell Duncan　　Stan Holmaas

Ray Jacobson　　Clifford Johnson　　Robert Knutson　　Ernest Miedema

Sheldon Mortrud　　Clarence Quanbeck　　Eldor Sorkness　　Olve Willand

The Male Quartet from New Luther Valley, McVille, ND, sang at the 1963 Conference Mission service in Fargo, ND: Alfred Haugen, Arnold Haugen, Rudy Rishovd, Albin Haugen

The Ambassadors Youth Caravan traveled to AFLC churches during the summer of 1963: Fran Monseth, Alan Hendrickson, Terry Simonson, Roger Strom, Dave Johnson

Resolutions Committee Meeting at the 1976 Conference in Hancock, MI

Coordinating Committee Meeting 1980

Schools Corporation Meeting at AFLBS 1969

**1974 Annual Conference
Our Saviour's Lutheran, Thief River Falls, MN**

1969 Annual Conference at Medicine Lake
Rev. Harry Molstre and
Stenographer Mrs. J. C. Eletson

Rev. John P. Strand
preached the sermon at the
closing service of the 1963
Annual Conference in Fargo, N

The Association of Free Lutheran Congregations
Aerial View of the Campus in Plymouth, MN

AFLC CHURCHES on these pages represent the Lutheran Free Church congregations that were not certified into the ALC as of February 1, 1963. They were among the first congregations that made up the AFLC and continue today. *(See chapter 3, page 39.)*

UNITED
BETHANIA (Org. 1896) merged into United in 1972
Greenbush, MN

BADGER CREEK
Badger, MN Org. 1896

OUR SAVIOUR'S
Thief River Falls, MN Org. 1951

DOVRE
Winger, MN Org. 1895

GREEN LAKE
Spicer, MN Org. 1883

LANDSTAD
Shevlin, MN Org. 1895

MAPLE BAY
Mentor, MN Org. 1894

NORLAND
Salol, MN Org. 1940

OILAND
Greenbush, MN Org. 1897

REINER
Goodridge, MN Reorg. 1935

ROSE
Roseau, MN Org. 1888

SELL LAKE
Shevlin, MN Org. 1900

SPRUCE
Roseau, MN Org. 1925

TRINITY
Wilton, MN Org. 1899

UNION LAKE
Winger, MN Org. 1896

WESTAKER
Newfolden, MN Org. 1887

LEBANON
Leeds, ND Org. 1897

NEW LUTHER VALLEY
McVille, ND Org. 1882

BETHANY
Binford, ND Org. 1901

NORMAN
Tioga, ND Org. 1908

BEAVER CREEK
Tioga, ND Org. 1895

ZION
Tioga, ND Org. 1906

ZION
Valley City, ND Org. 1888

ZOAR
Hatton, ND Org. 1898

PUKWANA
Pukwana, SD Org. 1920

BETHEL
Faith, SD Org. 1917

EMMANUEL
Eagle Butte, SD Org. 1957

ST. OLAF
Chamberlain (Ola), SD Org. 1909

FAITH OF RUNNING VALLEY
Colfax, WI Org. 1863

TRIUMPH
Ferndale, WA Org. 1967
FIRST (Org. 1903) and GOLGOTHA (Org. 1908)
merged to form Triumph in 1967

While the congregation is free, it is constrained by the Spirit of God to work with others building God's Kingdom. There is to be inter-congregational unity and fellowship. Congregations working together can do such tasks that congregations alone cannot do. The task of missions, the training of pastors, and the publications of literature, fall in these categories. A congregation's freedom does not exempt it from responsibilities in these tasks. As a matter of fact, it heightens the responsibility.

—John P. Strand

8

The Annual Conference

Next in Importance to the Local Congregation

Loiell O. Dyrud

Two years after the AFLC was organized, Rev. Raynard Huglen, the editor of *The Lutheran Ambassador*, made this observation concerning the Annual Conference:

> Now, to have free congregations is one thing, but they cannot be what they are meant to be by themselves. They must have outreach and fellowship or they become spiritual monstrosities. For this reason the Guiding Principles–blueprint of "free" congregations–devotes considerable space (Principle 5-11) to discussion of the relationship of free congregations to each other. It assumes and declares the need of mutual work for God's Kingdom.
>
> It should be obvious, then, that in a fellowship of free congregations the annual meeting or conference is next in importance to that of the local congregational program.[1]

That Rev. Huglen places the Annual Conference "next in importance to that of the local congregational program" may seem an overstatement to some, but his stand squares fully with Georg Sverdrup's understanding of the importance of local congregations cooperating with each other through the Annual Conference. According to Sverdrup, congregations were to be independent, but they were not to be islands unto themselves.

They were not to exist in isolation. Sverdrup stressed the importance of "mutual assistance" between congregations as demonstrated in the New Testament: "the New Testament shows us a fellowship of congregations that stand free and independent beside each other, and yet intimately connected by the same gospel, the same baptism, the same Lord's Supper, the same Lord, the same Spirit."[2] In fact, he seems to indicate there is as much to fear from congregations failing to cooperate with each other as there is to fear from a synodical hierarchy over them. This point is made clear by James Hamre in *Georg Sverdrup: Educator, Theologian, Churchman:*

> Sverdrup held that two great dangers threatening the development of church work in America were hierarchy and individualism. The only thing that could offer protection against them was restoration of free congregations that would associate with one another in Christian work.[3]

Eugene L. Fevold comes to much the same conclusion regarding Sverdrup's views on this subject in *The Lutheran Free Church: A Fellowship of American Lutheran Congregations, 1897-1963*: "free and independent congregations need one another and ought to be of assistance to one another. A congregation does not exist in solitary isolation but lives in a fellowship."[4]

In Articles 7-11 of the *Fundamental Principles*, Georg Sverdrup and Sven Oftedal speak directly of the necessity for cooperation among congregations. Three main ideas operate in these five Articles. First, congregations may assist each other spiritually through conferences and meetings. Second, cooperating as a fellowship, congregations can further the cause of education, missions, and other Christian activities that individual congregations could not do on their own. Third, these cooperating congregations cannot force their wishes on individual congregations.[5]

On the other hand, where the work of the congregations is led by the Holy Spirit, cooperation becomes a natural by-product, and this cooperation is best demonstrated through the

Annual Conference. It is through the Annual Conference that the mutual efforts of the free congregations are channeled. Without conference coordination and direction, ministries such as missions, schools, and parish education would have difficulty succeeding. Only when like-minded congregations work together in a Spirit-driven atmosphere can these larger ministries be accomplished.

Yet, how is it possible to operate an Annual Conference of free congregations? How do we maintain larger ministries involving individual congregations without becoming heavy-handed and coercive? How do we create a unified national effort without impinging on the congregation's freedom? This is the task of the Annual Conference in a non-synodical setting. It is a supreme balancing act put into practice by Georg Sverdrup and Sven Oftedal that relies more on the Spirit of God than the cleverness of man. Furthermore, we believe that God prompts like-minded people from like-minded congregations to gather each year in early June for a convention, without the aid of delegates or binding resolutions, and guides them through His Spirit to accomplish the work of the AFLC at large.

The AFLC is a continuation of the Lutheran Free Church founded in 1897 by Sverdrup and Oftedal and still follows its *Fundamental Principles* and practices. Thus it is helpful to see how LFC historian Clarence J. Carlsen explains the function of the Annual Conference some sixty years ago in *The Years of Our Church:*

> Our Annual Conference does not operate under a representative system whereby a limited number of delegates are chosen to act for the congregations. Congregations may, if they so desire, send representatives from their midst to the Annual Conference. But the number from any one congregation is not limited. The annual convention of our church is not a legislative body, the decisions of which are binding upon the congregations of the Lutheran Free Church. It is intended rather as an assembly of Lutheran Christians from our various congregations, gathered for the purpose of counselling

together concerning Christian life and work and making recommendations in regard thereto to the church at large. It is assumed that spiritually-minded and spiritually-interested members of our congregations will come to these annual meetings of their own volition in order that they themselves may be edified thereby and may assist in making the decisions which will in their common judgment best advance the work in the kingdom of God entrusted to us as a church. It is further taken for granted that the congregations will accept the decisions that are thus made and referred to them, though it is not legally or otherwise incumbent upon them to do so. Much time during these meetings is devoted to inspiration and edification, and the members of the convention are expected both to give and to receive in this respect.[6]

This is the blueprint, but how does it work in practice? It is completely different from other conventions or annual meetings with which most people are familiar. If people come to an AFLC Annual Conference expecting to muscle through resolutions, push through earthshaking projects, and make sweeping changes, they will be sorely frustrated. But if they have patience, they will see the beauty of a church body organized for spiritual renewal, not church politics, for the AFLC is a spiritual movement, intentionally organized loosely in order to be led by the Spirit of God.

The Role of Committees

To a first time conference attender, one of the most confusing parts of a conference is the role of "the committees." On the morning of the first full day of the conference (traditionally Thursday) after the president's annual report and some additional reports, the president calls for the reading of the resolutions from Committee 1. At this point the committee secretary comes forward and reads Resolution 1 from a sheet of resolutions that has been handed out on the conference floor. These resolutions are then debated and voted, up or down, until all the resolutions for that committee are finished. More reports are read, and then we move on to resolutions from Committee 2, and the process begins all over again.

This writer remembers sitting in total confusion through much of his first Annual Conference. Two burning questions kept arising: "Who or what do these committees and their numbers represent? And from where do these resolutions come?"

First, who or what are these committees? Five committees representing areas of work within the AFLC are elected the previous year to serve during the conference. Committee 1 is responsible for resolutions pertaining to administration. This includes the office of the president, all general resolutions to the conference, and the Coordinating Committee. (The Coordinating Committee is the oversight administrative board that is responsible for the clergy and congregational rosters, the AFLC Administration Building, *The Lutheran Ambassador*, as well as for organizing the annual conferences.) Committee 2 is responsible for the Bible School and Seminary. Committee 3 is responsible for World Missions, Home Missions, and Evangelism. Committee 4 is responsible for Parish Education and Youth. Finally, Committee 5 is responsible for Stewardship and Pensions. All the ministries of the AFLC are represented by one of the five committees.

The day before the conference business sessions begin, members of these five committees meet to study the annual reports from chairpersons, directors, and boards that are under their respective jurisdictions and to formulate resolutions (recommendations) to be considered on the conference floor.

This basically answers the second question: "From where do the resolutions come?" But at the same time this answer raises some even more troublesome questions. If the resolutions come from the reports of the chairpersons, directors, and boards, doesn't this system seem to be a closed circuit, a system that perpetuates the ideas, desires, and whims of the establishment which includes the directors and boards? Even in the most positive light, it seems to be a contradiction of "free" church freedom. On the other hand, who is more aware of the needs of these endeavors than the directors and boards? Yet, even here is a balance that tends to prevent abuse of power. Complete freedom to bring up resolutions from the floor is always in order and is encouraged as evidence of the Holy Spirit's prompting.

In a recent change, the order of committee reports and resolutions is now on a rotational basis to prevent Committee 5 from always being pushed to the last item of business on Saturday afternoon. Once one grasps the relationship between reports, committees, and resolutions, one is better able to understand the operation of the business sessions of a conference.

The Historical Role of Corporations

Why all these corporations and their endless elections? In a synod, the General Council or Church Council basically "owns," is responsible for and exercises authority over the congregations, schools, and missions of "the church." But the AFLC as a free church is congregational in its polity. We are not incorporated as a legal entity, nor do we have an organizational constitution. The AFLC does not own property, and the so-called "headquarters" exercises little authority over congregations, schools, and missions. Thus much of the work beyond the congregation must be done by individual corporations legally organized in the states in which they began their operation. We have four major corporations–Missions, Schools, ARC (Association Retreat Center), and the Coordinating Committee. (The Coordinating Committee Corporation owns the administration building property and as a legal entity can accept legacies for the AFLC at large.) Each corporation is legally separated from the others with no oversight corporation to bind them together. The only tie between them is a spiritual one.

The existence of these corporations goes back over a hundred years to the experiment of the Lutheran Free Church, and they have evolved as a necessity for maintaining congregational freedom.

The Lutheran Free Church, established in 1897, was an outgrowth of the Conference for the Norwegian-Danish Evangelical Lutheran Church. Called a "conference" to distinguish itself from a synod, this small Midwestern Lutheran body forbade decisions of the Annual Conference from binding the congregations and constitutionally guaranteed their freedom. Augsburg Seminary, organized in 1869, became the seminary for the Conference. Since the Norwegian-Danish Conference was not operating as a synod, it could not "own" Augsburg Seminary; thus Augsburg was operated by an independent corporation made up of its Board of Trustees. In the 1870s Georg Sverdrup and Sven Oftedal became leaders of that institution and champions of "free and living congregations" in the Norwegian-Danish Conference.

As the spirit of unionism grew, Sverdrup and Oftedal worked toward a union of the Norwegian-Danish Conference with two other small synodical groups to form the United Norwegian Lutheran Church in 1890. Both men firmly believed that through their influence, this new church would be structured in a free church manner similar to the Norwegian-Danish Conference.

However, on the conference floor, Sverdrup and Oftedal watched resolution after resolution pass, essentially binding the free church concepts in a synodical vise. Not only was it apparent that the congregations would lose their freedom, but Augsburg was also in jeopardy. Augsburg would have to be turned over to the new United Norwegian Lutheran Church Council, and Augsburg's operating corporation and board would be dissolved. Furthermore, the United Church vision was to have St. Olaf College, Northfield, Minnesota, as the official college while Augsburg would be the official seminary only. Sverdrup and Oftedal revolted. They felt that in order to have free congregations, the church had to have "servant pastors." And in order to have servant pastors, the training had to begin in college. Otherwise, they believed, there was a danger of turning out pastors who could become as dictators in the congregation.

As Sverdrup and Oftedal watched the first annual conferences of the United Church, they became convinced that the United Church was not interested in free congregations. Furthermore, Augsburg under synodical control would have to acquiesce to the will of the Annual Conference delegates.

Fortunately, Augsburg could still lay claim to its independent corporate status. Thus when Sverdrup and Oftedal and thirteen congregations officially separated from the United Church in 1897 to form the Lutheran Free Church, they brought Augsburg with them. The United Church, however, still claimed control of Augsburg. A court case followed that went all the way to the Minnesota Supreme Court where the 1898 decision ruled that the rightful owner of Augsburg was, after all, its independent corporation. The decision was critical. Had the court ruled in favor of the United Church, Sverdrup and Oftedal would not have had the institution from which to launch the Lutheran Free Church, and the AFLC as we know it today would not exist. The separate corporation structure that saved Augsburg became the model for holding property and institutions in the LFC, and we have continued this practice in the AFLC to this day.

How Corporations Are Elected in a Conference Setting

Corporations, then, are a time-honored part of our heritage as well as an absolute necessity for retaining our status as a free church. Nevertheless, their operation is a constant source of confusion for many.

First of all, there is no set number of corporations or members in each corporation. In the original Augsburg Corporation, there were only five members, and they doubled as the Board of Trustees as well. In other words, each corporation member was also a board member. Later Annual Conferences increased corporation membership numbers. Our Missions Corporation, for instance, consists of one hundred members, while the Schools Corporation and the ARC Corporation have fifty members each. (The Coordinating Committee is a corporation made up of only seven members who double as board members. Their function will be discussed later.)

All corporation members are elected to five-year terms. The terms are staggered so twenty percent of the corporation's members are up for election each year. The Nominating Committee for the Annual Conference—made up of one member from each of our AFLC districts—nominates twice the number to be elected. This means that forty people will become nominees for the twenty positions open each year on the Missions Corporation, and twenty people will become nominees for the ten positions open each year on the Schools and ARC Corporations. These nominees are presented to the Annual Conference where more names may be added from the floor before the Annual Conference votes to narrow down the list. But the important thing to remember is the Annual Conference only narrows down the number of nominees. Conference attendees do not actually elect corporation members. That is the duty of the corporation itself. For according to Rev. Raynard Huglen,

> The nominee approach used in the AFLC is to appease the legal requirements of a corporation since only a corporation can vote on who becomes a member. Yet, the opportunity to nominate 20 members from the congregations and narrow them down to ten by a vote of the annual conference fulfills the notion of church control. These ten nominees are really just that, nominees to be officially elected by the corporation at its annual meeting in a sort of "rubber stamp" vote. However, technically speaking, the corporation would not have to accept the nominees though it almost always has in the past.[7]

The reason corporations may choose not to accept a nominee sent by the Annual Conference is because the corporation may feel the nominee would not serve in the best interests of the AFLC. Corporations, then, may exercise what is their legal right by state statute.

Each corporation is registered as a legal entity and holds all property entrusted to its ministry and is responsible for all activities of that ministry. Each corporation elects officers at its annual meeting held at a specific time during the annual conference. There are no term limits for corporation members. (See Figure 1)

ELECTING MEMBERS TO CORPORATIONS

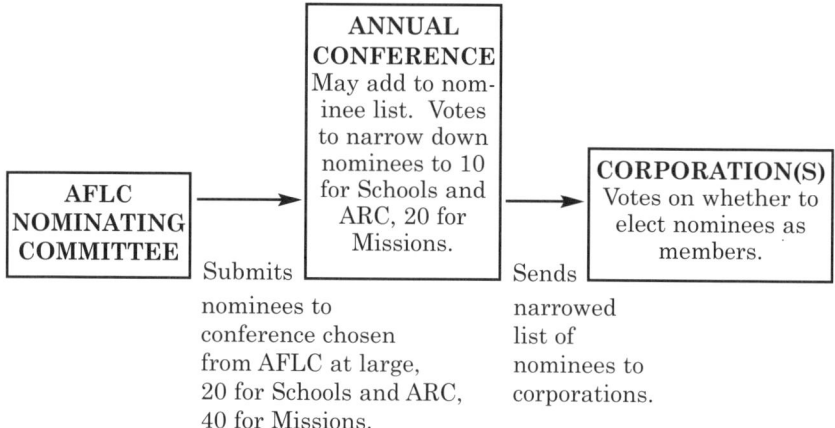

FIGURE 1

Electing Board or Committee Members from the Corporations

Since most of the corporations are too large and unwieldy to handle the day to day activities of the endeavors entrusted to them, they elect boards or committees usually made up of seven members–three pastors and four lay members. (The emphasis on the laity is to avoid clerical domination.) But the important thing to remember is that in order to be a member of the Schools Board of Trustees, World Missions Committee, Home Missions Committee, or ARC Board, *one must first be a member of that corporation.* Furthermore, the Nominating Committee should always keep in mind when nominating members to the corporations that these nominees should be viewed as potential board members.

The election process for members of boards and committees that operate under these corporations works something like this. The Annual Conference Nominating Committee selects at least two members from the respective corporation membership list for each position open on the board or committee and presents them to the conference. The conference may nominate further members. But in the Schools, Missions, and ARC Corporations, these members remain "nominees," just as we have seen with the corporation nominees, until they are voted on in their respective corporation's annual meeting. Here the final vote is taken by the corporation, electing one or more individuals to each board or committee position. (See Figure 2)

ELECTING MEMBERS FROM SCHOOLS, ARC, AND MISSIONS CORPORATIONS TO COMMITTEES AND BOARDS

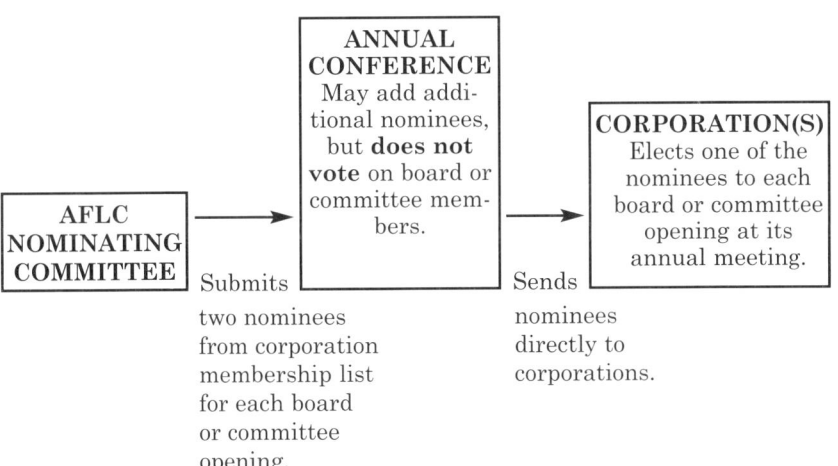

FIGURE 2

The process for electing members to the Coordinating Committee Corporation is somewhat different from the others because this corporation is made up of only seven members. These seven corporation members actually double as board or committee members much the same way as the original

Augsburg Corporation operated over a hundred years ago. One or two positions are up for election each year, and the conference nominating committee nominates at least two people from AFLC congregations for each open position and presents them to the conference floor where there may be further nominations. In this case, the Annual Conference "elects" the members that have been nominated, but here, too, one must remember that as a private corporation, the coordinating committee has the final say as to its make-up and can reject the conference choice. (See Figure 3)

ELECTING COORDINATING COMMITTEE MEMBERS

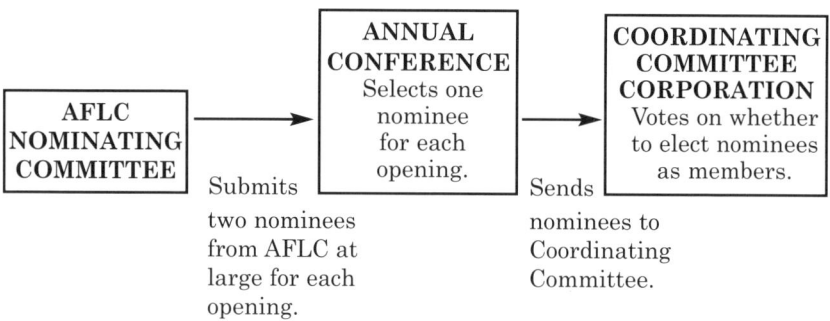

FIGURE 3

All board and committee members are limited to no more than two consecutive five-year terms, and no one can serve on two major boards or committees simultaneously.

Except for the Coordinating Committee, the corporation functions as follows: the ministry answers to the board or committee, and the board or committee answers to the corporation, which ultimately has the final say. Furthermore, the relationship of corporations to boards and directors of the AFLC is analogous to the way our local congregations are structured. The director is the servant of the board as the pastor is of the council, and the board is the servant of the corporation even as the council is the servant of the congregation. In all things, the corporation has the final say over its affairs even as the congregation has the final say over its affairs. The way corporations, boards and committees, and their ministries relate to each other is illustrated in Figure 4.

AFLC CORPORATION STRUCTURE

CORPORATION
The Schools and ARC Corporations are made up of 50 members. The Missions Corporation is made up of 100 members. Each corporation elects its own officers–president, vice president, and secretary. From its members, each corporation elects a board or committee to carry out its work.

↓

BOARD OR COMMITTEE
Each is usually made up of seven members–three pastors and four lay members. They are directly responsible for the operation and ministry of the schools, missions, and ARC and are under the jurisdiction of their respective corporations.

↓

MINISTRY
Bible School and Seminary, Home Missions and World Missions, and Association Retreat Center.

FIGURE 4

Conference Resolutions Cannot Bind Corporations

What control, then, does the Annual Conference have over a corporation? Very much spiritually–very little legally! We have seen how nominations can be overturned by a corporation, though rarely practiced. What about resolutions passed by the Annual Conference? The same applies here. The conference can recommend; it cannot dictate. No one says it better than Rev. John Strand, AFLC President from 1962-1978:

> The annual conference is a means by which the corporate works of the AFLC can be done. It has no legislative authority, however. [A] corporation is an independent body as are the individual congregations. The corporation elects its own membership and the Board.... The independence of each corporation and of each congregation must be guarded fiercely. If the corporation or the board can be bound by conference action, attempts can be made to bind congregations. This is completely contrary to our Fundamental Principles.[8]

There are both practical and historical reasons why Strand's comments make so much sense. On one occasion in the early years of the AFLC, the Annual Conference passed a resolution that the Mission Board should send out two missionary couples a year for the next three years. This never became a reality. The board had neither the finances nor the personnel to accomplish this task. In this case, the Missions Corporation was more aware of what it could do than did the Annual Conference in all its zeal. Obviously, the corporation could not be bound to such a resolution.

But there is, also, an historical reason and that deals with the heritage of our free church. A synod passes binding resolutions; a free church such as the LFC or the AFLC does not. And if the Annual Conference ever does start passing binding resolutions on corporations or congregations, we will be well on our way to becoming a *de facto* synod.

That seems to be why Rev. Strand's comments are so

emphatically stated. He had been a pastor in the Lutheran Free Church in the 1940s and 1950s and had experienced the centralization of power and the erosion of congregational freedom that led to the merger and the loss of the Lutheran Free Church. He had then struggled for sixteen years to rebuild and maintain another Lutheran church on the same *Fundamental Principles*, namely the AFLC. He was not about to see it happen again. Thus, his staunch stand is a reminder of the vigilance necessary to maintain a free church.

Just because the Annual Conference does not have binding authority on the congregations and corporations does not mean it is to be viewed as an anemic, powerless body. Far from it! The Annual Conference floor is where the work of the committees, corporations, and common endeavors can and should be evaluated. And though the conference cannot bind the congregations and corporations, it has always been the tradition, as C. J. Carlsen points out, that its wishes are generally accepted.

How Conference Resolutions Affect Corporations

Corporations are not to operate in isolation, as so many medieval fiefdoms, but as arms of the AFLC that perform tasks that cannot be accomplished by individual congregations. Whenever possible, it is understood that the corporations will follow the will of the conference, which represents the will of the individual congregations. The conference, then, provides guidance for corporations and boards through its resolutions, while at the same time the conference provides a forum for the needs of these corporations (schools, missions, retreat centers) to be aired and brought back to the congregations through the reports given on the conference floor.

Parish Education, Youth, Evangelism, Stewardship, Pensions, Budget Analysis, and Colloquy are all departments, committees, or boards that do not have separate corporations but operate under the jurisdiction of the Coordinating Committee. This gives them legal status to operate within the AFLC.

Electing AFLC Officers

The offices of president, vice president, and secretary of the AFLC are also elected by direct vote of the conference. In the first years after the AFLC was organized, the office of president received a great deal of attention. Should there be term limits or should a president be eligible for as long as he is willing to stand for the office?

Historically, the office of president in the Lutheran Free Church was a one-year term, and the president could only serve two consecutive terms. But as years went by, term limits were eliminated, and shortly before the merger in 1963, Dr. T. O. Burntvedt, an outstanding leader, had served for twenty-eight consecutive years. Some in the AFLC felt that was too long. Others felt term limits could hinder God's will in raising up leaders. Several letters were written to *The Lutheran Ambassador* on both sides of this issue. One writer makes a particularly interesting point: "a man who holds an office for a certain number of years shapes himself to the office, but a man who holds an office for a great number of years shapes the office to himself."[9] The Annual Conference worked out a solution by seemingly going down the middle of the issue. The president is eligible for three terms of three years each. Thereafter, he must receive 75 percent of the vote on the first ballot for any subsequent term he serves. This seems to have worked satisfactorily through the years.

In 1989 the "ecclesiastical" method of voting was first introduced for electing national officers: president, vice president, and secretary. In this process, conferees write down the name of a person for the office on a blank ballot and submit it. A large number of nominations are usually made. In some cases there have been more than fifty nominations. These nominees must be whittled down through several ballots to the final choice, but the process does not usually take long. The logic behind "ecclesiastical" voting seems to be that it removes the opportunity for politicking for offices before and during the conference and would hopefully allow more freedom for God's guidance in the selection process.

The Conference Is an Expression of Congregational Needs

Our fellowship also views the conference as a vehicle for establishing ministries or programs deemed necessary by the congregations when the operation of such cannot be accomplished by individual congregations. *Fundamental Principle 7* states, "A free congregation gladly accepts the mutual assistance which congregations can give one another in the work for the advancement of the Kingdom of God." *Fundamental Principle 8* states that this "advancement of the Kingdom of God" comes about through "Spirit-prompted cooperation of congregations for the accomplishing of such tasks as exceed the ability of the individual congregation." The conference, then, is the major vehicle for establishing these tasks or ministries. It is where new ministries and endeavors can be discussed and, if approved by the conference, brought into existence.

It is, however, understood that these new endeavors are to be discussed in a spirit of freedom. Sometimes well-meaning advocates present new ministries with such enthusiasm that conferees may feel coerced. If there is little balance in the presentation, conferees can be placed in the awkward position of appearing to be voting against the work of the Kingdom of God if they question the merits of the proposal. Though not officially elected delegates, conference attendees, nevertheless, are the voice of the congregations and should be encouraged to give prayerful direction as to whether or not these new ministries are, indeed, advancing the Kingdom of God.

It is worth noting what Rev. John Strand said regarding this matter in his "President's Report" to the 1977 Annual Conference:

> The officers and boards should regularly examine their work to see if they are really reflecting the congregations' concerns, seeking to develop the whole body. Am I sensitive for that which is good for the congregations? Are my decisions for their good? Are the congregations' actions and stewardship indicating this direction?

> Should there be a referendum of the congregations before pursuing this course? Will this build the whole body, or just be advantageous for one member of the body? Does this provide outlet for the congregations' expressed concern for outreach? Is this a challenge that the congregations understand? Am I trying to manipulate the congregations, or am I following their concerns? Is there a need for this in the Association? . . . The whole body must be served, not just one member of the body. The body must serve the congregations.[10]

Furthermore, the AFLC is no different from other religious organizations in that money is rarely in ample supply; therefore, establishing new programs often means tapping the same sources for money with the result that new programs can impinge upon already established programs.

For these reasons, then, it is more in keeping with our heritage to promote new programs in an atmosphere where the merits of the endeavor can be balanced against spiritual needs and financial resources in unfettered discussion. We seek to be a Spirit-driven association of free congregations. Care must be taken to maintain this freedom by remaining open to the quiet prompting of the Holy Spirit and avoiding the zealous salesmanship of man.

The Annual Conference Is Not a Political Arena

We have spent a good deal of time discussing the mechanical workings of a conference, but in a free church that is really the minor part. The major emphasis is spiritual.

AFLC Annual Conferences are never meant to be political arenas. Sverdrup felt politics in church affairs was the highest form of worldliness and should be absolutely avoided. Nor are our conferences structured to be debating forums for arguing fine points of theology in order to pass down "official stands" of the AFLC. After all, the only "official stands" we have in the AFLC are the Word of God; the three Ancient Creeds–Apostles', Nicene, Athanasian; *Luther's Small Catechism*; the unaltered

Augsburg Confession; and the *Fundamental Principles* and *Rules for Work*; and that's it.

According to Rev. Huglen, our LFC heritage

> never occupied herself much with doctrinal discussions. That is, she never overly defined or refined her theology. Georg Sverdrup, "patron saint" of the church, in those days prior to the unions of 1890 and 1893 insisted that it was enough that Lutherans agree on the Catechism (*barnelaerdom*)[11] and the Confessions. These were sufficient, he said, and series of theses were unnecessary, ambiguous and tended to stifle living Christianity.[12]

In fact, both Sverdrup and Oftedal had experienced enough theological wrangling in the 1870s and 1880s concerning the Election Controversy (predestination) and justification to last a lifetime. They had had their fill and knew what a spiritual toll it takes on Christians and congregations. The LFC conferences were structured to avoid theological debate and controversy. Our AFLC conferences continue in this tradition. When we forget this fact, problems may arise. Our Annual Conferences were not organized for theological debates and were never intended for such.

The Annual Conference Is to Be "The Great Spiritual Powerhouse"

Our Annual Conferences were intended to be every bit as much spiritual rallies as business meetings. Sven Oftedal referred to the Annual Conference as "the great spiritual powerhouse" (or drive wheel) where members come together to do the work of the church and be renewed for the common tasks that lie ahead in the upcoming year.[13]

Two things this writer will never forget after attending an entire conference for the first time were the singing and the prayer sessions. Music rising from hundreds of people singing joyously to the Lord is an inspiring experience. But the really astounding note that sets the tone for everything else is the prayer. Each session begins with a short meditation and prayer. Every morning at 11:30, all conference activities come to a halt as the conference turns to a half hour of prayer before noon. If the conference is to be the great "spiritual powerhouse," then the conference must constantly stay in touch with that power for guidance and renewal. Thus the joy that comes from being a part of hundreds of people praying in small groups on the conference floor–many on their knees–is hard to describe.

These prayer sessions were a tradition in the LFC annual conferences and continue in the AFLC. It was, therefore, no surprise when this letter appeared in *The Lutheran Ambassador* shortly after our first Annual Conference in 1963. Several people came to see what this fledgling group was about and went away blessed as this writer did:

> I attended your convention in Fargo this past summer, although perhaps I went there more for curiosity than any other reason. I left that convention with a conviction that a group of people who in their sessions took time out for a prayer session are going to be hard to stop.[14]

Whether the AFLC is a group that has been "hard to stop" is hard to say, but for people who come from church conventions where delegates "horse trade" votes and wrangle over resolutions for days, our conventions are a welcome change.

Rev. John Abel, our first AFLC missionary to Brazil, puts it another way in a letter of invitation to the 1963 Annual Conference: "This conference is not just another convention. It is to be a real spiritual retreat."[15] The tone of this "spiritual retreat" is set by the keynote address on Wednesday evening, the official opening of the conference. On that night, the speaker's sermon is based on the theme text for the conference.

Thursday night is designated Missions Night, and the program is put on by the WMF. Speakers are usually missionaries home on leave or home mission pastors.

Friday night is devoted to the laity with the sermon given by a layman followed by a time of testimonies where men and women share what God has done and is doing in the lives of His servants. Some years the sharing has gone on for more than an hour after the sermon, and what joyous fellowship these times are.

The business of the conference wraps up on Saturday afternoon leaving Saturday night Youth Night. Music is usually provided by "The Ambassadors," a team of young people from AFLBS that travels across the country during the summer proclaiming the Gospel through song and testimony in AFLC congregations.

Sunday, the last day of the conference, begins with a communion service at the host church followed by worship service at the convention site, which may include an ordination service.

These are the "planned" spiritual highlights of the Annual Conference, but there are many spontaneous times of fellowship–coffee breaks, meal times, and late night sessions in restaurants and motel rooms. It is a gathering of old friends in Christ. All year long we meet weekly to worship and fellowship with one another in our local congregations. But once a year in June we have the opportunity to meet as a church body to do the work of the church at large, worship our Risen Savior, and fellowship with each other. These are, indeed, blessed times.

Why Not a Delegate System?

The more we attend conferences the more we look forward to attending them, for it is then we see again the Christian friends we have not seen since the last conference. At times like these, we can't help but think of how sad it would be to limit attendance through a delegate system. Some members in our AFLC have left synodical churches that had conventions with delegate systems. Few of these people ever went to conventions because it was hard to get elected as a delegate, and to come to a convention just to sit in a "visitor" section was not too appealing. Before joining an AFLC congregation, many had never experienced the blessings of an annual conference like ours. Because we do not use a delegate system, no one is barred from taking part. Here we reap the benefits of people who feel led by the Holy Spirit to attend, for anyone who is a member of an

AFLC congregation can register and take part in the Annual Conference. Furthermore, even people who are not members of an AFLC congregation can register if they are willing to sign a statement saying they accept the *Fundamental Principles* and *Rules for Work* of the AFLC.

The freedom of an "open" conference has caused no little apprehension in the past, and to a degree, this fear still exists for some because of the potential to "stack" an annual conference. In other words, what is to prevent hundreds of people from one congregation or one district from filling the conference floor and pushing through some adverse legislation, or as some would say, "creating some mischief"?

Theoretically it may be possible, but it would be very difficult. First, resolutions are not considered binding. They are basically recommendations, so what serious problems could be created? Secondly, what about elections? What about the possibility of voting out existing corporation members and replacing them with members sympathetic to a minority group's cause in an attempt to influence the work of missions or schools, for example? This would not be easy. Since only twenty percent of a corporation's members are up for election on any given year, it would take five years to completely change the membership of a corporation–three years to have a majority. And since the conference is held in different districts each year, the chances are quite unlikely that the conferences would be filled with like-minded members who would stack a conference at different sites over several years.

The fears, then, created by a non-delegate system seem groundless, yet what could be created by installing a delegate system could be more troublesome. A delegate system was argued on several occasions throughout the early history of the Lutheran Free Church but was always rejected on the grounds that it could make us a synod, and we would lose our free church status. During the merger debates of the 1950s, the issue surfaced again. After losing two referenda votes in 1955 and 1958, the Annual Conference of the LFC passed a resolution in 1959 changing the *Rules for Work* in order to install a delegate system. The delegate system went into effect in 1960, and in 1961 the Annual Conference of the Lutheran Free Church voted to conduct another merger referendum. This referendum passed, and the LFC merged with the ALC, ending a sixty-five-year tradition of free congregations.

These referenda would undoubtedly have continued until a final merger had taken place even without the delegate system. The important thing to remember, however, is what happened shortly after the merger.

The congregations that did not merge, that wanted to remain true to the principles of the Lutheran Free Church and carry on the tradition of the LFC, chose as their name "The Lutheran Free Church (not merged)." Because property and wills were involved, the American Lutheran Church sued this group in an attempt to deny the use of the name. We lost. Minnesota District Judge Gordon McRae ruled that though its founders had originally organized the LFC as a fellowship of congregations and loosely connected corporations, and though the LFC did not exist in legal terms as an official synod does, in actual practice the LFC through the years had been operating more and more as a synod. In fact the judge used the adoption of a delegate system as a final example to show how the LFC had become synodical in practice. He ruled that at the time of the merger the two bodies–the American Lutheran Church and the Lutheran Free Church–were "substantially the same"[16] in the way they operated. He also ruled that the name The Association of Free Lutheran Congregations (AFLC) could be legally used, and we could continue using the *Fundamental Principles* and *Rules for Work* as long as we did not use the name "Lutheran Free Church" in any of our work.

For these reasons, then, AFLC members have been reluctant to accept a delegate system regardless of how appealing it might seem for attracting people from congregations who rarely send anyone to the Annual Conference. By limiting participation to delegates, we would not only be endangering our free church status but also our heritage of the Annual Conference as the spiritual "drive wheel" of the congregations.

Finally, this writer is convinced that anyone attending three Annual Conferences in a row will experience an irresistible desire to return each year to share in the work, rejoice in the fellowship, and be renewed in the Spirit. In fact, there is a story about an LFC layman who dearly loved the Annual Conference. So important to him was the conference that even when the profits from his farm were so meager that he could not afford to drive or take public transportation, he would pack his suitcase and hitch a ride with a cattle trucker!

The zeal is contagious. Indeed, it is similar to thousands who have come to agree with Rev. Huglen that the Annual Conference is truly next in importance to the local congregation.

NOTES

[1] Raynard O. J. Huglen, "An Intelligent Conference," *The Lutheran Ambassador* 3, no. 9 (May 4,1965): 10.

[2] Andreas Helland, *Georg Sverdrup: The Man and His Message* (Minneapolis: The Messenger Press, 1947), 219.

[3] James S. Hamre, *Georg Sverdrup: Educator, Theologian, Churchman* (Northfield, Minnesota: The Norwegian-American Historical Association, 1986), 142.

[4] Eugene L. Fevold, *The Lutheran Free Church: A Fellowship of American Lutheran Congregations, 1897-1963* (Minneapolis: Augsburg Publishing House, 1969), 104.

[5] Fevold, *The Lutheran Free Church,* 104-105.

[6] Clarence J. Carlsen, *The Years of Our Church* (Minneapolis: The Lutheran Free Church Publishing Company, 1942), 104-105.

[7] Raynard O. J. Huglen, interview by author, 29 May 1995.

[8] From an undated letter Rev. John Strand sent in winter of 1995 to Rev. Martin Horn, Chairman of the Schools Corporation.

[9] Name Withheld, "Letters to the Editor," *The Lutheran Ambassador* 5, no. 1 (January 10, 1967): 12.

[10] John P. Strand, "President's Report," *1977 Annual Report of the Association of Free Lutheran Congregations*, 5.

[11] The term *barnelaerdom* literally means "child instruction" and refers to the simple, basic teachings found in the *Catechism and Explanation.* According to Andreas Helland, the word *barnelaerdom* can also be used "in a

special sense, as an expression of the divine truth set forth in plain language, understandable to children and the uneducated, as over against the abstruse theses and theological formulae" found in some synods. Helland, *Georg Sverdrup*, 295.

[12] Raynard O. J. Huglen, "Our Heritage," *The Lutheran Ambassador* 5, no. 7 (April 4,1967): 10.

[13] Fevold, *The Lutheran Free Church*, 106-107.

[14] O. W. Wehlander, "Letters to the Editor," *The Lutheran Ambassador* 1, no. 17 (September 24,1963): 9.

[15] John H. Abel, "Welcome to Fargo," *The Lutheran Ambassador* 1, no. 9 (June 4, 1963): 3.

[16] Fevold, The Lutheran Free Church, 300.

Organizing Conference

1962—Thief River Falls, MN   Our Saviour's Lutheran Church   278
"Press on Toward the Goal" Phil. 3:1-16

AFLC Annual Conferences

Registration numbers are from Saturday 2:00 p.m. final Journal count.

YEAR	LOCATION	HOST CHURCH	REGISTRANTS

1. 1963—Fargo, ND   Mission Center (St. Paul's Free Lutheran)   378
"An Open Door" Rev. 3:8

2. 1964—Valley City, ND   Grace and Zion Lutheran   336
"Contending for the Faith" Jude 1:3

3. 1965—Minneapolis, MN   Medicine Lake Lutheran/AFLC Seminary   220
"Freedom in Christ" John 8:32

4. 1966—Thief River Falls, MN   Our Saviour's Lutheran   329
"Our Precious Faith" I Pet. 1:3-9

5. 1967—Fargo, ND   St Paul's Free Lutheran   256
"Our God is Able" II Cor. 9:8

6. 1968—Cloquet, MN   St Paul's Evangelical Lutheran   268
"Working Together With Him" II Cor. 5:20 – 6:10

7. 1969—Minneapolis, MN   Medicine Lake Lutheran   263
"Great is the Lord" Ps. 145

8. 1970—Valley City, ND   Grace and Zion Lutheran   274
"The Lordship of Christ" Col. 1:9-20

9. 1971—Cloquet, MN   St Paul's Evangelical Lutheran   321
"Christ, the Power for Today" Eph. 3:14-21

10. 1972—Minneapolis, MN   AFLC Schools   352
"His Truth is Marching On" Eph. 4:1-16

The Annual Conference 211

11. 1973—Ferndale, WA   Triumph Lutheran Church   263
    "Go Forth with Joy" Is. 55

12. 1974—Thief River Falls, MN   Our Saviour's Lutheran   382
    "Continuing in His Grace" Ps. 91

13. 1975—Minneapolis, MN   AFLC Schools/Medicine Lake Lutheran   380
    "For the Life of the World" John 6:41-51

14. 1976—Hancock, MI   Maranatha Free Lutheran (Houghton)   262
    "A Past to Remember–A Future to Mold" Deut. 8:18-20

15. 1977—Fargo, ND   St. Paul's Free Lutheran   403
    "We Are God's Workmanship" Eph. 2:1-10

16. 1978—Minneapolis, MN   AFLC Schools/Twin City Congregations   496
    "Walking Worthy of Our Calling" Eph. 4:1-16

17. 1979—Whitefish, MT   Faith and Stillwater Free Lutheran   274
    "God's Word for Today's World" II Tim. 3:14-17

18. 1980—Valley City, ND   Grace and Zion Lutheran   379
    "The Lord Always Before Us" Ps. 16

19. 1981—Minneapolis, MN   AFLC Headquarters and Schools   400
    "Behold the Multitudes" Matt. 9:36-38

20. 1982—Dickinson, ND   Our Saviour's Lutheran`   344
    "Abounding in the Work of the Lord" I Cor. 15:58

21. 1983—Osceola, WI   Association Retreat Center   385
    "Forward with Confidence" Heb. 10:19-25

22. 1984—Minneapolis, MN   AFLC Headquarters and Schools   413
    "Loyalty to Christ" John 8:31-32

23. 1985—Osceola, WI   Association Retreat Center   404
    "Strong and Courageous for the Lord" II Sam. 10:12

24. 1986—Stanwood, WA   West Coast Dist. Congregations (Warm Beach)   333
    "The Church Fervent in Prayer" Acts 12:5

25. 1987—Thief River Falls, MN   Our Saviour's Lutheran   673
    "His Kingdom is Forever" Ps. 145:13

26. 1988—DeKalb, IL Grace Free Lutheran 406
    "An Open Door" I Cor. 16:9, Rev. 3:8

27. 1989—Minot, ND Bethel Lutheran 535
    "Fields White Unto Harvest" John 4:35

28. 1990—Bloomington, MN Emmaus Lutheran 544
    "Partnership in the Gospel" Phil. 1:3-6

29. 1991—Osceola, WI Association Retreat Center 490
    "Encouragement of the Scriptures" Rom. 15:4

30. 1992—Osceola, WI Association Retreat Center 582
    "One in Spirit and Purpose" Phil 2:1-2

31. 1993—DeKalb, IL Grace Free Lutheran/Northern Ill. Congregations 359
    "Times of Refreshing" Acts 3:19

32. 1994—Valley City, ND Grace and Zion Lutheran 636
    "Stand Firm in the Faith" Eph. 6:10-20

33. 1995—Osceola, WI Association Retreat Center 740
    "Standing in the Gospel–Sustained by Grace" I Cor. 15:1-10

34. 1996—Stanwood, WA West Coast Dist. Congregations (Warm Beach) 309
    "Complete in Christ–Through His Word" Ja. 1:1-27

35. 1997—Thief River Falls, MN Our Saviour's/Abundant Life Lutheran 527
    "Where the Spirit of the Lord Is, There Is Freedom" II Cor. 3:17

36. 1998—Red Wing, MN Our Saviour's Lutheran (Zumbrota) 470
    "God's Word is Our Great Heritage" Ps. 119:89

37. 1999—Fergus Falls, MN Calvary Free Lutheran 523
    "No Other Foundation Than Christ" I Cor. 3:11

38. 2000—Osceola, WI Amery Free Lutheran/Assoc. Retreat Center 443
    "The Message of the Cross for a New Millennium" I Cor. 1:18

39. 2001—Williston, ND Emmanuel Free Lutheran 386
    "Looking to Jesus" Heb. 12:1-2

40. 2002—El Campo, TX Faith Lutheran 277
    "Exalted Among the Nations" Ps. 46:10

The church often lends itself to deceit. Wanting to be relevant and contemporary, it becomes worldly. Seeking success, it gives the people what they want, crave, and desire, instead of being the "salt" that smarts. Seeking to communicate, it ignores the message God commanded it to give. Instead of being a molder of human thought and life, it seeks out what is popular, and promotes it. Becoming over-involved with many good social issues, it neglects the Spiritual, for which it was created. As many look to the church, it thus becomes a tool of deceit, and people remain in their Spiritual need.

—John P. Strand

9

FREE AND LIVING CONGREGATIONS

Writings of Rev. John Strand
Selections from *The Lutheran Ambassador*

After the decision was made to continue the heritage of the Lutheran Free Church in the fall of 1962, much work lay ahead. Newly elected officers, board members, and other interested people met regularly at the Powers Hotel in Fargo, North Dakota. Much prayer and planning took place at those meetings.

One important decision was to begin an official paper to communicate with those LFC congregations who did not intend to merge with the American Lutheran Church as well as other like-minded congregations and individuals interested in affiliating with us. Rev. Raynard Huglen, at the time serving a parish in Roslyn, South Dakota, became the editor (a position he held for the next twenty-seven years), and the first edition of The Lutheran Ambassador *was published February 12, 1963.*

The tone of those early issues is remarkable. The struggles with the merger forces had been difficult and divisive, yet one would be hard pressed to find any tone of vindictiveness in these writings. Rev. Huglen and Rev. Strand constantly maintained a positive outlook.

The first three articles President Strand writes are basically position papers. "Fear" was published in the first issue of The Lutheran Ambassador *and is an attempt to calm the fears and worries of those who were about to begin this new venture. In "What Do We Want?" Rev. Strand answers the question by explaining our highest priority–the need for Spirit-led, awakened congregations. In order to properly understand "The Opportunity," one must view it in the context of the day. Rev. Strand is addressing a problem that was growing in our fellowship–those who wanted to affiliate with us for the wrong reasons.*

Fear

Fear is a powerful motive. It causes the destruction of health and robs people of the will to do. Fear is often incited to keep people cowed and immobile. Fear keeps many from heaven and imprisons them in a pit of uselessness.

Yet fear can be good. "The fear of God is the beginning of wisdom." When people have a childlike fear of God, a fear that impels obedience, God can use them for mighty works far beyond human attainments.

This is the first issue of *The Lutheran Ambassador*. It is the voice of a group of individuals and congregations who, for often-stated reasons, find it impossible to become a part of the American Lutheran Church. We aren't too good for the American Lutheran Church. We have been called to a task that demands that we stay out of the American Lutheran Church. Being convinced of that call, and fearing God, we cannot do otherwise. So help us, God!

Do we have other fears than a fear of God? Yes, I am afraid we have. Therefore we must remember our Lord's admonition "Fear not" as we enter upon the task set before us–a task we did not choose, we did not seek, that some have prayed to be spared from. We must fear no one, nothing but God, and God has manifested that He is with us in countless ways. There is no other explanation for so many things that have occurred and are occurring daily than that He is with us. And we believe that He will continue to be with us. And "if God is for us, who can be against us"? He who equips the Church by His Spirit so she is equipped for every good work, will equip us as we wait on Him. While at times we may lack various physical equipment, we know God gives His Spirit, the only really necessary equipment, to those who ask Him. And if He has called us, won't He equip us if we are obedient? This above all else is a spiritual movement.

We fear not because we have each other. We have been so impressed by the men, women, and congregations which make up our fellowship that we will never cease thanking God for the privilege of working with such people. We are sinners in need of daily grace. Sometimes individuals have done things that have been unwise. But as a group, the integrity has been kept. We renounce deceitful and underhanded ways and commend ourselves to God. Being bound together by the bonds of our common faith and common concerns, we move forward.

We fear not because of the good will towards us by thousands of our brethren who for different reasons find themselves in other church bodies. These have the same concerns and faith we have. They believe our cause and method are just and they stand with us in a real way. What an encouragement it has been to get their hundreds of letters, to speak with countless folk who inform us we are doing right, that we are needed as a separate church body, that they will pray for us and that they will support us with their means. Not a few have suggested they may be completely with us soon. There is such a deep concern over some of the trends in our beloved Lutheran church today amongst thousands of our people. It is humbling to know that they see in us a ray of hope. For this cause, too, we fear not.

We fear not because we have a job to do. If there was nothing to do, we would have reason to fear. It is truly a stupendous task. Some people are frightened by tasks, others are challenged by them. We have a task to do in foreign missions. Already several calls have come to us, several doors have opened. We have a task in home missions to help congregations in need, to reorganize parishes, to establish new congregations. We have a task in establishing a seminary. There is a desperate need today for a Lutheran seminary that will give young men a firm ground in the Scriptures and prepare them for a congregation-centered ministry. A seminary is needed that will inspire real faith in God's word as God's Word and open the eyes of the students to the lost souls about us who know not the Saviour. We have been much encouraged as we have begun moving into these fields. Because God has given them to us, we fear not.

To our brethren who will not be with us in our church, we wish you well as you go into the new church. We are still brothers in Christ. To say less would be to be tragically sectarian.

God bless you in your chosen vineyard. We will pray for you and we can covet your prayers. Brethren, contend earnestly for the faith!

Let us fear not. Only believe!

—The Lutheran Ambassador 1, no. 1, p. 3
February 12, 1963

What Do We Want?

Most congregations have recently entered a very busy fall and winter program. As we launch out, we ask ourselves, "What do we want to accomplish with our church this year?" Unless we have a goal, the work will not produce the results it should.

The question should not be, however, "What do we want to accomplish?" but rather, "What do we need in and through the church?" Sometimes our wants aren't very sanctified. God knows our needs, and we should seek the "higher good." Each congregation should examine itself to see what is really needed.

What is true for a congregation is also true for our Association. There are many things we want. It would not take long to make a long list of wants–and undoubtedly many of these wants are very wonderful. But we must be more concerned with what our Lord knows we need. Only as we make our goal what God knows we need will the greater blessings come our way.

There is one basic need in our Association, our congregations, and in our individual lives. This need is a spiritual awakening.

The Lutheran Free Church was born in the midst of an awakening in the 1890's. This awakening was felt throughout the Midwest and was the work of the Spirit of God. The awakening was so desperately needed in that day. The church strife had become very bitter. We hope the strife today won't come to that point in any place. But in the midst of this strife, very strangely, God poured out His Spirit, and a mighty awakening came. May God be pleased to do the same today.

A spiritual awakening will result in several wonderful blessings. I shall mention just a few.

A spiritual awakening will produce holier living on the part of the children of God. An awakening must begin among Christians. Christian living is very low among many today. Many Christians are so much of the world that no one can tell if they are Christians or not. God would have each of His children be a real witness for His Lord. The most effective witness is a consecrated life. We read in I Thessalonians 4:3: "For this is the will of God, even your sanctification." An awakening always results in a deeper awareness of personal sin, a sincere repentance and greater commitment to God on the part of Christians.

During a spiritual awakening, sinners are converted. Are all members of our churches Christians? We fear not. One of our Fundamental Principles draws attention to the fact that we must not consider all our people Christians. This is different from the approach of many today. While we believe in baptismal regeneration, because many are not taught God's Word in home and church as they ought to be, because many reject God's claims on them through the Word, they lose their faith and their souls. They need to be brought back. There ought to be a great burden on our hearts for the unsaved. II Corinthians 6:2: "Behold, now is the accepted time; behold, now is the day of salvation." During an awakening, sinners seek salvation. There is an urgency in preaching, an urgency in seeking.

During an awakening, eyes are opened to the task before the church. "Do you not say, 'There are yet four months, then comes the harvest'? I tell you, lift up your eyes, and see how the fields are already white for harvest" (John 4:35). Paul had an unceasing anguish in his heart as he thought of the fields, the task to do. Many are blind today. They see only very little of the tasks and opportunities. They need to be awakened.

An awakening results in better stewardship. Paul appealed to the Romans to present their bodies as a living sacrifice. Awakened people do that. They give of themselves, their time, their talents, and their treasures. And as they live giving lives, the fields white for harvest are entered in upon.

Are we prepared for an awakening? I don't know. Perhaps we would be genuinely frightened if one came. Regardless, this is what we need. Will you, too, pray this prayer, "Dear Lord, begin with me"?

—The Lutheran Ambassador 1, no. 17, p. 3
September 24, 1963

"The Opportunity"

Noah had a tremendous opportunity. Because of his position and time, he could give a noble direction to all of mankind after the flood. His was an unprecedented opportunity.

Our Association has a tremendous opportunity today. The world and the church are being engulfed with many different tides. We are in a position to give help to congregations and people who are deeply troubled. The dangers are many, however. We must exercise great care or we will fail. How we need the wisdom and love only God can give.

We stand in danger of becoming a "waste basket" for other groups or churches. Some may gravitate to us who for various reasons are unwanted or have worn out their usefullness in other places. There are those who may come to us to gain personal advantage instead of for conviction's sake. They would not be a blessing to us, nor we to them. Therefore we must exercise due care in this area. Accordingly, any pastor who would want to be on our clergy roster must let his desire be known to one of the officers. He must then meet with our Colloquy Committee. He may then be received into our Association on a fellowship basis, serving with us for one year. At the end of that time, if all is well, he will be placed on our regular roster. All, of course, can see the necessity of this procedure. The Colloquy Committee has been busy, and has many waiting to meet with them. We are thankful to God for sending needed laborers to us.

We are grateful, too, that congregations are desirous of joining our fellowship. We want them, too, to have a thorough understanding of our Principles and polity. They should communicate with our officers whenever possible when they contemplate associating with us. We want them to know us well. We want them to understand the freedom we enjoy and the sound Lutheran theology we believe in and practice.

There are those who look with suspicion on anyone that does not belong in their synod or association. Some folks who claim to be very ecumenical are very unbrotherly to those who for conviction's sake cannot be in the same outward church body. All believers are one in Christ, and herein lies the essential unity of the church. This truth we would voice in our day. While we are not aligned with any other group or groups, we extend the right hand of Christian fellowship to believers wherever they are. We renounce sectarianism as a tragic sin of this and any day.

There are many theological winds blowing today. It is possible to go off on tangents very quickly. There are those who go overboard about tongues, their church body, ecumenicity, liturgy, church architecture, methods, procedures, gimmicks, etc. We would make a serious attempt to "try the spirits," to have a program emphasizing sound evangelistic preaching, lay activity and responsibility, as our Principles emphasize. We refuse to be sidetracked into lesser tasks, no matter how they may be clothed.

The road will not be easy. We are not "wrestling against flesh and blood." Discouragements and misunderstandings will be many. We also believe joys and blessings will continually come. Believing that God has called us to this task, relying on Him, knit together with a common faith, and seeing the opportunity, we faint not.

—The Lutheran Ambassador 1, no. 20, p. 3
November 5, 1963

The next five articles deal with, perhaps, the most important distinctive of the AFLC, our Fundamental Principles. Using Georg Sverdrup's ideas written sixty years earlier, Rev. Strand attempts to explain what makes us different. What does it mean to be a free and living congregation? What does it mean to be an "association" and not a "synod"? The first of these, "The Difference," begins the explanation. In the next articles, he writes about each Fundamental Principle.

But he only finished five. In the summer of 1964, he moved from his parish in Tioga, North Dakota, to Minneapolis to assume the dual role of AFLC president and dean of the newly established Association Free Lutheran Theological Seminary. Administrative and teaching duties in the seminary as well as official duties as president of the AFLC consumed his time, and he was unable to finish the articles on the remaining seven Fundamental Principles. We are the poorer as a result, yet we are fortunate to have his insights on the first five.

The last article in this series is on stewardship, "The Price of Congregational Freedom."

The Difference

The question if often asked, "How is the Association different from other church bodies?" To many, the differences are obvious; to others, there are no differences. I will attempt to point our some of the differences in this and several succeeding articles.

During the Church struggle in the 1890's, a set of Fundamental Principles came into being which set apart the Lutheran Free Church from other church bodies. These Principles set forth basic teachings of the congregation and the kingdom of God which were very different from the prevailing church thought of that day, and certainly today. These Principles came to be ignored by some later, but were never abandoned as such by the Lutheran Free Church. Today the Association continues to work under the guide-line of these

Principles. Most of the congregations in the Association have always done this. They have never decided to abandon them. They still are The Guiding Principles of the Lutheran Free Church, and the free Congregations of the Association.

There are twelve of these Principles. We will consider the first briefly in this article. It reads, "According to the Word of God, the congregation is the right form of the kingdom of God on earth."

In the desire to build God's kingdom, the Word of God must be the authority. This is immediately stated in this the first principle, as well as in other principles. The Word of God must be the authority in all that pertains to the congregation and all church matters. It is with childlike faith we seek guidance from God's Word, not with worldly wisdom or critical analysis. Therefore, every Christian has a right to arrive at a conclusion as to God's kingdom. The truth is not reserved for the formally trained theologian. And after the question of the salvation of the soul, the next most important question concerns itself with the Christian congregation. To the Word we look for guidance.

Georg Sverdrup, a man God so mightily used, and a man with a burning love for God's kingdom, had this to say in articles which appear in Volume III of "Skrifter i Udvalg, "God's Kingdom has its inner side, which is righteousness, peace, and joy in the Holy Spirit. It has its outer form, which is the congregation, the Spirit's people in the world."

Christ came to establish God's kingdom. This kingdom was not only a spiritual reality in the heart, but it was also a new community, which He called a congregation.

All the apostles and all the first Christians, driven by the Spirit, worked for this form of God's kingdom, the congregation. There is no other form of God's kingdom mentioned in the New Testament. There is no mention of church departments, synods, or councils of synods. When efforts were made not long after the apostles' day to find a better form for God's kingdom than the congregation, we see unmistakable signs of failure and decay, continues Sverdrup. You must have a congregation if you are to have God's kingdom. But you do not need another organization over the congregation.

It is a principle in our Association that the congregation is the right form of God's kingdom on earth, according to the Word. The Church body, the synod, the council, is secondary to the congregation. The congregation is number one. This is radically different from many other churches where the dominant authority lies with the synod or church body rather than in the congregation. We seek to build Christian congregations, not a super-church organization. The Association seeks to serve the congregations, not the congregations serve the Association. To some, if they are not in a particular synod, they are not in the Church. They would accuse those who are not in the same Church body as they are of not being in the Church. This is contrary to Scripture, and sectarianism to the nth degree. We emphasize what is good for the congregation, rather than what is good for the Association.

There is such a desire to have a super-church organization today. We may see in our day the establishing of the World Church, which will not be the handiwork of God. We would work rather for living congregations. Many seek to belong to a certain church body, rather than to a living congregation. They join congregations with little spiritual life, in order that they may belong to a certain church body. They should seek rather to belong to a living congregation, living according to God's Word. More on this later.

—The Lutheran Ambassador 2, no. 1, p. 5
January 14, 1964

Is It Really Wrong?

"Is it really wrong, then, when the days are evil and the night is approaching, to lift up our eyes and minds from the confused and dwarfed present, and to turn to the true, real picture of the congregation which the New Testament gives us?" This is a familiar quotation from Georg Sverdrup who understood the Christian congregation as few have done. Yes, we must look to the Word for guidance if we would build the church. It is not wrong in these days either to emphasize the Scriptural concept of the Christian Church.

The first of the Fundamental Principles of the Lutheran Free Church emphasizes that the Christian congregation is the right form of the Kingdom of God on earth.

Principle No. 2: "The congregation consists of believers who, by using the means of grace and the spiritual gifts as directed by the Word of God, seek salvation and eternal blessedness for themselves and for their fellow men."

The Christian congregation is the fulfillment of the prayer and longing of Moses in Numbers 11:28, David's song in Psalm 110:3, and Jeremiah's prophecy in Jeremiah 31:33. The congregation is also the fulfillment of Joel's prophecy in Joel 3:1, 2, as given by Peter in Acts 2:17, 18: "And it shall come to pass in the last days, saith God, I will pour out of my Spirit upon all flesh: and your sons and your daughters shall prophesy, and your young men shall see visions, and your old men shall dream dreams: and on my servants and on my handmaidens I will pour out in those days my Spirit; and they shall prophesy." On Pentecost the Christian Church, a Christian congregation, was born.

The Christian congregation consists of believers. There are unbelievers in most, if not all organized congregations, as principle No. 4 states, but the real congregation in the sight of God is only made up of believers. Here we come to the Scriptural teaching of the Church visible, and the Church which is often called invisible, though the living believers certainly are visible. The goal and pattern of each congregation must be that all members be children of God, just as all believers must strive to be like Jesus. We will never attain to the ideal in this world, but nevertheless we must strive for it.

The weapon of the congregation is the Word and the Sacraments. These means of grace sustain the congregation and call unbelievers to the fold. The congregation must make use of all the spiritual gifts given the members. These gifts must be used according to the Word, and subject to the Word, which is not always done.

The goal of the congregation is salvation, salvation for themselves and for all men. This makes the congregation a tremendous force of evangelism. Seeing men with love, hearing God's command to make disciples, the congregation seeks to win souls for Christ. There must be a great burden that men be saved.

In our day, terms like "being saved" are frowned upon. These are good Scriptural terms. Men are going lost today. They need to be saved. They need to experience sin and grace. They need to know Christ is a personal way unto salvation. The local congregation has this as its great responsibility.

All men are to be saved. It isn't enough that the congregation be living because there are members who have a living faith, but the congregation must have a living compassion for missions throughout the whole world. The congregation takes seriously our Lord's mission command.

It is so easy for congregations to take comfort in the fact that their church body has a mission program. But this should not be a comfort to them. Each congregation must ask herself if she has a mission program. How many of her young men and women have gone into full-time Christian service? How much of the local budget is for missions outside of the local community?

The congregation seeks eternal blessedness for themselves and for their fellow men.

—The Lutheran Ambassador 2, no. 4 , p. 5
February 25, 1964

Organization

This is the age of organization. Organization is needed today. There is, however, a grave danger of over-organization. When this occurs, the individual ceases to be a real person, and becomes a number or a part of a large machine. The dignity of man is thus lost and tasks are not completed. The struggles in the Communist world are ample examples of this.

The Christian congregation becomes and lives through the

work of the Holy Spirit. The Spirit works through the Word and the Sacraments. But some organization is necessary, too. This is clearly taught by the New Testament. The danger is, however, that many will expect the organization to do the necessary work of the church, instead of the Word and the Sacraments. While this may not be said, the program carried out reveals this to be true.

Organization can become a hindrance to the work of God's Spirit. Therefore, it is essential to follow the teachings of the Scriptures about organization in the church.

Principle No. 3

"According to the New Testament, the congregation needs an external organization with membership roll, election of officers, stated times and places for its gatherings, and other similar provisions."

Where is the basic organization in the church supposed to be? According to the New Testament, it should be in the local congregation. This is contrary to the trends of our day.

We have seen in our day the growth of strong church bodies and synods with complex organization. To these complex organizations, many look for an effective church.

Congregations are considered effective if they carry out faithfully the directives that come from the central or head body. This is foreign to the New Testament, as pointed out by Principle No. 3. The main organization must be in the local congregation.

The congregation needs outward organization, but not in the same way as it needs the Word and Sacraments. The congregation needs a membership roll, officers, stated times and places for gatherings, etc. The early Christian Church elected deacons, etc., in order that basic responsibilities in and of the congregation would be met. Paul, writing to the Corinthian congregation, in I Corinthians 14:26, urged that things be well planned and done decently and in order. There was to be no binding by high-churchliness, nor were there to be disorganized programs giving room for personal glorying. Everything was to be done for the edifying of the church.

The organization in the church is well outlined in the New Testament. We do not have to dream something up that will fit our time or day, as we hear so often. We in our day would put a greater stress on the organization of the local congregation than on the synod. Many would want the congregation to be "free" by depending on the synod to do the task. This is not what is means to be "free." Others would have each member to be so "free" as to have no feeling of responsibility to the congregation. Again, this is wrong. Both of these tendencies would destroy the congregation, which is the right form of the Kingdom of God on earth. The right organization would have each person doing his task to build the Christian Church. When organization takes away individual responsibility and initiative it becomes a destructive force and an evil. When it becomes so loose as to encourage the feeling of irresponsibility, it is also wrong.

The Association of Free Lutheran Congregations has no strong organization as an Association. Because our congregations are free and independent, basic organization is their responsibility. We trust that every member will feel deep responsibility for God's Kingdom. This alone is good Scriptural organization.

—The Lutheran Ambassador 2, no. 6, p. 7
March 24, 1964

Cleansing the Congregation

Are all the members of the congregation Christians? This is a very important question, for the answer will determine the approach the pastor makes to his people.

God would have all members of the organized congregation to be Christians. He intended that believers are to make up the church. We know that as far as God is concerned, His Church is made up only of believers. But in the organized church in the world this is rarely true. Our Fourth Principle calls attention to this fact.

"Members of the organized congregation are not, in every instance, believers, and such members often derive false hope from their external connection with the congregation. It is therefore the sacred obligation of the congregation to purify itself by the quickening preaching of the Word of God, by earnest admonition and exhortation, and by expelling the openly sinful and perverse."

Here we have stated something that sets our Association and congregations apart from some other church bodies and congregations.

Some pastors today approach their ministry as though all their people are Christians. They believe that it is unscriptural judging to believe that some of their members may not be Christians. They forget it is just as much judging to call a man a saint as it is to call a man a lost sinner.

Judging is not necessary. The pastor can approach his congregation as though some are lost, without judging anyone. Believing that some are lost puts an urgency and a purpose to the ministry, which will be lacking if the pastor feels that all his people are saved.

Are there lost sinners in our churches who believe they are saved? Are there those whose hope rests in something other than the finished work of Jesus Christ? Are there those who believe that because they are members of the organized church they are also members of the body of Christ? We are completely unrealistic if we say there are no people like that in our congregations.

People fall away from grace. Apostasy is to be especially great in the last days. Paul was concerned that, even though he had preached to others and had had a successful mission career, he himself might go lost. There was a tragic falling-away even among the disciple band. This happens today too. The power of the evil one is great.

Principle Number Four points out that it is the sacred obligation of the congregation to purify itself. Now, how can a congregation purify itself? There is but one way and that is through the quickening preaching of the Word of God.

It is not enough to preach the Word of God. Today we fear

there is much preaching which has very little Word in it. There is much of social gospel or Christian ethics, but the whole counsel of God is lacking. There is a spirit which would appeal to one part of man, perhaps his intellect, and neglect the rest of the total man. There also are those who would appeal to the emotions, and not to man as he really is. The whole counsel of God must be preached if the church is to be built.

Not only must the Word be preached, but it must be preached in a certain fashion. Principle Four calls it "quickening" preaching. This is preaching with an urgency about it; it has a sincere call to repentance of sin and to faith in Jesus Christ. This kind of preaching destroys false hope, awakens the slumbering, and calls the faithless to Christ. This kind of preaching is disturbing to the unbeliever. Many will not come to such a church. If humble love is evident, however, this drawing power compels many to come in. We must remember, however, that the preaching of the cross of Christ will always be foolishness to many people. If we would please all men, we may be denying men the truth that alone can set them free.

Are there those who are unfit for membership in the organized church? Yes. Those who persistently oppose the truth of the Word and make effective preaching impossible ought to be dropped from the congregation. Great care must be exercised that all that is done be motivated by love and led by the Spirit. The principal cleansing of the congregation ought to be done by the preaching of the Word of God.

—The Lutheran Ambassador 2, no. 8, p. 5
April 21, 1964

The Congregation Under the Word of God

This month we will return to a consideration of the Fundamental Principles of our Church. Other matters caused us to drop these considerations some months ago.

God's Word witnesses that a true congregation consists of believers in a locality who are working for God's kingdom. The first of our Fundamental Principles emphasizes that the congregation is the right form of the kingdom of God on earth. The child of God must, therefore, be most concerned that his congregation is what it ought to be. The child of God must conduct himself in a manner that helps his congregation, not harms it. All aspects of the church on earth must seek to serve the congregation. It follows, therefore, that the congregation ought to direct its own affairs. The fifth of our Fundamental Principles emphasizes this scriptural truth.

5. The congregation directs its own affairs, subject to the authority of the Word of God and the Spirit of God, and acknowledges no other ecclesiastical authority or government over itself.

The importance of the local congregation is being lost sight of in our day. In the desire for vast worldwide programs, the simple scriptural truth that the local congregation is most important is forgotten. The needs in the world demand that the congregations be directed, we are told. Only as congregations are directed will they reach their maximum accomplishments. The congregations, therefore, ought to willingly give away some of their freedom, or delegate away some of their authority, that a more efficient world program can be carried out, and they themselves be blessed. In the process, however, the congregations themselves lose some of their real life and scriptural position. As a result, instead of progress, there may be spiritual deadness. For those who have espoused the "social" gospel, with its primary concern for the bodies of men, this is not bad, but for those who are concerned primarily with the needs of the soul, this is tragic. It is the living congregation that must minister to the souls of men. Nothing else can take its place. Each congregation, therefore, has a tremendous responsibility.

Each congregation is responsible to God. It must be what God intends it to be on earth. Each congregation is bound to Him, and each congregation is free in Him.

The congregation directs its own affairs. These affairs have to do not only with the local program, so-called. These affairs have also to do with the worldwide responsibility of every congregation. The congregation is commanded to evangelize the world. It is so easy for congregations to leave such matters up to others, or to give such responsibility to others. When they do, they cannot be properly called Christian congregations.

A Christian congregation directs its own affairs, is responsible for, makes decisions concerning, all aspects of its position as the right form of the kingdom of God on earth. The pastors are not to be directors, but shepherds who lead. They are responsible to the congregations, not the congregations to them. The church body is to have no authority, in any way, over the congregation. The congregation disciplines and cleanses itself. It is not to be dependent on the good graces of the church leaders. It directs its own affairs. Cooperation, yes, but not delegation of power and responsibility.

There is an authority over the congregation, but not an earthly authority. The only authority over itself that the Christian congregation ought to recognize is the Word and Spirit of God.

Can there be a greater evil than to destroy the authority of God's Word and Spirit over mankind? Is there a greater sin than to substitute human authority over the congregation in place of the divine? This is being done today. Is your congregation as sensitive to the divine authority as it ought to be?

A congregation must conduct itself according to God's Word and Spirit. God's Spirit never contradicts or goes contrary to God's Word. When your congregation makes decisions, does it seek to make them in the light of God's Word? Is it more apt to do things as others have done, instead of following in simple faith the Word of God? A congregation can no longer be called a Christian congregation when it refuses to follow God's Word and Spirit as the authority over itself. A Christian congregation chooses its officers and plans it program according to the principles and truths of the Word.

Has your congregation submitted itself to the authority of the Word of God? Is your congregation submitting itself to other authority? Remember, only as your congregation is true to the Word are you in the exalted position God has given the congregation.

Only as a congregation is true to the Word, will it be fruitful in God's sight. The directed people of Russia have not been able to produce as free men can and do. Free congregations, as free men, bear most fruit for God. The world is in need of what only those submitted to the Word can give.

—*The Lutheran Ambassador* 3, no. 1, p. 15
January 12, 1965

The Price of Congregational Freedom

Freedom and liberty are always costly. The easiest and cheapest road leads to bondage and death. This is also true in the life of the church.

As an Association we prize our freedom. It has been costly for us as individuals and congregations to cling to our principles. It would have been far easier to conform and forget our heritage and convictions. Some have had to pay a higher price than others. It perhaps is true that those who have paid the most, appreciate and value their freedom the most. The opportunities to sacrifice are not over, however.

We face a critical test now. Are we to forget the principles of congregational freedom and life now that the opportunity to be free has been extended? Are we going to grow lukewarm in our commitment to that which shaped our actions the last few years? If so, our Association will soon be nothing but a remembrance.

Yes, it costs to be free. It costs time, a great deal of it. It costs talents, the wise use of God-given abilities for His kingdom. It costs money, money that God has placed in our hands for awhile to test our faith, love, and obedience. It is on this last that I would write something now.

Last year we as members and friends of the Association gave about $90,000 to the three main items of our general budget. We oversubscribed our budget of $53,700 in a joyous manner. The money was needed, and made it possible to do more than we originally intended. It made the future for the Association more promising.

Our conference in June, 1964, adopted a budget for February 1, 1965 to January 31, 1966, of $87,093.62. This budget is a trifle less than the receipts of the 1964-65 year. Needless to say, we need this sum, and more could be wisely used.

The budget can be divided into three headings:

1. General Fund, including Board of Publications, Youth Committee, and Stewardship Committee — $31,765.62
2. Theological Seminary — $23,328.00
3. Missions — $32,000.00

Why should we give to the Association budgets? Simply stated, that you and your congregation can be free. This is a basic and underlying reason. You want to be free, not for selfish reasons, but so that you and your congregation can serve your God in freedom, according to the Word and Spirit of God. If the Association cannot expand in obedience to God through missions, it will soon die. If pastors are not trained in the seminary to have a godly respect for the congregation, and to be servants of the congregation, your freedom will soon die. If the total work of the Association is not coordinated on behalf of all the congregations in freedom (general fund), one by one the congregations will fall by the wayside.

A free congregation and individual is not forced to give. A free congregation and individual will want to give because it or he is free, and wants to remain so. Constrained by God's Spirit, and not by synodical machinery, we will do better even than last year in our support. That is our confidence, hope, and prayer. Remember, too, free men enjoy giving, and receive a blessing. "God loveth a cheerful giver."

The Lutheran Ambassador 3, no. 11, p. 11
June 1, 1965

The officers and boards should regularly examine their work to see if they are really reflecting the congregations' concerns, seeking to develop the whole body. Am I sensitive to that which is good for the congregations? Are my decisions for their good? Are the congregations' actions and stewardship indicating this direction? Should there be a referendum of the congregations before pursuing this course? Will this build the whole body, or just be advantageous for one member of the body? Does this provide outlet for the congregations' expressed concern for outreach? Is this a challenge that the congregations understand? Am I trying to manipulate the congregations, or am I following their concerns? Is there a need for this in the Association? etc.! etc.! The whole body must be served, not just one member of the body. The body must serve the congregations. The congregation is the right form of the Kingdom of God on earth. Principle Number 1. It is easy to forget this. Is the Association serving the needs and desires of our congregations?

—John P. Strand

10

FREE AND LIVING CONGREGATIONS

Writings of Rev. John Strand
Excerpts from AFLC Annual Reports

Two passions are apparent in Rev. John Strand's Annual Conference "President's Reports"–his belief in the congregation's freedom and the correctness of Lutheran doctrine.

Leading the AFLC through its first sixteen years was a difficult task. When the AFLC was organized in 1962, it was with the express notion of perpetuating Sverdrup's dream of "free and living" congregations. Those who gathered in Thief River Falls that fall were convinced this could only be done by continuing the polity of the Lutheran Free Church through the Fundamental Principles *and* Rules for Work.

This, however, was not an easy task. In the early years of the Association, several pastors and congregations affiliated with the AFLC, but not all understood who we were. Some had come from synodical backgrounds and had little understanding of our polity. Some had come with the notion that the AFLC was a totally new, evangelistic Lutheran organization and were more than willing to "help" mold this new group to "their" liking. Some even came with a low regard for the Lutheran view of the sacraments and felt our polity would somehow allow them the freedom to do much as they pleased.

President Strand faced these problems on an almost daily basis as well as a myriad of others. So it is understandable that he repeatedly stresses the importance of our Fundamental Principles *and Lutheran doctrine in his reports.*

But these excerpts reveal a good deal more. They also reveal his uncanny, almost prophetic, ability to foresee many of the trends we are struggling with in our congregations today. Yet, above all, they reflect his unrelenting, evangelistic concern for the lost.

Though some of the reports are long, they are well worth reading in their entirety. But because of space constraints and the nature of this book, we are limiting our choices to excerpts that deal primarily with his concern for the congregation and our Lutheran heritage.

1963 Annual Report
(First Annual Conference of the AFLC)

Last year when the Lutheran Free Church gathered in Annual Conference in Minneapolis it was to have been the last conference. According to plans formulated by others, we should have been for some months now "an integral part of the new church." But here we are in another annual conference, in the friendly city of Fargo, that has known many Lutheran Free Church conferences. We are meeting, thank God, continuing to work under the Fundamental Principles of the Lutheran Free Church.

It is necessary that we meet to take a good look at our world, a good look at our Church, and a good look at our Lord. (p.8)

We are a congregation-centered church. There are some real struggles taking place in many of our congregations. Some have been split over the merger question. We are sorry but we must report that often the constitutions of the congregations, and the principles of our Church, have been forgotten or ignored. This naturally causes confusion. Advice has often been given by church leaders that has also added to the confusion. Some congregations have been treated as pawns to be manipulated, instead of as a part of Christ's Body. Some pastors have assumed authority over congregations, instead of being servants of the congregations. Our laymen have been very long-suffering, too longsuffering in many places. Perhaps they should have insisted on their rights provided by their constitutions and the Principles of The Lutheran Free Church. Each congregation must make these decisions, of course.

The Fundamental Principles of The Lutheran Free Church

The Fundamental Principles of The Lutheran Free Church is a precious document. Our congregations must get better acquainted with these principles and compare them with synodical constitutions. They will then have a greater appreciation for the Principles of our Church.

There is need for an evangelistic thrust in our congregations. The Church's main task is evangelism and fellowship. (p.12)

June 13, 1963

1964 Annual Report

As we meet, we are concerned about our congregations. They are the hub, or center. Our Conference and Association are nothing, if our congregations fail to be real Christian congregations.

We believe in living congregations, where the Spirit of God does His gracious work of creating saving faith in the hearts of repentant sinners, and calling them to use their gifts for Christ.

We believe in **free** congregations, congregations that are free to serve their Lord as they are guided by the Spirit though the Word of God. The Word and Spirit are the only authority over them.

We believe in a simple yet orderly liturgical service with the emphasis on the prophetic ministry of the Word.

We believe in personal piety, where the believer is encouraged to live a life separated unto his God. . . .

Congregations may be tempted to legislate living congregations, and personal piety, by laws or rules in constitutions, or by other means. Freedom, which we prize so highly, can easily be destroyed this way, and legalism will take its place. We are grateful that two model constitutions have been prepared which will give guidance to congregations preparing or modifying constitutions. These documents, especially when the Fundamental Principles are made a part of them will give good guarantee to congregations, and not destroy the freedom we need and want. (p.6)

June 11, 1964

1965 Annual Report

The church, Sverdrup went on to say, is not an assembly of people which men may compel by the exercise of worldly or superstitious power to maintain a priestly caste; nor is a church a gathering of ignorant, perhaps even immoral, people among whom the clergymen are to be teachers or masters, for the purpose of restraining them and thus strengthening civil order or the power of rulers. Nay, a Christian congregation is an assembly of volunteer men and women, brought together and united by the Spirit of God through the Word of the Lord and the Sacraments, one body with the Lord, Who lives in them and in Whom they live, the household of God and the dwelling-place of the Spirit. This assembly of believers should all be workers in the vineyard of the Lord; they should all show forth the excellencies of Him Who called them out of darkness into His own marvelous light; they should all be priests of God, and there should be no "gracious sir" among them, nor should any even be referred to as such. . . .

Very little is written or taught of the Christian congregation in our day. There is much concern of Christian fellowship, evangelism, doctrines of God, the Father, Son, and Holy Spirit, missions, ecumenism, denominations, the Word, history, eschatology, Christian education, youth work, liturgy, stewardship, etc., but little real concern for the congregation as such. This seems strange for the Christian congregation is so central in the New Testament. It was for the sake of the congregation, Paul suffered and labored: it was to strengthen, lead and build up congregations, he wrote his epistles: it was the congregations that he expected to carry the Gospel, to be God's house on earth, the pillar and foundation of truth. It was the congregation he considered to be Christ's body, Christ's bride. We stand in awe as we consider Christ and the congregation. Should we not be more concerned with the congregation than we are? Truly much more attention needs to be given this great subject. Living congregations are the life giving stream for our society, for the world.

It is easy to become so concerned with Christian doctrine, apart from the congregation, that we forget the congregation. I am a firm believer in a good emphasis on correct doctrine. This is so necessary in our day. But we must not forget the congregation. It was for the sake of the right concept of the congregation that the Association was formed. Let us never forget that. And people are generally more interested in the congregation, their congregation, than any other phase of the kingdom. When we help them build the congregation we will have their support. If we get side-tracked, much more than the Association will die. I believe that the one main task of our Association is to hold up the Scriptural pattern of the congregation. God grant that we be faithful. Not all evangelical Lutherans agree with us. Many simply do not understand our position. To be evangelistic is not always the same as being of free church mind and spirit.

The congregations are to be free. Freedom is the key word in so much of our founding fathers' writings. The congregations are to be free from ecclesiastical domination of all kinds, whether from the church body and/or official bodies, or the local pastor. The only authority above the congregation is the Word and the Spirit of God. If they do not recognize the authority of the Word and the Spirit of God, they are not a congregation. Here, too, they are free to interpret the Scriptures, interpreting Scripture with Scripture, not being bound by the interpretations of others. The larger church body is to be the servant of the congregation, not its master. The pastor is to be the servant of the congregation, not its overlord. . . .

The congregation is the right form of the Kingdom of God on earth. The congregation is the bride of Christ. Only true believers are true members of the Christian Church. A congregation is still a congregation when it has unbelievers in it, however. Such conditions prevailed in the apostolic congregations and the Apostle Paul still addressed them as congregations. They were not to be content with this situation, however, but were to seek to win the unbelieving church members to the new life in God. This is done through the preaching of the Gospel. Here Sverdrup quotes from the catechism, "I believe that I cannot by my own reason or strength believe in Jesus Christ my Lord, or come to Him; but the Holy Spirit has called me through the Gospel, enlightened me with His gifts, and sanctified and preserved me in the true faith; in like manner as He calls, gathers, enlightens, and sanctifies the whole Christian Church on earth, and preserves it in union with Jesus Christ in the one true faith."

Through the preaching of the Gospel a congregation becomes living. Laws and rules cannot create freedom and life, but only take it away. God alone, through the Gospel, can create life. As the Gospel is preached, people in freedom will come to the Christian congregation and to Christ. They are not to be coerced, but drawn by the Gospel and their own needs. No one else is to determine their worthiness or unworthiness. Those that desire the Gospel and are drawn by the Gospel are to come. There must be the quickening preaching of the Word that the lost be saved, the lost within and without the congregation. . . .

As a congregation becomes living, it serves. It has a concern that the lost be saved, and the Gospel be preached. This concern is to be had by all, not only the clergy. Laymen too have the responsibility to proclaim the Gospel. They are encouraged to work, using all the gifts God gives them, for the salvation of souls, for the edification of the church.

While the congregation is free, it is constrained by the Spirit of God to work with others building God's Kingdom. There is to be inter-congregational unity and fellowship. Congregations working together can do such tasks that congregations alone cannot do. The task of missions, the training of pastors, the publications of literature, fall in these categories. A congregation's freedom does not exempt it from responsibilities in these tasks. As a matter of fact, it heightens the responsibility.

The common task of the congregations are given guidance by the congregations through boards and committees elected by the annual conference or by corporations elected or nominated by the conferences. The conference itself, and various boards and corporations, have no authority over the local congregations. They can only recommend to the congregations. The conferences, institutions, and corporations are to serve the congregations and to work on their behalf. Certainly the theological seminary supported by Free Congregations must train pastors with the right understanding of the congregation.

Is a free church practical today? Will it really work? We believe it is most practical, and the Biblical way of church work. It is dependent on Spiritual life in the congregation. Without it, it will not succeed. (pp.8-10)

June 10, 1965

1966 Annual Report

Much has happened since 1962. I am sure that most of us are amazed at God's blessings showered upon us since our beginning as an Association just a short three and one-half years ago. Instead of the 40 congregations originally foreseen, we are about 100 congregations and groups. . . .

Much else could be said. But, the greatest value is in the souls that have been brought into God's Kingdom through the teaching and preaching of the Word and the administering of the Sacraments. These things cannot be measured. The value of our Bible camps and conferences, to say nothing of congregational work, no man can measure. Yes, much more could be said. And, all this since October, 1962. To God alone belongs the Glory. "This is the Lord's doing: It is marvelous in our eyes." (p.6)

June 9, 1966

1967 Annual Report

Spiritual life is a product of the means of grace. Spiritual life cannot be legislated nor brought to pass by constitutions or congregational decisions. Only the Word and the Sacraments can make a congregation holy. When other means are employed, there are splits and broken fellowship. Only the Word and Sacraments can make congregations free and living. Thank God we have the means of grace today.

There is always a need for the reawakening of Christian life in our congregations. The standards of Christian conduct are very low in many so-called congregations today. The spirit of permissiveness permeates much of society. There is often little concern for the spiritual needs of man. This dearth of concern should cause real concern.

A living congregation is to be a witnessing congregation. Many of our people are not witnessing as they ought to. Some may have no personal experience with the Lord to bear witness of. The remedy for them is repentance and faith. There are many real Christians, however, who would witness if they knew how. A witnessing laity is absolutely essential if the task of proclaiming the Gospel is to be done. . . . We believe in lay activity and we rob our laity of real joy by not training them in the Christian obligation to be witnesses for Christ. (pp.8-9)

June 15, 1967

1968 Annual Report

In the fifth chapter of I John, we are told of the three who bear witness to Christ. They are the Spirit, the water, and the blood. They bear witness that life is in the Son of God. "He who has the Son has the life; he who does not have the Son of God does not have the life." Salvation is only in Christ. You can have and use the Means of Grace without experiencing salvation. The Means of Grace must never be an end in themselves.

The people of Israel had allowed the ceremonies and the sacrifices to become an end in themselves. In Isaiah 1, the Lord speaks to them, rejecting their sacrifices, offerings of the blood of bulls, lambs, and he-goats. The Lord was weary of them. Instead of their being a means to know God, they had become an end in themselves. Unfortunately for many in our day, too, the Means of Grace have become an end in themselves. If this is to be avoided, there must always be what our Fundamental Principles call the "quickening" preaching of God's Word.

We as an Association are also committed to the building of a certain kind of congregation, a congregation that is free and living. Where God's Word is rightly preached and the sacraments rightly administered, such congregations ought to come forth. We cannot say that they always will, however. The Means of Grace must fall on the right kind of soil. Personal Christian faith and free and living congregations are our basic goals, however. Towards this end we must work and pray. (p.9)

June 13, 1968

1969 Annual Report

As an Association, we cannot enter every opportunity as a larger fellowship might. We cannot hire every teacher that may want to teach, send out every one who may want to go to Brazil, enter every home mission field, hire all the personnel we could use at our offices, nor print all that could be printed for distribution. We must establish priorities as to what will build the Association most effectively. Surely the entire work is aimed at the saving of souls, and building God's Kingdom. A well-balanced program for the entire Association ought to be the goal.

A budget that is beyond our attaining is discouraging. One of the main reasons for the merger of the Lutheran Free Church with the ALC was the high budget the LFC was not reaching. Let us not get trapped into a similar situation. Let us rather have a program that will challenge our people but that they will not find burdensome. If more monies come in, it can be used for added opportunities. I am confident there will be more progress this way. (p.12)

June 12, 1969

1970 Annual Report

We believe that the Bible is the inerrant Word of God to which all man's teachings, theories, beliefs, and practices must bow. We believe that believers are united in Christ to each other in a spiritual bond, and that the present human efforts of organic unity are of limited value and dangerous to true spirituality. We believe in pietism, that the believer must live a separated life apart from worldliness and the works of the flesh. We believe that the proclamation of the Word of God is the essential task of the church and that liturgies, dialogues and forms should not replace preaching in importance in the church service. We believe that men must know Christ by a personal faith and therefore the church must be evangelistic in approach. (p.37)

June 11, 1970

1971 Annual Report

The church often lends itself to deceit. Wanting to be relevant and contemporary, it becomes worldly. Seeking success, it gives the people what they want, crave, and desire, instead of being the "salt" that smarts. Seeking to communicate, it ignores the message God commanded it to give. Instead of being a molder of human thought and life, it seeks out what is popular, and promotes it. Becoming over-involved with many good social issues, it neglects the Spiritual, for which it was created. As many look to the church, it thus becomes a tool of deceit, and people remain in their Spiritual need.

Evangelism is at the heart of the church. The church is so anxious to succeed in this. Evangelism is not free from danger, however. Instead of leading men to a sincere and deep repentance over sin, and a really new life in Christ, some "evangelism" only leads to a new worldly life style. We have instant evangelism with shallow repentance, and more form than commitment. We have evangelism without a personal cross, but with only a shallow "joy." This kind of evangelism can almost always point to some temporary successes, but does not build the true church. Not all that glitters is gold.

Let us, in these days of deceit, exercise Scriptural caution. Let us trust the Sword of the Spirit, the Word of God, to continue to do its work. Let us remember that the Kingdom grows silently and unobtrusively as a seed. Let us remember that only *some* of the Seed falls in good ground. Let not our craving for success make failure certain. Let us not underestimate the enemy. (p.42)

June 10, 1971

1972 Annual Report (Tenth Anniversary)

It was a fearful and bewildered group that gathered in Thief River Falls, Minnesota, in October 1962. They had some convictions, but little experience, and were empty handed. Fearful of merger developments taking place, they determined to proceed to build a fellowship of free congregations. Was history to show them to be fools, or would they know some measure of success under God's blessing? No one knew with any great degree of certainty. With simple faith in God, the decision to organize the Association was made. The results bear witness that this decision was under God's grace and blessing, and according to His Will. (p.1)

The basic aspect of the congregation is Christian fellowship. It is not enough that people come to know Christ. They must also become a part of a "living" congregation, and through fellowship and service in and through the congregations reach out to a needy world. We never build the Kingdom of God more effectively than when we build living congregations. . . .

It is through the "foolishness of preaching" that God saves some. It is only as God's Word is effectively preached and taught that the Kingdom of God comes to men. The "quickening" preaching and teaching of the Word of God is the primary task of the Christian church. To give adequate emphasis on the Word and Sacraments, non-liturgical and simple "orders of service" are encouraged.

Not all people are Christians. There is need for preaching and teaching the Word of God in such a way that people see their sins and need of The Savior. Through an evangelistic emphasis, the people are to be faced with the claims of Christ, and are challenged to receive Him. There must be repentance over sin, and personal faith in Christ for salvation. . . .

The standards of Christian living are at a low ebb. Christians are to be different, because Christ dwells within them. "All things have become new." They are strangers and sojourners on earth. They cannot live as worldlings. Their fellowship is centered in the things of God, not in the things of the world. The Word of God and not their old nature determines their conduct. The institutions of the church and the life within the congregations reflect this same separation. "Faith without works is dead." (p.3)

The Association of Free Lutheran Congregations is intended to be above everything else, a spiritual movement. The Association is dependent on God's Spirit to lead, guide and provide, as human strength is weakness. The Association has no other means of operation. If the Association should become something else than a spiritual movement, she would immediately cease to be. We thank God for this. Our concern must constantly be that we be obedient to our Lord and His Word. If we are faithful, God will provide. (p.4)

June 15, 1972

1973 Annual Report

The power and inerrancy of the Scriptures is not accepted today in much of Christendom. Some church denominations are in great struggles over this issue. If men compromise on this question, all is lost. Faith believes that which is beyond human explanation, understanding, and possibility, if God's Word says so. Much of Lutheranism has apparently forsaken this historic Lutheran conviction. And faith dies when God's Word is stripped of its credibility as being Truth. (p.4)

June 14, 1973

1974 Annual Report

Scriptural worship is a lost reality to most individuals and many congregations. The center of their religious experience is what they do, not in adoration and submission to God.

Many attempts at worship are man-centered, man-pleasing, not God-glorifying. Because they want to please men, they are always experimenting with liturgies and forms, trying to arrive at that which people enjoy.

Church music is changed. Instead of having a Word-centered message, the emphasis is on "beat," on that which is easy, and a shallow sentimentality appealing to man, often unconverted man. This is justified as an attempt to win the world. We must remember, however, that it is just as possible for the church to gain the world and lose its soul as it is for an individual.

Some desire to prepare their own forms of various services. God and His church are expected to adapt to their likes and dislikes, to their condition. "Take me as I am," is interpreted, "I'll come the way I want to." We must come to God on His terms, because He is God. He demands humble submission. He is to be worshipped. May true worship be at the center of our lives as individuals and congregations. (p.2)

June 13, 1974

1975 Annual Report

A common error of our day is to confuse awakening to the realization of spiritual need with conversion. When this is done, the Gospel is often applied to folks still in ignorance of their sin and depravity. Faith then becomes only a good work instead of surrender to Christ. A psychological peace is achieved without conversion. The law must kill before lasting peace can come. We must preach and teach the whole counsel of God, that thorough conversions take place, and not take human and evasive shortcuts. (p.2)

We are a congregation-centered fellowship. Our Fundamental Principles and our practices give emphasis to the truth that the congregation is the right form of the Kingdom of God on earth. The Association lives to build up congregations and to establish new ones.

We are a fellowship of Lutheran congregations. Our Lutheran heritage is precious. Our doctrinal position is Scriptural.

To be a Lutheran does not mean much among many so-called Lutherans today. Lutheran doctrines and distinctions are sacrificed to syncretism and well-meaning neo-evangelicalism.

As Lutherans we understand the centrality of worship in Spirit and Truth, in the life of the congregation and Christian individual. Worship is not a program that is personality-centered, talent-centered, gift-centered, or even mission-centered, even though it may be enjoyable and entertaining. These things often go for worship. Worship must always be Word-centered and Christ-centered, raising our thoughts from the earthly and human to the heavenly and eternal. Worship is not always successful to those caught up with programing and numbers, but nothing succeeds in the church without it. Worship meets our needs as nothing else does. Entertainment is replacing true worship in many congregations today. God thus becomes human, understandable, and small, not One Who inspires awe and surrender.

So much programing and evangelism available today is talent and personality centered, much given to entertainment and appealing to the old nature. They boast of their successes, abilities, and callings. They promote themselves and their talents, and need generous financial support. It is questionable stewardship to support such efforts. The fruits of this kind of religious activity do not abide. The ofttimes slower and humble, steady work of pastor and congregation is what really counts. This Godly work is often really hindered by the "Word-peddlers" with their musical and emotional extravaganzas.

The congregation is to meet the truly spiritual needs of people. The world cannot be won by worldly methods and forms. The old nature is not changed by things enjoyable to it. It is the "foolishness" of humbly preaching the Word that counts for eternity. (p.3)

June 12, 1975

1976 Annual Report

God has chosen to reach the world with the Gospel through the work of the Christian congregation. The work of the Association as a group of congregations must not dominate over the individual congregation. The Association is not to grow at the expense of the congregation. What is good for the congregation is good for the Association, not vice versa. We must not build the institutions and missions of the Association at the expense of the congregation. The individual congregation must come first in all our planning and programming. The Association and all her "arms" must serve our congregations. (p.2)

Convictions, unless discussed and taught, die. We have

much to do in the area of explaining, "Why the Association?"

Our congregations have the initial responsibility in the area of teaching our positions. When our positions are rightly understood, they are loved and command good support from most people. Our people should all be able to give eloquent answers to the question, "Why the Association?" These answers should not pertain to failures of others, but to the Scriptural positions that are held by our church.

The Bible School and the Seminary have a great responsibility to promote the Association doctrines and practices. Unfortunately, the temptation is real to have academic programs patterned after other schools or to let practices and standards of other institutions determine our methods, instead of that which meets the needs of the A.F.L.C., and makes our positions more familiar. A pastoral concern that each student become grounded in the Word of God and Lutheran doctrine wedded to A.F.L.C. polity and piety must be the goal of our schools. The procedure of other institutions must be very secondary. (p.3)

We thank God for our Bible Camps. They must maintain an emphasis on the teaching and preaching of the Word of God. Psychological motivation must be avoided at all costs. We all need to be grounded in the Word of God. Only then can young and old mature in Christ. (p.8)

June 10, 1976

1977 Annual Report

What was it God brought into being in the fall of 1962? It was a body. Scriptures speak of the church as a body, Christ's Body, no less, with many members. While we believe each congregation is the body of Christ, we also believe that congregations working together in those works they cannot do alone, are also a manifestation of the Body of Christ. (p.2)

The Association is a body, a body of congregations. This body is to do what the congregations cannot do individually, that congregations be born and nations be discipled. Agencies and/or boards have areas of responsibility on behalf of the congregations, acting on behalf of the congregations in the corporate areas.

Not only are the agencies and/or officers of the A.F.L.C. to carry out policies and decisions in these areas of responsibility, but they are to work with each other that the entire body may prosper. We think of what we are taught in I Corinthians 12. One member of the body is not to be exalted over the others. All areas are important. Each member of the body is to have care for the other members of the body. The body is one, and is to be developed into a beautiful whole. Individuals may have gifts or interests in specific areas. They will naturally emphasize these. The church, however, is one body, and should develop as a healthy body, without abnormalities. Sometimes the church grows like Topsy of *Uncle Tom's Cabin*, just grows without apparent respect for plan or normal development. It becomes awkward, without beauty, and inefficient. Unusual growth in one area may be cancerous.

The officers and boards should regularly examine their work to see if they are really reflecting the congregations' concerns, seeking to develop the whole body. Am I sensitive for that which is good for the congregations? Are my decisions for their good? Are the congregations' actions and stewardship indicating this direction? Should there be a referendum of the congregations before pursuing this course? Will this build the whole body, or just be advantageous for one member of the body? Does this provide outlet for the congregations' expressed concern for outreach? Is this a challenge that the congregations understand? Am I trying to manipulate the congregations, or am I following their concerns? Is there a need for this in the Association? etc.! etc.! The whole body must be served, not just one member of the body. The body must serve the congregations. The congregation is the right form of the Kingdom of God on earth. Principle Number 1. It is easy to forget this. Is the Association serving the needs and desires of our congregations? (p.5)

June 9, 1977

1978 Annual Report

The evangelical churches are enjoying increased respect and position. Evangelicalism is popular today. This may not be all good, as we remember that the soundest growth is often when the church is in tribulation. A large percentage of Americans claim to be evangelicals. Over one half of our people claim to have had a "born again" experience. This is strange when we see the conditions of life about us. A truly "evangelical" and "born again" people would have a greater influence of righteousness than is apparent today. A true Christian is a new person; "old things are passed away, all things have become new." (II Cor. 5:17) A real child of God is "salt and light" and changes the quality of life. Just what do the statistics and the modern mores of society tell us?

Evangelism and soul winning are popular themes. There is a great deal of evangelistic activity. Some of these programs can quote startling statistics of success. They enjoy tremendous financial support and spend money lavishly. Yet the Christian influence for righteousness in our nation is not stronger. While we are an evangelistic fellowship, and love the cause of evangelism, perhaps there ought be a critical look at popular evangelism and soul winning. According to the scriptures, at the last judgment some will say that they cast out demons and did mighty works, but the Lord will say, "I never knew you." (Matt. 7:22-23)

There is a great deal of evangelism effort through the "electronic church" (radio, T.V., and electronic gadgets). There is growing unrest concerning the overall result of much of this work. Almost universally the "electronic church" ignores the sacraments as "Means of Grace." The same can be said of some programs of personal evangelism. The result is often that the people reached do not get involved in the worship and fellowship of a Christian congregation, and may actually feel they do not need the church. They continually look back to what they think was a "born again" experience, and at times the false teaching of eternal security, instead of being grounded in the Word of God, nurtured in a true church thus looking to Christ alone for salvation. Soon there is little spiritual reality in their lives (Matt. 13:19-23) and they may actually be worse off than if they had not responded to the appeal (II Peter 2:20). The appeal is not always Word centered (sin and grace, and pointing to Christ)—but is overwhelmingly people centered, talent centered, name centered, program centered, gift centered, and volume centered. We must remember that the Spirit comes as a still, small voice (I Kings 19:10-12). (pp.2-3)

The Association lives to build congregations. Congregations do not live to build the Association. In this we differ from many churches. (p.7)

At the last annual conference I informed the church that I was not available for the presidency beyond this term. . . .
It has been a privilege to serve as your president. There have been joyous times, and times of heartache and tension. Through it all God has been good. I have kept a low profile as your president believing that to be in the best interests of the Association. There have been many inabilities, weaknesses, and mistakes. Basically, however, if I were to do it over again, I would make the same decisions and pursue the same course.
I love the A.F.L.C. I ask your forgiveness for my failings as your president. In spite of my lack, you have been most supportive. I trust that the Association will move on to greater usefulness in the sight of God. Thank you very much for the privilege that has been mine these past soon sixteen years. We have a great God, a loving Savior, a patient Holy Spirit, and a fine church. Let us, as our theme suggests, be worthy of our calling. (p.10)

June 15, 1978

We face a critical test now. Are we to forget the principles of congregational freedom and life now that the opportunity to be free has been extended? Are we going to grow lukewarm in our commitment to that which shaped our actions the last few years? If so, our Association will soon be nothing but a remembrance.

God has chosen to reach the world with the Gospel through the work of the Christian congregation. The work of the Association as a group of congregations must not dominate over the individual congregation. The Association is not to grow at the expense of the congregation. What is good for the congregation is good for the Association, not vice versa. We must not build the institutions and missions of the Association at the expense of the congregation. The individual congregation must come first in all our planning and programming. The Association and all her "arms" must serve our congregations.

—John P. Strand

11

Historical Documents of the AFLC

Fundamental Principles
(Guiding Principles of the Lutheran Free Church)
Since 1897

1. According to the Word of God, the congregation is the right form of the Kingdom on earth.

2. The congregation consists of believers who, by using the means of grace and the spiritual gifts as directed by the Word of God, seek salvation and eternal blessedness for themselves and for their fellow men.

3. According to the New Testament, the congregation needs an external organization with membership roll, election of officers, stated times and places for its gatherings, and other similar provisions.

4. Members of the organized congregation are not, in every instance believers, and such members often derive false hope from their external connection with the congregation. It is therefore the sacred obligation of the congregation to purify itself by the quickening preaching of the Word of God, by earnest admonition and exhortation, and by expelling the openly sinful and perverse.

5. The congregation directs its own affairs, subject to the authority of the Word and the Spirit of God, and acknowledges no other ecclesiastical authority or government above itself.

6. A free congregation esteems and cherishes all the spiritual gifts which the Lord gives for its edification, and seeks to

stimulate and encourage their use.

7. A free congregation gladly accepts the mutual assistance which congregations can give one another in the work for the advancement of the Kingdom of God.

8. Such assistance consists partly in the mutual sharings of spiritual gifts among the congregations through conferences, exchange visits, lay activities, etc., whereby congregations are mutually edified, and partly in the voluntary and Spirit-prompted cooperation of congregations for the accomplishing of such tasks as exceed the ability of the individual congregation.

9. Among such tasks may be mentioned specifically the training of pastors, distribution of Bible and other Christian literature, home missions, foreign missions, Jewish missions, deaconess homes, children's homes and other work of mercy.

10. Free congregations have no right to demand that other congregations shall submit to their opinion, will, judgment, or decision; therefore, domination by a majority of congregations over a minority is to be rejected.

11. Agencies found desirable for conducting the joint activities of congregations, such as conferences, committees, officers, etc., cannot in a Lutheran Free Church, impose any obligations or restrictions, exert any compulsions, or lay any burden upon the individual congregation, but have the right only to make recommendations to, and requests of, congregations and individuals.

12. Every free congregation, as well as every individual believer, is constrained by the Spirit of God and by the privileges of Christian love to do good and to work for the salvation of souls and the quickening of spiritual life, as far as its abilities and power permit. Such free spiritual activity is limited neither by parish nor by synodical bounds.

Rules for Work
(As finally adopted at the Annual Conference in 1967)

1. The name of this association shall be "The Association of Free Lutheran Congregations."
2. Its aim shall be to work towards making Lutheran congregations free and living, so that, according to their calling and ability, they may work in spiritual freedom and autonomy for the cause of the Kingdom of God at home and abroad through such agencies and institutions as the congregations themselves may designate.
3. It endeavors to realize this aim in particular by training men and women for Christian work in and for the congregations, by conducting larger and smaller conferences, by distributing suitable literature, by organizing committees and societies, by sending out evangelists, and by any other means which from time-to-time will be found necessary or advisable.
4. The AFLC consists of congregations which, in their constitutions, unreservedly subscribe to the ancient ecumenical symbols, Luther's Small Catechism, the Unaltered Augsburg Confession, Fundamental Principles, and Rules for Work of the AFLC and report the same to the secretary of the Co-ordinating Committee.
5. The AFLC shall hold an Annual Conference which usually opens the evening of the second Wednesday in June and which shall elect the necessary committees and officers, and determine what church activities in particular it shall recommend to the congregations.
6. The right to vote in the Annual Conference of the AFLC shall be held by all ordained pastors and lay-pastors in regular standing in the AFLC and by all voting members of congregations affiliated with the AFLC. Individual Lutherans who are not members of a Lutheran congrega-

tion, but who are interested in supporting the work of the AFLC, may be granted speaking and voting privileges by the Co-ordinating Committee after said committee has received and approved their credentials. Voting members of other Lutheran congregations may be granted the right to vote in the Annual Conference providing they have at least two (2) weeks previously signed and sent to the secretary of the Annual Conference the special blank provided for that purpose, signifying that they approve the Fundamental Principles and Rules for Work of the AFLC and will work for aim set forth in Paragraph 2 of the Rules for Work.

7. The officers of the AFLC shall be a president, a vice-president, and a secretary, who shall be chosen from the membership of the AFLC and elected by the Annual Conference. Voting shall be by ballot.

    a. The president shall be elected for a term of three years and shall devote all of his time to the service of the AFLC. He shall preside at the Annual Conference and shall report to it on the work of the AFLC in general, on church dedications, installations, celebrations, etc. He shall be an advisory member of all Boards and Committees. He shall assist congregations and pastors by giving counsel and guidance when this is desired, and he shall also, as Ordainer, assist the congregations in ordaining men with the proper and adequate training who have been duly called as pastors. His salary shall be determined by the Co-ordinating Committee and shall be paid out of the AFLC General Fund.

    b. The vice-president shall be elected for a term of one year and performs the duties of the president in the latter's absence.

    c. The secretary shall be elected for a term of one year. he shall keep the minutes of the Annual Conference and is the custodian of the archives.

d. The term of office of the officers of the AFLC shall begin October 1, and shall expire September 30.

e. The executive officers after having served three (3) consecutive terms can be elected for additional terms only by a three-fourths majority vote.

8. The Annual Conference shall nominate members of the Co-ordinating Committee. This committee shall consist of seven members: three (3) pastors and four (4) laymen chosen from the membership of the AFLC. The number of those whose terms expire shall determine the number to be nominated by the Annual Conference each year. No member can serve more than two (2) consecutive terms.

9. Duties of the Co-ordinating Committee.

    a. The Co-ordinating Committee shall seek to make the Fundamental Principles and Rules for Work of the AFLC and further the discussions of the same throughout the congregations, so that the task of the AFLC, in an ever increasing degree, may be more clearly understood and more generally put into practice.

    b. It shall seek to have the congregations as fully and as generally represented at the Annual Conference of the AFLC as possible.

    c. When desired, it shall assist congregations and pastors by giving counsel and guidance.

    d. It shall compile parochial statistics and report thereon to the Annual Conference. It shall maintain the clergy and congregational rosters of the AFLC.

    e. It shall have charge of the AFLC General Fund from which shall be paid the salaries of the president, secretary, transportation secretary, traveling expenses, and expenses incurred in connection with the Annual Conference.

    f. It shall elect the editor of the church organ.

    g. Any duty not assigned to any other committee shall be

the responsibility of the Co-ordinating Committee.

10. The Annual Conference shall nominate members for the following boards and corporations of the AFLC: Co-ordinating Committee, Board of Trustees and Corporation of the Free Lutheran Theological Seminary, Board and Corporation of Missions, Board of Publications and Parish Education, Youth Board, Stewardship Board, and Pension Board. The editor of the church organ shall also be nominated by the Annual Conference.

   a. No member can serve for more than two (2) consecutive terms.

11. Reports shall be given by the following at the Annual Conference of the AFLC: The President, the Co-ordinating Committee, Board of Missions, Schools, Board of Pensions, Board of Publications and Parish Education, Youth Board, Luther League Federation, special committees elected by the Annual Conference, and by such institutions and activities within the church as may be given permission to report to the Annual Conference.

12. The president and secretary shall constitute the Annual Conference Committee, whose duties shall be: To fix time and place of the Annual Conference in the event that the last Annual Conference did not do so, arrange the program for the Conference, prepare the calendar for the business sessions, and to make any other arrangements that are necessary for the conduct of the Conference. The Conference Committee shall announce the Annual Conference at least two (2) months previous to the date of the meeting. It shall publish the Annual Report of the AFLC.

13. The manuscript for the Annual Report shall be kept on file by the secretary for at least two (2) years after the publication of the report. The president and secretary shall determine how much of the manuscript of the Annual Report shall be kept on permanent file.

14. The Secretary shall send notices to all concerned as to res-

olutions passed by the Annual Conference, election of committees, etc., By September 1.

15. These Rules for Work may be amended in the following manner: A motion to make an amendment shall be presented in writing to the Annual Conference and shall be voted upon at the following Annual Conference. For the adoption of the motion, a two-thirds majority of the ballots cast is required. All amendments must be in agreement with the Fundamental Principles, especially 5 and 10.

16. These Rules for Work of the AFLC shall take precedence over all other orders and decisions in effect.

Declaration of Faith

Having a common purpose and seeking one goal, we join together as free congregations for Christian fellowship, mutual edification, the salvation of souls and whatever work may be necessary that the Kingdom of God may come among us and our fellow men. No bonds of compulsion bind us save those which the Holy Spirit lays on us.

No man fully understands the times and the situations in which he lives. At best we see through a glass darkly. Nevertheless, each Christian must decide in the light of God's Word and the evidence which he has what course of action he should take and to what causes his life should be given. It is the same for the Christian congregations. Imperfect as it is, it must decide in what fellowship of other congregations it can best live out its purpose for being. Out of considerable soul-searching and prayer we have come to choose to continue as Lutheran free churches.

As we stand at this particular moment of time we give thanks for the heritage of the past. We recognize and confess our indebtedness to many noble souls of the faith, both the relatively unknown who are faithful in their places and the ones on whom God placed the mantle of leadership. Even as it is true that before the Cross of Christ there are no self-made men, so it is true that we have shared in blessings from many and are debtors.

It seems good to us as we join together for common work and fellowship to state our beliefs in regard to the following matters.

I. Doctrine

1. We accept and believe in the Holy Bible as the complete written Word of God and preserved to us by the Holy Spirit for our salvation and instruction.
2. We endorse the statement on the Word as found in the United Testimony on Faith and Life and would quote here the following: "We bear witness that the Bible is our only

authentic and infallible source of God's revelation to us and all men, and that it is the only inerrant and completely adequate source and norm of Christian doctrine and life. We hold that the Bible, as a whole and in all its parts, is the Word of God under all circumstances regardless of man's attitude toward it."
3. We accept the ancient ecumenical symbols, namely, the Apostles', the Nicene, and the Athanasian Creeds; Luther's Small Catechism and the Unaltered Augsburg Confession as the true expression of the Christian faith and life.
4. We reject any affiliations or associations which do not accept the Bible alone as definitive for the life and practice of man and the church.
5. We submit all religious teaching to the test of II John 7-11.
6. We endorse no one version or revision of the Bible to the exclusion of others. We recommend all which are reverent and true translations.

II. Christian Unity

1. He who believes in and accepts the sufficient work of Jesus for his salvation and is baptized is a child of God.
2. The Christian is united by the strongest bonds to those who share this faith with him whether they come from his own denomination or another.
3. We believe that Jesus in His High Priestly Prayer prayed that those who believe in Him might find and accept each other.
4. In some situations and in some times it is possible that unions of groups of congregations may be desirable.
5. We recommend that our congregations cooperate with like-minded Lutheran congregations and movements in programs of evangelism and witness.
6. We envision opportunities for our congregations to cooperate with other Protestant churches in the area of evangelism and witness to their communities. However, care must be taken not to compromise the Lutheran understanding of the Scriptures.

III. Church Polity

1. We believe that final human authority in the churches is vested in the local congregation, subject to the Word of God and the Holy Spirit.
2. Scripture does not command or forbid any particular organization for fellowship of congregations. In the absence of this we believe it is most safe to operate in a democratic way.
3. Conferences of the congregations of our fellowship do not enact law for the congregations, but simply recommend actions and practices to them.
4. In a free association of congregations such as this, neither its officers or conferences can negotiate the union of any or all of the congregations with another fellowship of congregations. This is an individual matter for the congregation.
5. We accept the Guiding Principles of the Lutheran Free Church as a true statement of our belief in regard to church polity.
6. The Holy Christian Church consists of those who in their hearts truly believe in Jesus Christ as Lord and Savior.
7. A free congregation selects and calls its own pastor, conducts its own program of worship, fellowship and service, and owns and maintains its own property.

IV. Practical Life

1. The Christian seeks to refrain from those acts, thoughts and words which are against a stated law of God.
2. Where actions and practices are neither forbidden nor encouraged in Scripture by name, the earnest believer will search the Scriptures for principles to guide his decisions and conduct.
3. He is aware that there is a separation which is necessary between the Christian and the world.
4. Ultimately every Christian makes his own decisions as to life and practice in the presence of His God. But he welcomes the sincere counsel of fellow believers.
5. Every Christian is responsible for his witness by life to others

and will govern himself, with the Lord's help, accordingly.
6. The Christian will refrain from belonging to organizations which practice a religion without Christ as the only Saviour. Belonging to such a group places the believer in a hopelessly compromised position and destroys his witness for Christ.

V. Church Life

1. We make no recommendation as to the use of liturgy and vestments except that we encourage simplicity in worship.
2. We believe the earliest Christians were extremely simple in their order of service. Whatever is added to the service carries the danger of becoming only form.
3. Even the simplest parts of the service may become only form.
4. The preaching of the Word of God must be the central part of the service.
5. True Gospel preaching endeavors to meet the needs of all who hear: the believer who desires to grow in his life with God, the seeking and uncertain souls who want to see Him, the hypocrite who must be awakened from his self-righteousness, and the hardened sinner who must still be called to saving faith.
6. The Sacraments must always be met by the response of faith in the heart of the recipient to be efficacious.
7. Hymn books should be such as will give honor to the Word of God and the Sacraments.
8. Congregations will cherish opportunities for Bible study and prayer fellowship.
9. Congregations are encouraged to have fellowship with one another in various activities.
10. The Lord has given talents and gifts to Christian lay people as well as pastors, and opportunity should be given for the practice of these gifts in the life of the congregations, also in meetings of fellowship outside the congregation, and in service to a needy world.

Submitted to the Special Conference of Lutheran Congregations at Thief River Falls, October 25-28, 1962

A Statement on the Historical Situation

> *Presented at Thief River Falls, Minnesota, on October 25-28, 1962, at a special conference of the Lutheran Free Church congregations and other interested persons and congregations who, having chosen not to enter the American Lutheran Church, gathered for the purpose of continuing the Lutheran Free Church. This is a presentation of reasons for remaining apart from that larger fellowship.*

Whenever a minority disagrees with the majority opinion, and particularly to the extent of taking the action we propose, it devolves upon that minority to explain the reasons which cause it to dissent. We, a minority of the Lutheran Free Church fellowship, do hereby present some of the issues which bring us to this convention for the purpose of continuing an association of Lutheran congregations to which we invite other Lutheran congregations which may desire, to join us. It should be understood that of the reasons for our actions which follow, not all may be accepted as equally valid by every person who joins this association. Nevertheless, these are submitted as a fairly comprehensive statement of the factors which make the American Lutheran Church unacceptable to us and cause us to continue a fellowship which will guarantee us the freedom to which we are accustomed, the emphases we believe are needed in our time, and a program for which we can work for the furtherance of God's kingdom.

Also in the nature of a preface, we want it clearly understood that we do not hereby condemn the American Lutheran Church as such or any Lutheran body. Most, if not all of us, have had many fine relationships with pastors and people of the American Lutheran Church. Many of us, if not all, have members of our families, other relatives and friends who are or will be a part of that synod. We would not cut ourselves off from them in taking this action. We do not judge any person or his decision in being a part of that fellowship, nor will we do so in the future. We are not precluding the possibility that much good will be done in and come out of the American Lutheran Church. We believe there will be.

We are saying that for us it seems necessary to take this action, for we are acting out of the understanding which we have of our time and situation. There are factors within the American Lutheran Church which we believe would make it difficult for us to work whole-heartedly in the total program which they have. To be with the majority would be much more comfortable than to be in the smaller fellowship we envision, if only the outward is considered. To be with the minority will be more satisfying to us if we feel that in so doing we are being true to ourselves and our understanding, which is also the result of much prayer and study, and this is, we trust, the spirit in which we take this course of action.

Now, the objections which we have raised against the American Lutheran Church. They cannot be taken up in any great detail, but we set them before you.

I. *Her membership in the World Council of Churches.*

This is an issue which many of us have become increasingly aware of only in these last few years. Some of us are still young enough so that we were not really aware of the importance of the beginning of the World Council in 1948 in Amsterdam. This is also an issue which has aroused much strong feeling and opinion. Certain it is that anything we say here today will be answered by arguments which to those who speak them will be more valid to them than what we say. And yet we speak with what to us seems as at least equal conviction. Is it not true that we, both sides, shall have to submit the matter to the judgment of time, and in time one opinion shall have been proved right? This we are willing to do and in the meantime do hope to work outside the framework of the World Council even as others will find their place in it.

It is true, as Dr. Alvin Rogness, president of the Theological

Seminary of the American Lutheran Church, wrote recently, that the member churches assure one another that they "confess the Lord Jesus Christ as God and Savior according to the Scriptures and therefore seek to fulfill together their common calling to the glory of the One God, Father, Son and Holy Spirit." This, by the way, is the basis for the World Council. But it has been pointed out by a number of Lutheran theologians that the phrase, "according to the Scriptures" does not mean to many in the World Council what it means to us, as expressed, for instance, in the United Testimony or the Augsburg Confession. As an example, there are those within the World Council who do not see in the Bible the Virgin Birth of Jesus, the physical resurrection of Jesus, His real presence in the Sacrament of the Altar, or the bodily return of Christ to judge the quick and the dead. We do not see how we can with these make a united witness to the world for Christ. There are many situations we can envision wherein a Lutheran pastor might be unfrocked for teaching wrong doctrine and then reappear as a member of some other communion within the World Council and be embraced by his erstwhile Lutheran companions as a "dear brother in Christ."

Do we not have to make up our minds as to whether we can continue to hold that we have true doctrine as Lutherans, and instructing people in this doctrine before permitting them to join our churches and at the same time through the World Council saying to fellow members, "We are not really sure if we have any more truth than you do"? In other words, we believe a contradiction is involved here. This is not to say that we do not recognize truth in other denominations. Lutheran Free Church congregations have generally been more lenient in fellowship with other church groups than perhaps any others of the Lutheran family. But these fellowships have existed where there has been a oneness of spirit in a local community and an opportunity for witness. It is quite another thing to give a more blanket recognition to denominations, some of whose ways and teachings we are not at all sure about and some we really can't accept.

We believe a greater witness for Biblical truth can be made

apart from the World Council. After all, where Christianity is going to make its greatest impact is where it is lived out in the local community, where the world sees the Christ-life in an individual, and not in the pronouncements of world councils of churches on disarmament, the United Nations, etc., although we do not rule out the possibility of good coming through these in the proper place.

We fear that there will be a movement to organize a one-world church. This argument is highly debated, but there have been statements by some leaders which certainly favor this idea. Perhaps they have spoken only for themselves, but at least it indicates some are thinking in this direction. And following is a statement to be found in the study booklet for the Third Assembly of the World Council of Churches held in New Delhi, India, soon a year ago. We quote, "The churches, and that means the people of Christ gathered in their various congregations and communions, have created the World Council of Churches. They have created it so that one day they might dispense with it. The World Council of Churches lives to die. If the churches ever become content with it or concerned solely to perpetuate it, then they will be disobedient to the heavenly vision. The World Council is a tabernacle of pilgrim people to serve only until God fulfills His promise and purpose for them to make them one in Him and for Him." End of quotation.

No doubt you may find different interpretations of this paragraph. What does it mean, "The World Council of Churches lives to die"? Do they mean it will come to an end when this world ends? We do not think so. Rather they seem to envision a day when the word "Council" may be dropped and all churches become one church. It is not wrong to long for the day when God's people shall be gathered in one place and in one time. The Bible speaks of Zion and the new Jerusalem. But we do not look for this in the present world, but beyond. Did not Jesus say, "When the Son of man comes will he find faith on earth?" This hardly seems in keeping with the hope expressed in the study booklet, of millions and millions of believers, using the statistics of member churches. Nor do we share the optimism of those who equate these membership statistics with the true people of

God. Would God it were so, however.

Another matter about the World Council which bothers us is its relationship to the Communism issue. Generally, we opposed the entry of Communist nation churches into the Council. We doubt whether they represent the true Church in those lands. In a report coming back from New Delhi we heard Archbishop Nikodim, head of the Russian Orthodox delegation, say that his church could work without interference in his homeland. Then we read the statements by non-Russians that the church in Russia must labor under many handicaps placed by the government. The reports were conflicting.

But we may be wrong in our assessment of the church situation in Russia. We would not lay any added cross on our true brethren in Christ there. We are sure God has His witnesses in that benighted land. However, the entrance of Russian and satellite country churches into the World Council has added a new problem for this body. This was vividly set forth in the recent statement of Bishop Otto Dibelius of Berlin. He pointed out that a report on world affairs presented at a summer meeting in Paris of the World Council's Central Committee went over many world problems not connected with the Communist world conspiracy and then before he closed, as a kind of addition, Dr. O. Frederick Nolde mentioned the Soviet threat to Berlin, setting forth the hope that consultation might ease the problem. The bishop's warning was this, that perhaps the World Council will not now feel free to speak against the evils of communism for fear of endangering and embarrassing Russian and satellite country delegates to the Council. We think, too, that the Council may "pull its punches" in regard to the evils of Communism while feeling quite free to point out the sins of capitalism, of which, we must confess, there are many. We call upon those who choose to be members of the World Council to keep close watch to see whether the charge and warning of the venerable bishop are true.

Another decision which the American Lutheran Church must soon face is membership in the National Council of Churches of Christ in the United States of America. It cannot long be consistent to belong to one and not the other. The

National Council bears some real question marks as to its work and witness and we would rather not be a part of it.

In summary of this first objection to the merger, let us say that we feel our testimony to Christian and Biblical truth can best be given outside of the World Council which, because of its divergent views, can only represent a confused theology. We fear the efforts of some to make the World Council one church, and we believe the Council's witness against communism may be muted dangerously because of the membership of Russian and satellite country churches. Therefore, we do not wish to belong.

II. *Theology*

We are conservative theologically. We are, most of us, reared in this tradition and wish to continue in it. We are living in a time when rapid changes in thought regarding the Word of God are taking place. Those who are moving with these changes, people in college and seminary work, in parish education and Lutheran League activity, or as pastors and laymen, are deeply convinced that they may do so with no lessening of their faith and devotion. Rather, they would say, these are strengthened. We, on the other hand, see the time-honored principle of "let Scripture interpret Scripture" endangered in the new approaches to the Bible. If present trends continue, most Lutheran Sunday school and confirmation materials will soon have to be rewritten. Some of it has already been done. They will be replaced by materials which may be intellectually acceptable, but in that acceptability miss the voice of God. We must not be against scholarship. We must guard against this temptation. But we will want, generally speaking, to hold the line at a defensive position further out than some others will.

In our day we are also confronted with changing attitudes toward Roman Catholicism. The changes within the last ten years have been almost beyond imagination. Certainly, with others, we rejoice in every lessening of hatred and bigotry between members of one faith and another. However, we do not share the optimism of some in regard to the Roman Church.

The main objections to Roman Catholicism which Martin Luther had 400 years ago and which caused him to be excommunicated are still present today; namely, his belief that justification is by faith alone, and that the Bible must be the supreme religious authority of man. If the Roman Catholic Church should accept Luther's position on these, then we would have an entirely different situation.

In the absence of such a change, however, the gulf still runs deep. We wish our Roman Catholic neighbor well and we watch his church council with keep interest, but we can have no real fellowship with him. We shall be no part of a "back to Rome" movement. All of this has nothing to do with merger except that in maintaining our own fellowship we will not be responsible for more favorable assessments of the Catholic-Protestant situation than we think are right.

III. *Church Polity*

The passage of time has dulled some of our criticism of the polity of the new church. That is, we would not make as much of an issue of some points as we would have a year or two ago. But what were the points in regard to church government to which we objected and which we still do not like? One is the smaller size General Convention of 1,000 delegates (500 pastors and 500 laymen) with no mandatory system of rotation for congregations. Roughly speaking, if a system of rotation were used for lay delegates, a congregation would have such representation only once in about 20 years. Also, some pastors under the present setup will likely never be delegates to the Convention. We objected to the involved procedure for the withdrawal of a congregation from the synod, and to the fact that in the American Lutheran Church the congregational referendums such as we have known them would not be a part of the system of government. Still another is the threat of bureaucracy.

Mention should be made of the district presidents. Our opinion of them and their place has changed somewhat. We see that they do play a vital role in a large church body. Many of them will serve the cause of Christ with real distinction. However, we still do not feel that it is necessary for these presidents to sign all letters of call to pastors. The point we have tried to make is that we do not believe it is the same to say "a congregation calls its own pastor" and "a congregation calls its own pastor and each letter of call must have the signature of the district president on it." Surely this regulation ought not to be necessary to protect the congregations from the few clergymen who would be under church discipline at any one time. And, what protection is guaranteed to the pastors and congregations against a district president who may have a vindictive spirit? We can see where every congregation seeking a pastor in a large church body will want to consult its district president, but we have objected to this new regulation which seems to impose a restriction on congregational freedom.

IV. *The American Lutheran Church, the Lutheran Church in America, and the Lutheran Church-Missouri Synod, all represent the Lutheran Church as being high-churchly.*

We think this is unfortunate. Is there not something to be said for the low-church emphasis? The Articles of Union for the American Lutheran Church state, "We deem it advisable that the American Lutheran Church strive for unity in practice, and therefore we recognize the responsibility of the Church to recommend appropriate practices relating to"–among other things–liturgy, a common hymnal and vestments. So far as we know, this statement has not been superseded by anything in the constitution.

The question we ask is, "Is it necessary to strive for unity in these matters?" We do not think so. Many of us come from a low-church tradition and do not feel we are any less Lutheran for that reason. In our new fellowship we must not lay down any restrictions for others in regard to these matters, but we do hope to preserve and propagate the idea of and opportunity for simplicity in worship among Lutherans in the United States and Canada.

V. *And now finally, we object to merger with the American Lutheran Church because it does not represent the pietism we believe is needed and is right for our day.*

Pietism has different meanings to different people and so we speak of "the pietism we believe is needed and is right for our day." We think of pietism as an emphasis on personal Christianity, and in which emphasis the Christian does not use all his Christian liberty both because of his own weakness which may lead to occasions of the flesh, and because he must watch his example and not cause a weaker brother to fall.

We assert and defend the right of each Christian to make his own decisions as to what is right conduct for him, assuming that he will do so after searching the Scriptures for principles of guidance, speaking to the Lord in prayer and, if it should be helpful, consulting friends and superiors who give evidence of having the mind of the Spirit. In this way he determines his stand in regard toward those things which Scripture neither commands nor forbids by name, but which in the nature of things have been questioned as suitable Christian conduct.

In the Lutheran Free Church, together with some other Lutherans, we have been very skeptical of the social dance and social drinking of alcoholic beverages. Incidentally, together with all churches we recognize drunkenness as a sin. But to get back to what we just said, we have not wanted to give any encouragement toward these things because we have felt that they carried particular dangers. Rather, we have warned against them on the basis that the Christian must not jeopardize his faith or witness and would better exercise personal discipline by refraining. Therefore, it stands to reason that we have consistently opposed social dancing in churches, at church-sponsored functions, and in other church-owned properties and institutions.

In the proposed merger of the Lutheran Free Church with the American Lutheran Church we were brought face to face with an entirely different outlook. We find in regard to the social dance that it is permitted in a number of the senior colleges of that church. In the Lutheran Free Church we have always considered Augsburg College and Seminary as the "heart" of the church. In fact, the Lutheran Free Church was born in struggle over Augsburg. In a recent statement released by the Board of College Education of the American Lutheran Church called "The Case for College Education," this sentence is found, "The colleges and schools of the church are at the heart of her program." Therefore, the two churches have had the same idea. The point is that if something is good enough and right for what is at the heart of the church, it is good enough for the congregations, too.

We believe it is wrong that this sanction be given to the social dance. The dance has long been a symbol of the worldly spirit. It does not foster a deeper life with Christ, but bears the likelihood of encouraging spiritual indifference. From the early days of the recent merger discussions among Lutherans, two of the compelling reasons given why Lutherans must get together were to resist communism and the secular spirit of the age. Secularism is another word that can be defined in many ways, but it is correct to also call it the worldly spirit in the bad sense of the term. We fail to see how secularism is being combatted by the merger at the same time as more and more Lutheran colleges and congregations are embracing the social dance as a legitimate function in their programs. Last Saturday night a well-known late evening WCCO dance program originated from the student union of one of our Lutheran colleges in Minnesota, not of the American Lutheran or Lutheran Free Churches. Was not this an uncertain trumpet sound coming from a school which bears the proud name of the Lutheran Church?

We do not want to support these schools which we believe have compromised their witness. We are interested in supporting Christian education and will do what we can for those schools in which we can believe. Within the American Lutheran Church we would have no choice but to support all. Outside of it, we will have the right to be selective in our support.

We note the action of the recent convention of the American Lutheran Church in asking the Board of College Education to review the policy of permitting each college of the church to decide for itself as to whether or not social dancing shall be allowed. We are not sure just what the issue involved here is, but we welcome the study and would be pleased at action which would prohibit dancing at the church institutions, or, if that is not possible, at least grant the congregations the right of protest.

In regard to social drinking we ask, "What is more a symbol of secularism or the worldly spirit than the alcoholic beverage, the corner tavern, the cocktail party, and the beer can or bottle lying by the curb or in a highway ditch? Whatever the status of wine was in the time of Christ, we believe that in modern American life the liquor industry and its products stand condemned and have nothing of value to contribute to life, and have rather left a vast wreckage of human hopes in their wake. We do not believe it is the job of the churches to preach moderation in the face of the situation in which we live and have lived.

From statements printed in *One* magazine and the *Lutheran Standard*, not editorially perhaps, we have sensed a different attitude toward these things. Not in a defense of drunkenness, to be sure, but in promoting the idea that if one can drink for the right reasons he may do so. We consider this an unwise approach in view of the American and Canadian scene of today. We believe that any total statement made on the subject by the American Lutheran Church will not be acceptable to us, but will resemble those given by some other Protestant churches. Such broad-minded pronouncements do not meet the needs of this day against what we believe is a real enemy of American and Canadian life.

We are concerned about the policies of publications for youth among Lutherans in regard to social dancing and social drinking. We have already mentioned *One* magazine. In addition we find the same approach to dancing in *Youth Programs* and in the *Weekday Church School* series published by Muhlenberg Press and recommended for use by other Lutherans. We raise our voice in protest about these and ask, "Who speaks today for the pietism we knew just five and ten years ago?" We do not believe it is out-moded, but has its place today and is needed. We would like to speak for it.

Conclusion:

And now in conclusion, let us say that we have stated these things so that people might know our thinking and the factors which cause us to take the action we do here in Thief River Falls during these days. We speak out of the world view which we have and in light of the Scriptures as we have read them. We are subject to error and human failing, and our work must be exposed to the test of time. This we are willing to have done.

We have tried to speak in Christian love. To speak otherwise would be to break the commandment to "love your neighbor as yourself." By saying what we have, we have not wanted to charge others with sinning against their consciences in taking a course unlike ours. We have said, "This is what we believe we must do and for these reasons, in the sight of God."

We have not cut ourselves off from the Lutheran faith or the Lutheran family. We are ready to work together with our fellow Lutherans when we can do so without compromising the principles mentioned in this statement and in the Declaration of Faith which is to follow and to be found in the Guiding Principles of the Lutheran Free Church, and at the same time maintaining a separate identity and certain freedoms and emphases which, to our way of thinking, we can better do alone. We realize that we have no claim to the right of this fellowship with those from whom we outwardly separate now, but for our part will stand ready to act in common witness wherever we can.

This entire statement has been the negative statement of this convention. It is given in the hope that this will speak for us all, and that we might go on from here to the positive and refrain from belaboring the objections we have toward the merger, and airing old grievances toward persons and churches. If we succumb to these temptations, we will doom whatever organization we form here to a useless and unblessed future. Let us now confess our sins, let us do what we can to heal the wounds, let us be willing to forgive;

where we must differ with others, let it be done in love. And if we can go on to think positively about the work we would like to do together in God's kingdom, we have the chance of doing something which can have a real value in the world and which would carry God's blessing. The committee hopes and prays that this may be so.

For Further Reading

Batalden, Abner B., ed. *Our Fellowship*. Minneapolis: Messenger Press, 1947.

Carlsen, Clarence J. *The Years of Our Church*. Minneapolis: The Lutheran Free Church Publishing Company, 1942.

Chrislock, Carl H. *From Fjord to Freeway: 100 Years–Augsburg College*. Minneapolis, 1969.

Christensen, Bernhard. "The Idea of the Lutheran Free Church." In *Freedom and Christian Education*, ed. John A. Houkom, 33-46. Minneapolis: Board of Trustees, 1945.

———. "What Is the Lutheran Free Church?" *The Lutheran Messenger* 24, no. 12 (April 10, 1941): 5.

Dyrud, Loiell. *The Quest for Freedom: The Lutheran Free Church to the Association of Free Lutheran Congregations*. Minneapolis: Ambassador Publications, 2000.

Evjen, John O., ed. *Veiledning i Den Lutherske Frikirkes Principer*. Minneapolis: Free Church Book Concern, 1914.

Fevold, Eugene L. *The Lutheran Free Church: A Fellowship of American Lutheran Congregations, 1897-1963*. Minneapolis: Augsburg Publishing House, 1969.

Hamre, James S. *Georg Sverdrup: Educator, Theologian, Churchman*. Northfield, Minnesota: The Norwegian-American Historical Association, 1986.

———. "Thanksgiving Day Address" in *Norwegian-American Studies* 24. Northfield, Minnesota: Norwegian-American Historical Association, 1970.

_____. "Georg Sverdrup and the Augsburg Plan of Education" in *Norwegian-American Studies* 26: 160-183. Northfield, Minnesota: Norwegian-American Historical Association, 1974.

_____. "Georg Sverdrup's Concept of Theological Education in the Context of a Free Church." *Lutheran Quarterly* 22 (May 1970): 199-209.

_____. "Georg Sverdrup's Concept of the Role and Calling of the Norwegian-American Lutherans: An Annotated Translation of Selected Writings." Ph. D. dissertation, University of Iowa, 1967.

_____. "Georg Sverdrup's 'Errand into the Wilderness': Building the 'Free and Living' Congregation." *Concordia Historical Institute Quarterly* 53 (1980): 39-47.

_____. "Georg Sverdrup's Expression of A Lutheran Restorationism in America." *Lutheran Quarterly* 14 (Spring 2000): 53-78.

_____. "The 'Augsburg Triumvirate' and the *Kvartalskrift*." *Luther Theological Seminary Review* (November, 1972): 21-30.

Hanson, E. M., Ludvig Pedersen, E. E. Gynild, Elias P. Harbo, Andrew Olson. *Menigheten: Foredrag holdt under bibelkonferansen i Eagle Lake menighet, Willmar, Minnesota, 19de til 21de mars, 1918 (The Congregation: Lectures at the Bible Conference in Eagle Lake Church, Willmar, Minnesota)*. Minneapolis: Folkebladets trykkeri, 1918.

Helland, Andreas. *Augsburg Seminar gjennem femti aar, 1869-1919*. Minneapolis: Folkebladet Publishing Companys Trykkeri, 1920.

_____. *Den Lutherske Frikirke og dens Fællesgjøremaal*. Minneapolis: Frikirkens Boghandls Forlag, 1914.

_____. *Georg Sverdrup: The Man and His Message 1848-1907*. Minneapolis: The Messenger Press, 1947.

_____. "The Lutheran Free Church." *The Lutheran Quarterly* 57 (July 1927): 373-386.

Helland, Andreas, ed. *Professor Georg Sverdrups samlede skrifter i udvalg*. 6 vols. Minneapolis: Frikirkens Boghandels Forlag, 1909-1912.

Helland, Melvin, trans. *The Heritage of Faith: Selections From the Writings of Georg Sverdrup*. Minneapolis: Augsburg Publishing House, 1969.

Huglen, Raynard O. J., ed. *The AFLC at 30: Growth and New Challenges 1962-1992*. Minneapolis, 1992.

Kleven, Bernhardt J. "The History of the Norwegian-Danish Evangelical Lutheran Church in America." Master of Arts thesis, University of Minnesota, 1930.

Lee, Robert Lloyd. *A New Springtime: Centennial Reflections on the Revival in the Nineties Among Norwegian-Americans*. Minneapolis: Heirloom Press, 1997.

Lillehei, L., ed. *Augsburg Seminary and The Lutheran Free Church*. Minneapolis, 1928.

Lutz, Charles P. *Church Roots*. Minneapolis: Augsburg Publishing House, 1985.

Monseth, Francis W. *Georg Sverdrup: Champion of the Free Congregation*. Minneapolis, 1997.

Nelson, E. Clifford and Eugene L. Fevold. *The Lutheran Church Among Norwegian-Americans: A History of the Evangelical Lutheran Church*. 2 vols. Minneapolis: Augsburg Publishing House, 1960.

Nydahl, J. L., Johan Mattson, and H. C. Caspersen, eds. *The Lutheran Free Church Handbook*. Minneapolis: The Lutheran Free Church Publishing Co., 1928.

Oftedal, Sven and Georg Sverdrup. *Aand og Liv: Praedikener over alle tre tekstraekkers evangelier*. Minneapolis: Free Church Book Concern, 1898.

Pederson, M. A., and Andreas Helland, eds. *Bibelkonferentsen i Belgrade, Minn. fra 2den til 6te November 1898* (*The Bible Conference in Belgrade, Minnesota, from the 2nd to the 6th of November 1898*). Minneapolis: den Lutherske Missionar's Trykkeri, n.d.

Quanbeck, Warren A., Eugene L. Fevold, and Gerhard E. Frost, eds. *Striving for Ministry*. Minneapolis: Augsburg Publishing House, 1977.

Rodvik, Johann. *Legem- og hustenkerne hos Paulus*. Minneapolis: Lutheran Free Church, 1927.

Saugstad, C. *Augsburgs historie*. Minneapolis, 1893.

Stensvaag, John. "Are We Hypocrites?" In *Freedom and Christian Education*, ed. John A. Houkom, 55-58. Minneapolis: Board of Trustees, 1945.

_____. *Do You Really Want The Congregation? . . . Georg Sverdrup For Our Day*. Reprinted, Minneapolis: Ambassador Publications, 1987.

_____. "The Living Congregation: Georg Sverdrup's Views on Lay Activity in the Church." Seminary thesis, Augsburg Theological Seminary, n.d.